AN ORDINARY WHITE

AN ORDINARY WHITE

My Antiracist Education

David Roediger

FORDHAM UNIVERSITY PRESS

NEW YORK   2025

Fordham University Press also publishes its books in a variety of electronic formats. Some content that appears in print may not be available in electronic books.

Visit us online at www.fordhampress.com.

Library of Congress Cataloging-in-Publication Data available online at https://catalog.loc.gov.

Printed in the United States of America

27 26 25 5 4 3 2 1

First edition

To my mother and father

Contents

Preface

BECOMING FATHOMABLE

In 1993, I began teaching at summer schools on race and class for industrial workers around St. Louis. Socialists organized some of them. The New Directions reform caucus of the United Automobile Workers (UAW) convened others. One was so mainstream that the incoming international president of the steel workers attended. He was terrific, as a student anyhow. Not knowing how to begin, I jotted down a possible question and a follow-up: "Why would anybody want to identify as a 'white worker'?" and then "Why not just as a worker?" Two concerns made me hesitate to ask these questions of that first class of UAW members. The first was that the whites would shut down, leaving the question to Black students to answer. This happens frequently enough in university classrooms when race comes up. The second worry anticipated that some of the white workers would say that affirmative action and other reforms that addressed race were what forced them to identify as white. I took the questions with me without deciding whether to ask them.

I opted for those big, hard questions because the workers who came, perhaps 70% white, seemed so familiar to me. I'd grown up about a dozen miles from St. Louis, closer still to the big suburban Chrysler plant. Lots of my friends had taken industrial jobs right out of high school. The ones in good unions and working overtime were still making considerably more money than I was. I knew such friends to be clever and to have lots to say. I'd just turned 40 and the summer school students' age averaged around there. Such familiarity ruled out any supposing that the whites in the class would be without racism. I knew them, and myself, as people formed by some of the worst ideas and prejudices in US society. But they were not only that and I wanted to hear what they had to say in an integrated, union-based setting, exactly the sort of place that Bill Clinton's pollsters had scrupulously avoided in setting up focus groups to find out what white "middle class" workers thought in the then-recent 1992 presidential election. I wanted to learn if they'd speak.

When I posed the question, white workers immediately answered with a catalogue of the white advantages that anchor a white worker identity: "You get better home loans." "You have a shot at getting into the skilled trades and making lots more money." "You can live in any neighborhood, ones with better schools." "The cops don't get after you as much." The workers who were white thus explained how white advantage persisted long after legal equality, much as those of us contributing to the developing field of Critical Race Theory did. They knew a lot.

Broad conversation across color lines then occurred. From that time on, the "Why be a white worker?" question figured in almost every labor workshop I taught. In one steelworkers' school I taught, a childhood neighbor turned up. He'd proven a rank-and-file leader across the color line in his local union. He didn't learn that in our little, aggressively all-white town, I would once have said. But in talking to him after the class it became clear that he did learn some of his anti-racism there, every bit as much as I had.

Such encounters introduce a central point of this book: the insights of what is sometimes called Critical Race Theory (CRT) and sometimes Critical Whiteness Studies do not require sinister injections of "Soros money," plotting intellectuals, popular culture influencers, the allegedly liberal media, or indoctrination by schools. They can arise—alongside, it is true, other and contrary ideas—from experiences and observations of everyday life by ordinary whites. As much as my thoughts about pervasive white advantage came later in my life to involve study and struggle, they originated with plain observations of the settings in which I lived and worked. Had they contradicted what I saw, I'd have discarded them. The same is true regarding the views of the many tens of millions of whites who, however unevenly, have reached antiracist conclusions. The fierce attacks from white nationalists on what they caricature and vilify as Critical Race Theory mean to prevent teaching about deep patterns of white supremacy. They attempt to stop whites with interracial experiences from thinking about what those experiences mean because those thoughts sometimes lead to solidarity.

Finding the Right Words

Very late in writing this book, I found the right word for understanding my own story and that of the workers speaking as whites in those summer schools. It is the strange word *fathomable*. In the end those workers needed not so much to be familiar to me and each other as fathomable. Likewise, I had to be fathomable to them, enough so that we could speak to one another. More important than showing that CRT is correct, or is unjustly maligned, is to show that it is at least possible—fathomable—based on knowledge and experience many whites already hold.

Fathomable, or initially *unfathomable*, and *ordinary* found me when I needed them. The words came when the former Freedom Rider Joan Constance Browning spoke in early 2023 on the University of Kansas campus. She looked back on her experiences, including incarceration resulting from her 1961 participation in nonviolent direct action (when she challenged federal authorities to confront Southern states disobeying court decisions outlawing segregation of passengers traveling across state lines on buses and trains). Telling stories of heroism against brutal violence, she insisted that hers was a movement of "ordinary" people who were both African American and, like herself, white. She described her own family as landless farmers, coming later to buy a tiny farm on credit. Only late in the talk did we learn that some in that ordinary white family, including her father, abandoned contact with Browning partly over the Freedom Rides.

I suspect some in her audience found Browning's association of bravery and moral vision with the ordinary to be confusing. Her use of the work of the historian and freedom fighter Howard Zinn, whom she met in the Georgia freedom movement, explained why she would insist on the point. She recalled that Zinn's essays from the civil rights movement, published as *The Southern Mystique*, began with a long first section answering the awkward question "Is the Southern White Unfathomable?" Zinn, a fierce and suitably impatient critic of Southern racism, argued the case for rejecting over-simplifications that place

white racists beyond understanding. I would too, where workers racialized as white today are concerned. To declare large white swathes
of the working class irredeemable or deplorable, he reasoned, invites
disaster and timidity. It disappears complexity. We start by regarding
poor people with some terrible ideas as fathomable as humans capable
of making better choices or we do not start at all, Zinn realized.

Something additional mattered to Browning. In connecting her own
experiences in retrograde places with what she became—she once described a segregated rural church as her first "beloved community"
though not one that she could directly connect to civil rights—her own
radicalism became fathomable. I want to claim as much for my radicalism
too, and to argue for a grounded white anti-racism as itself fathomable.

In arguing that working-class everyday life can animate radical egal-
itarian positions—in fact that no radicalism of enduring consequence
can come from anywhere else—I am not pretending that my life is
typical. Still less do I claim that there are *enough* whites raised in very
racist settings who are poised to become revolutionary opponents of
white supremacy, and rejoin humanity, as James Baldwin hoped they
would do. They are certainly not bound to become readers and advo-
cates of CRT. The good fortune I had in in learning what harm whiteness was doing to myself as well as everyone else sometimes resulted
from uncanny recurrences of dumb luck. However, I would insist that
elements of a deep-reaching antiracist position—knowledge of white
advantage, attraction to cultural forms created on the other side of
color lines, and a strong feeling that the present order makes even the
advantaged miserable—does suffuse the ranks of working-class people
racialized as white. It is certainly true that such sentiments cohabit with
many others, and many of those whites cling to those large and small
advantages. The holders of such contradictory views are nevertheless
fathomable, even ordinary in many ways.

What made me a radical are things lived by the millions with whom
I share a generation. These experiences reached beyond, but also happened to, huge numbers of people whom society calls "white Americans." They were and are everyday experiences of what the South
African historian Neil Roos calls "ordinary whites." I grew up in a
strictly segregated town with no presence of "diversity"—meaning

no people of color—at all. This was true of many upper Midwestern towns. Sometimes I lived in a small city far south in Illinois that was half African American but adhered to strict Jim Crow segregation, as did most Southern towns. I come from a so-called broken home—a divorce when I'd barely begun grade school between parents who'd been in a "mixed marriage," as they thought of it, because one was Catholic and the other Lutheran. Anomalous earlier, these phenomena too happened by the millions in the fifties and sixties. The Catholicism enforced in my single-parent home grudgingly became a post-Vatican II one, leaving cracks for guitar masses, reforms, anti-racism, and eventually liberation theology to enter.

When I joined Students for a Democratic Society (SDS) at the end of the sixties, polls showed many young people identified as radicals rather than as Democrats or Republicans. The massive disapproval of the war against Vietnam plus support for freedom movements of women, gays, and people of color made the oppositional politics and dissenting ideas I gravitated toward popular positions. I'd witnessed strikes of family members from childhood forward, again a commonplace drama in the fifties and sixties. Public education provided all my schooling through age 22. I loved African American sports heroes and musical stars and my racist schoolmates did likewise.

CRT, Me, and Autobiography

For this book to exist it also had to become fathomable for me to write autobiographically. And it's the venom, effectiveness, and durability of white nationalist attacks on Critical Race Theory, the critical study of whiteness, Black Studies, and Ethnic Studies that helped call the book into being. I identify as a critical race theorist despite believing that CRT is mainly the good work of legal scholars and lies somewhat beyond my expertise. Those scholars have wanted to provide rigorous and creative reminders that judicial precedent and everyday practices beyond the courts systematically deliver racially unequal results, absent tough-minded critiques of what structures inequality. The work of my late friend Derrick Bell provided the best example. A historian of labor, I did not belong in Bell's company where legal studies were concerned, except that he wanted me there.

Explaining to my older son Brendan, a law professor, why I would embrace CRT but be reluctant to center my contributions to it drew an unexpected response from him. He reminded me that my work on the critical study of whiteness got generously sampled in Richard Delgado and Jean Stefancic's *Critical Race Theory*, a 1995 collection announcing the creation of that area of study, as well as their later collection, *Critical White Studies*. In any case, the censors of CRT entertain little doubt that their opposition extends to those who critique the harm done by a political alliance based on identifying with the "white race," which is central to my work. Legislative efforts against CRT attack "whiteness studies" as well. Indeed, some express desires to outlaw anything with the potential to make white students uncomfortable. So, I'm in on the side of CRT.

The book details how I came to be an antiracist activist and intellectual, after growing up in what might seem like settings hopelessly inhospitable to such commitments. Its autobiographical emphases startled me almost every time that I sat down to write. Thirty years or so ago my wonderful editor Colin Robinson, then at Verso Books, suggested that I write a book about my life. It is true that in Colin's native Britain, low-key well-known left intellectuals sometimes write such books, but I couldn't think of a single such a memoir by a similarly positioned US writer. Nor did my life seem weighty or long enough to justify writing such a book. The left autobiographies that I knew anchored themselves in political groups. They alternated between triumphalism and a sense of betrayal, each delivered with an authority that eluded me. They imparted lessons and I had few. My favorite pages of them talked about work, though very seldom about academic work.

Several changes opened me up to writing about my life. My mother's living so long and well—she only recently died at 100—had me thinking about the course of a life, the changes she saw in a half-century of K–12 teaching labor, and moments when ordinary Americans regard themselves as middle class and when as working class. Having grandchildren also made the preservation of life stories more compelling. Feminist theory had taught me the importance of situating oneself and one's standpoint in scholarly work. More and more I came to wonder what it would look like to practice history from below in thinking about myself and my ordinary family.

As those whom I struggled alongside and learned from passed away—Susan Porter Benson, Franklin Rosemont, Margaret George, Martin Glaberman, John Bracey, Sterling Stuckey, Maurice Berger, Mike Davis, Noel Ignatiev—I saw how others appreciated their lives, spent well outside of even the left political mainstream. Initiatives in which I worked, from surrealism to anti-fascism to revitalizing the radical Charles H. Kerr Publishing Company, proved durably able to recreate themselves. Those whom I knew and worked with more episodically, including Ted Joans, Toni Morrison, Leonora Carrington, Lawrence Ferlinghetti, Grace Lee Boggs, Jayne Cortez, Philip Lamantia, Raya Dunayaskava, Tariq Ali, H.L. Mitchell, Stan Weir, and Dennis Brutus wrote important books and had books written about them.

Still the main attraction of writing autobiographically has remained conveying how everyday life animates radical critiques of racial capitalism. Far from being the product of the hothouse of academic life, my work often provoked fierce opposition there. Social movements, in their waning as well as waxing, shaped what I thought about. Nor did pro-Democratic party electoral machinations, assumed by critics to drive CRT support, animate my activism. I had begun while I was still in high school to doubt that the Democrats would put on offer anything capable of sufficiently addressing the miseries of humanity.

A prefatory word on method also seems in order. For a historian to write about their own past is to be tempted constantly by further research. I have needed to do so to check memories, dates, and spellings. Reentering the historical record, whether from my own records, or those of the Chicago Surrealist Group, or by reading accounts of experiences I have lived through, has proven useful. It interrupts the stories I have come to repeat, often with little variation, in many published and archived interviews about my life. I offer no apology for the repetitions or the didacticism. I have often stood on the other side of gathering what my friends Staughton and Alice Lynd called "personal histories" and appreciate their logic. It goes with the process of remembering to hone the same stories and their lessons. It's in the old-timers' Bill of Rights.

Such performances of memory construct our traditions. In interviewing the labor radical Fred Thompson decades ago for a book on his long life, I heard him draw on what he learned as a youth from an older worker who had in turn been a Chartist in mid-nineteenth century Britain. Connecting Fred's memory of the Chartist to my life constructs a chain stretching over 200 years. That tradition is happily not an academic one; nor do I claim that "further research" validates my opinions.

The very form of the writing, as autobiography, ensures that those to whom I am most indebted are credited in the text so that a separate acknowledgments section becomes superfluous. Long ago I took to heart the advice that a mentor, the historian George Rawick, relayed to me from his mentor, the revolutionary theorist C.L.R. James. James urged writing for an actual list of a few flesh-and-blood people whom one hopes to move—I think George urged a half-dozen names—and "everyone else in the world." I have never managed to actually write down a short list of interlocutors in imagining a book but came close in this instance. That is, I described the project, or sent parts of it, to Betsy Esch, Kevin Mumford, Niels Hooper, Maya Delmond, May Fu, Brendan Roediger, Donovan Roediger, and George Lipsitz, coaxing responses designed to tell whether or not it was a hare-brained scheme. Their encouragement licensed my proceeding. Delmond served as my graduate research assistant supporting the writing, and funding for time to write came from the Huntington Library's Avery Fellowship. Help with the illustrations and with my memory came from Jean Allman, Don Stahlheber, Tammy Smith, and Penelope Rosemont. Esch and Hooper offered detailed responses to the text and the former rescued me from stopping writing when I worried my story was just too slight. Thanks, too, to the wonderful Richard Morrison and others at Fordham University Press for their expertise and confidence in the book and to Lee Bebout and Lisa Lowe whose reports on the book for the Press greatly improved the manuscript.

A central lesson in this autobiography is that we learn to fathom our own place in history not simply through individual mentors but also through social movements. Thanks particularly go in my case to the movements for working-class emancipation, Black freedom, women's and queer liberation, environmental justice, decolonization, Palestine, immigrant rights, Indigenous sovereignty, and prison abolition.

The starting-point of critical elaboration . . . is "knowing thyself" as a product of the historical process to date, which has deposited in you an infinity of traces, without leaving an inventory.

—Antonio Gramsci in *Prison Notebooks*

1

BORN AND RAISED
Abandoned Cities and a Sundown Town

I learned racism about when I learned to walk. The learning laboratories in my childhood were classic ones. I mostly lived in the "sundown town" of Columbia, Illinois. "Sundown" derived from the social fact that Black people had to be out of town by dark or face legal and extralegal consequences. The sundown spatial arrangement of white supremacy dominated in much of the Midwest. It drew upon the example of the region's colonial settlement, one featuring rapid and nearly total ethnic cleansing of Native people. It followed too on the peopling of the states of the Old Northwest around the exclusion of not only slaves but also of Black people in general. In calling their towns "sundown" ones, Midwesterners created an illusion of being without a race problem, even as they betrayed a deep commitment to white supremacy.

But my birth and parts of my childhood took place in other cities much more like those of the South in racial geography. Black people were present in my life in East St. Louis and Cairo, Illinois, but under threat of removal and confined, often by Democratic Party politicians and brutal policing, to their "place." Both Cairo and East St. Louis also became in my youth thoroughly "abandoned" cities, forsaken by employers, state aid, the white population, and ultimately much of the Black population. This pattern created a popular association among whites of African American self-government, as things finally changed, with failure. This seemed to true believers in whiteness to justify the view that Jim Crow needed defending. I suffered exposure to variants of the white supremacy bacillus—from sundown town to abandoned city—finding their clashing forms puzzling but later appreciating that they cohered.

Accounting for a geography that schools whites in meaningful *an-ti-racism* gets trickier. If, as Marx once wrote, "Consciousness does not determine life: life determines consciousness," escape from the racial ideology of the sundown down and the Jim Crow city must ground itself in something more than reading even the best of books. Such books were in any case unavailable to me, K through almost 12. Sundown towns and abandoned cities enforced material facts of life that provided whites with real advantages relative to the Black population.

It's tempting then to write this chapter as the one where I learn racism and sections that follow—describing when I begin to escape my hometowns—as narrating the learning of anti-racism. I hope to resist that temptation. I have not lived yet in any US town or city that embodies opposition to racism. Least of all do the several college towns where I have taught fill that bill. What I experienced in Columbia, East St. Louis, and Cairo did teach racism but the very nakedness and variety of their racist practices also trained me to appreciate fissures in the system and to seek out resistance to it. That process took a long time and it took me longer still to connect miseries among whites with a commitment to what James Baldwin has called the "lie of whiteness."

Born in East St. Louis?

I steer clear of that "Where were you born?" cyber-security question. My responses have been so varied that I have had to guess what I might have set as the answer when I was first prompted to do so. My birth certificate says East St. Louis, Illinois, a weighty place to be from and one that has only grown more urgent to understand. As my parents approached the hospital there before my birth in 1952, the city limits sign would have placed its population at 82,366, the total from the 1950 census. An important railway center, its massive packinghouses attracted diverse immigrants in the early twentieth century. The murderous 1917 white riots against Black workers failed in their attempt to create an all-white city. Black institutions soon thrived again.

The year I arrived newborn also saw Chuck Berry launch his career on electric guitar at the city's Cosmopolitan Club. Trumpeter Miles Davis, raised partly in East St. Louis, released his second album that year. The trumpet came to be closely associated with the city because, as the poet and critic Quincy Troupe observed, marching bands thrived there, often led by German American directors. Shortly after my birth the bright star soon to be known as Tina Turner began singing with Ike Turner's Kings of Rhythm at the city's Manhattan Club. A decade later the dancer, choreographer, teacher, and anthropologist Katherine Dunham—the *Washington Post* once called her "Katherine the Great"—moved to the city.

East St. Louis now has 16,671 people, though its traditions of Black creativity and athletic excellence continue. Its tragic decline came fast but could hardly be called unexpected. As the fifties ended, the Armour meatpacking plant and Alcoa's nearby aluminum ore facility phased out production. Even before they helped make East St. Louis what the sociologist Jennifer Hamer has called an "abandoned" city, these industries structured its problems. The companies created company towns outside of the city's tax base. National City hosted the packinghouse tax dodge and Alorton (get it? Aluminum Ore Town) did that for aluminum production. Bordering the city's south end was Sauget, the multi-company town serving the chemical and rubber industries. Inadequate infrastructure remains a pressing current problem, in an East St. Louis chronically under threat of flood, especially given toxic waste left by the industries. Though proximate to perpetually redeveloping downtown St. Louis, even relatively good housing on the Illinois side attracted little interest among those who might have replaced residents losing industrial jobs. Whites in surrounding areas remark on abandoned private homes as the index of all that is wrong with contemporary East St. Louis, but such victim-blaming seldom acknowledges the fact that the stockyards have stood for decades as depressing and dangerous "ruins," unaddressed by capital or the state.

White residents, with greater choices for relocation, abandoned the city comprehensively and fast. As late as 1960, about 45,000 of the city's just over 80,000 residents were white. In 2022, about 300 whites remained. Born into East St. Louis two months after me was tennis legend Jimmy Connors, whose family stayed until his sophomore year of high school. He attended the mostly white, but integrated and excellent Catholic Assumption High School for a year. (I'd have played against him in high school if he had stayed at Assumption and not gotten too good to play much high school tennis). In earlier decades, Catholic high schoolers in my hometown had taken a school bus to Assumption. Public schools in East St. Louis remained minimally desegregated as white officials found various subterfuges to avoid implementing state laws, even after appearing to agree to changes in response to a militant National Association for the Advancement of Colored People protest in 1949.

My family eagerly consumed and created whitelore surrounding the image of East St. Louis. We participated in, and witnessed, the city's abandonment, in a modest way. As it became a Black city, grownups taking me on family shopping trips to the big Sears store there issued solemn warnings as we entered the city. They insisted that we ritually roll up car windows and lock doors, not where the short trip started, but where East St. Louis began. This bit of tutelage in racism—Aimee Sands' important 2008 film *What Makes Me White?* begins by dramatizing just such a scene from her childhood—mattered especially as our cars lacked air conditioning and St. Louis–area summers sweltered. Soon we did not go on such trips. We had donated to, and shopped at, a big St. Vincent de Paul Catholic charity situated where the Great River Road entered East St. Louis. My mother took me as a pre-teen to roam the halls of the wonderful Southern Illinois University-East St. Louis branch campus, the most convenient place for her to finish a degree and to earn raises by enhancing her teaching credentials. The first college I ever set foot in, it disappeared in 1965.

Regional meetings of the teachers' association in which my mother was active sometimes gathered in downtown East St. Louis, once featuring the famous futurist R. Buckminster Fuller, who wanted to enclose the city inside a geodesic dome. The militancy of unionized teachers in East St. Louis helped set an example for my mom and her coworkers to organize more as workers and less as professionals.

Baptized in Cairo

East St. Louis taught me about race indirectly and episodically. I grew up though partly in Cairo, Illinois, where white supremacy carried arms, and mostly in Columbia, Illinois, where police and realtors prevented African Americans from living altogether. Before and after becoming a single parent, my mother got help caring for me during summers and on school vacations by returning to her family where the Ohio and Mississippi Rivers joined, in Cairo. When we drove there the city limits sign first reported a population of 9,100 and then, in the sixties, 6,300. That dip reflected a larger drop, from a high in 1920 of 15,000.

Nevertheless, compared to the small town where I lived most of the year, Cairo did seem a city: a movie theatre, a swimming pool, a public address system at its Little League field, a newsstand, soda fountains, a drive-in, and a tamale vendor. The storied *City of New Orleans* train stopped there. So did luxurious riverboats. Cairo featured overbuilt structures, including a palatial library, a stately Catholic church, an imposing federal courthouse and customs house, and a Millionaires Row of Southern-style manor houses, surrounded by magnolia trees.

Geography and history burdened Cairo. I grew up hearing that the city sat further south than Louisville and Baltimore. The rehearsal of facts regarding latitude underwrote white supremacist claims to a Southern "way of life" and a "natural" racial order. As white resistance to civil rights stiffened, the preferred white way to put it specified that Cairo lay south of Richmond, the capital of the Confederacy. Cairo's hinterlands looked Southern. The region, as far as perhaps fifty miles north, sat within the Mississippi Delta geographical area. Our trips entered the city through cotton fields where, as I later learned, welfare authorities connived with planters to coerce Black labor, including child labor, during the harvests. Two facilities ginned cotton, and a plant processed cottonseed oil. Postcards sold in the city featured cotton fields. The area included vast wetlands, habitats for creatures and plants more associated with areas quite further south. Bald cypress trees, some of them 800 years old, as well as Tupelo gums and swamp cottonwood trees, joined festoons of Spanish moss to announce proximity to Cairo. "Illinois Bayou" names part of the countryside.

Cairo sometimes seemed tantalizingly and tragically close to being connected to liberation. Its name, derived from associations with Egypt and the Nile—pronounced however as CARE-oh by whites in the region and more like KAY-ro by some local African Americans—conjured biblical stories regarding bondage and emancipation. One of the great touches of some of the freedom movement leaders in Cairo involved refusal to call the state's chief executive "Governor," opting instead for "Pharoah." That fortuitously rhymed with Cairo. Positioned geographically at the exact point where prohibition of slavery began to apply on one side of the Mississippi, if approached from the south, it was therefore likewise the very spot the river began to run through nothing but enslavement, traveling from the north.

US literature acutely appreciates the city's drama. In Mark Twain's classic imagining of white solidarity with resistance by the enslaved, *Huckleberry Finn*, Cairo stands as the goal as Huck and the fugitive slave Jim raft down the Mississippi. When he thinks he's spotted the city, Jim enthuses, "We's safe, Huck, we's safe! Jump up and crack yo' heels! Dat's de good ole Cairo. . . ." Except, not quite. Cairo figured in the novel less as the promised land than as a turning-off point, a place to hop a steamboat heading up the Ohio River to other places symbolizing real freedom. Southern Illinois did not itself signify a refuge to Jim. If it had, he could have disembarked from the raft long before reaching Cairo or just crossed the river to freedom in Illinois from his hometown of Hannibal, Missouri. Even ascending the Ohio River would have left Jim situated as before, between slavery on one shore and nominal freedom on the other.

Herman Melville's under-appreciated novel of the Mississippi, *The Confidence Man*, similarly played with Cairo's ambiguous relation to freedom. As the riverboat on which it is set approaches that city, a pair of white characters frivolously dispute weighty issues concerning slavery. One overstates, "come from Maine or Georgia, you come from a slave-state, and a slave-pen, where the best breeds are to be bought up at any price."

Cairo's ambiguities grew from being in a state where slavery was prohibited, but where exceptions were at times made for labor in downstate salt mines, for slaves already present, and for seasonal labor needs. It was a state where authorities and vigilantes opposed and surveilled any free Black presence. The Illinois Black Law of 1853 staked out the most aggressively racist policies toward exclusion in any Northern state. Black emigrants became subject to steep fines for their very presence and, if they could not pay, to forced labor. The law enshrined what Nikhil Singh calls "whiteness as police" by encouraging white vigilantes to join in enforcement, incentivizing the process through bounties. Some white vigilantes took the logic a step further, calculating that the real payoff lay in kidnapping Blacks and selling them into slavery in a "reverse underground railroad." It was in this context that some whites in Cairo hoped to remove the small African American population in the 1850s and to recreate the city as a sundown town. Ink was scarcely dry on the 1853 statute when Joseph Spencer, a prominent Black businessman and gambler, avoided being held for trial by using a gun and a keg of gunpowder. He escaped to his boat, resisting further against a mob approaching by land and river. His vessel torched, Spencer attached a weight to himself and plunged into the river to his death, escaping at least the atrocities accompanying many lynchings.

In 1857, when a kidnapping and attempted sale into slavery ended in the escape and return to Cairo of one victim, outraged whites began pogroms that featured burned-down Black lodgings and bloody street confrontations. Mobs drove many Black residents away from the city but some persisted. Having tried lawlessness, the mob followed up with concerted efforts to enforce anti-Black Illinois laws and to collect bounties, soon able to cite the Supreme Court's Dred Scott Decision as endorsing the view that African American rights need not be respected. Cairo's status as a hub on rivers where many African Americans labored and as a railroad center would have made enforcement of sundown restrictions difficult. Still the outcome was uncertain. In 1860 only 47 of Cairo's 2,168 residents were African Americans.

The Civil War shifted matters remarkably, reconnecting Cairo with freedom. The base of General U.S. Grant's operations on the Mississippi, the city's total population quadrupled in wartime, but the African American population rose nearly twenty-fold. The city hosted the Cairo Contraband Camp, sustaining those who had moved or been out of slavery, but were not yet emancipated. Grant encouraged placing the fugitives in jobs and by 1870, and with emancipation secured, 1,849 Black Americans remained. Cairo had suddenly become 30 percent, and by 1900 at least 40 percent, Black. A boom in Black institution-building matured. By the turn of the-century one Illinois African American in twenty lived in Cairo. It remained unclear which race constituted most of the population, though censuses through 1960 tended to produce official results roughly indicating a 60/40 white majority.

As in East St. Louis, extraordinary Black cultural production issued from Cairo. The confluence of rivers and intersection of rails also proved a nexus for the exchange of musical ideas. Luminaries included the fabulous bluesmen Henry Townsend and George "Harmonica" Smith, blueswoman Mama Yancey, and actor Rex Ingram. Perhaps the most vivid depictions of slave resistance by a US artist came from Cairo's Hale Woodruff, creator of the breathtaking *Amistad* mutiny murals. One of the great pleasures of my years with the Chicago Surrealist Group was to meet and speak alongside the marvelous surrealist artist, trumpeter, and beat/jazz poet Ted Joans, also a product of Black Cairo. "Jazz is my religion," Joans insisted, "and surrealism is my point of view."

As late as 1910, some Cairo whites floated the idea that total exclusion remained possible. In 1909 the city had become the site of one of most notorious mass "spectacle" lynchings in US history. Anna Pelley, a young white woman who had left work in a Cairo shop, was raped and murdered. Press accounts emphasized a violation of white womanhood and supporters raised contributions for a monument to the victim. Police focused on two Black suspects. One evaded them for a time, but the other, William James, suffered arrest. Perhaps the sheriff took seriously the need to at least appear to adhere to Illinois' recently passed anti-lynching law. Perhaps he realized—as investigations by the crusading Black journalist Ida B. Wells later showed—that authorities lacked evidence against James. In any case the lawman, a deputy, and the accused fled together into the woods. Tipped off, a mob of 300 commandeered a train north, confronted the sheriff, and seized James, returning him to Cairo just after dark. In the woods the lynchers had had time to plan and publicize. A crowd of 10,000, equal to two-thirds of Cairo's population, gathered in a bustling downtown area, hanging James from an arch over the city's brightly lit Commercial Avenue, where the street railway ran. Accounts have an elderly white woman issuing the fiercest call for blood and children running through the crowd.

After the noose gave way, assailants riddled James' body with bullets, decapitated it, and set it afire. His charred head, displayed on a pole, became one of an extensive set of postcards documenting the lynching. The dismembered body itself, carved into pieces, furnished its own relics. In a 2012 documentary on Cairo one historically minded white resident reported that he knew people who still privately displayed pieces of the body. My own family did not traffic in such horrors but having sites of white terror pointed out was part of my youth in Cairo. My great aunt, who put me up, passed almost daily the site of James' murder as she got to work. The brutality of the mob had commingled with a convivial and festive atmosphere, and in her award-winning 2006 book-length poem on the lynching Martha Collins mixes images: "roast the body. in another place, / the barbecue we had . . . ."

In 1910, attempts to lynch two African Americans around the alleged theft of a purse ended only when authorities fired into the crowd, killing the son of a former mayor. Termed by one organizer a "holiday," mob action had the grim goal of "lynch[ing] enough to scare the rest of the negroes out of town." That same year John Lansden, a Cairo lawyer and politician sympathetic to civil rights, published the first modern history of Cairo. He acknowledged that James' lynching was anything but regrettable to most of white Cairo, who disdained the allegedly "worthless and debased negroes in our population."

The Black population persisted, too large to be displaced. Cairo's elites had moved instead to destroy African American political power, very much on display in struggles over the disciplining of the sheriff who had failed to protect James. The city soon replaced ward-based voting, in which Black voters could elect representatives, with an at-large city commission under which white voters could choose one of their own in every contest. Oddly, the connection of the James lynching to a hardening policy of blanket racial exclusion took place just to the north, in Anna, Illinois, where the memorial monument to Pelley eventually materialized. There, exclusionary patterns had begun before 1909 but gained a fiercer edge after 1909. The town's name was said to stand for "Ain't no [n-word, plural] allowed."

It is tempting to regard Cairo as having been cursed by the James lynching. Its population peaked around that time. Subsequent decline baffled locals, who reflected on the good fortune of their location and who had at times believed their city would surpass St. Louis and Chicago, maybe even become the nation's capital. The idea of a haunted city has surfaced regularly in popular memory.

But material realities provide better explanations for the city's down-fall than James' ghost. Some of what burdened Cairo had little to do with race. Amid changes in transportation systems, geography failed to deliver on its promises. While Cairo's advantages seemed to turn mostly on rivers, the city had also profited as a center of railroading. When the Illinois Central opened in the 1850s, it linked Cairo, Chicago, and the lead mines in the state's northwest corner. That route underwrote the railroad's brief claim to be the longest in the world. At its completion, the 1889 railroad bridge across the Ohio River set records as the world's longest such metallic structure. However, just before the James lynching a modern railway bridge at Thebes, twenty miles up the Mississippi, began carrying traffic. This change, plus mechanized and sped-up river traffic, meant fewer layovers due to cold weather. Barges could now break through ice jams, lessening Cairo's advantage as a warmer place where river traffic could move and workers could stay awaiting thaws upriver. The city's large ferrying industry fell victim to the proliferation of bridges, including by the thirties those carrying wagons, pedestrians, trucks, and cars across both the Mississippi and the Ohio. The huge mill cutting lumber for the celebrated Sears prefabricated home kit, shipped by rail and built on site, thrived for a time in Cairo after opening in 1911 but ended operation within three decades. Lumber manufacturing in the city also declined because of the over-harvesting of nearby forests.

The most direct economic impact of James' lynching was to the vice industry. Although he earned his living as a teamster, some in Cairo imagined James as a product of the underworld of gaming and pros-titution in a wide-open river town. The crowd that lynched him was termed a "sporting" one, supposed to be involved in the city's nightlife. Moral reform attempts to clean up Cairo followed. According to some local narrations, they deprived the city of a big chunk of its economy, though it can hardly be said that the Cairo of my youth was without its underworld influences and vice districts. Some were what historian Kevin Mumford has called "interzones." These hosted pleasure, crime, and contact across the color line. In his wonderful reporting from Cairo in 1971, the late journalist J. Anthony Lukas, whom I later came to know and treasure, found an old-timer who recalled the street numbers of a dozen houses of prostitution to which he had delivered customers from the river, with one vice district serving ordinary workers and another the aristocrats of river labor.

The culture of civic lawlessness went far beyond vice, with the city functioning in defiance of federal and state laws to enforce Jim Crow. Despite Illinois legislation in 1874 and 1885 barring segregation, Cairo maintained Jim Crow public schools for a century after the Civil War. Challenges to those disobeying the law first came in the form of legal cases seeking equal pay for teachers in segregated Black schools. A 1911 suit argued by Lansden, the local historian, seemed to win that right. Nevertheless, in 1946 the Negro City Teacher's Association was in federal court over just the same issue, with a young Thurgood Marshall arguing their side and enduring open race-baiting from the defense. In 1952—I was born that year and baptized in Cairo the next—the National Association for the Advancement of Colored People (NAACP) hoped that Illinois law could finally be enforced using school funding mechanisms. Dozens of Black families applied to send their children to white schools and, seemingly out of legal options, authorities processed those applications. The NAACP met Cairo's school board and in February Black students desegregated Cairo's schools.

When the law briefly held sway, "White Cairoites responded with cross burnings and shotgun blasts," according to a *Time* magazine reporter. Attorney David Lansden, representing a new generation of his family's lonely white witness to civil rights in Cairo, suffered arrest along with NAACP members and two mothers unaffiliated with the NAACP. Charges focused on "conspiring to cause or permit children to be placed in such a situation that their lives and health were endangered"—that is, encouraging them to exercise their civil rights. In short order, the homes of two Black dentists came under gunfire and that of a Black doctor was firebombed, as was the business of a tire dealer who served as the NAACP's vice-president. Within a week, only thirteen Black students stayed in white schools. The legal case and simultaneous use of extralegal threats are continuing features of white supremacy's rule in Cairo. In the early seventies the younger Lansden found his home illuminated by a neon arrow, mounted in the next-door yard. The neighbor who installed the light explained that he wanted vigilantes to know which house to bomb.

De facto school segregation managed to survive in Cairo long after the 1954 Brown decision in which the US Supreme Court ordered schools to desegregate. It only ended in 1967. As the Time reporter noted, Jim Crow also applied at the city's whites-only public pool, built by a New Deal Agency, at its Gem Theater, its gorgeous library, its restaurants, and its manicured uptown St. Mary's Park, home to an impressive baseball diamond—in short at all the places that made life in Cairo bearable to me.

When legal and political challenges to segregation matured, white leadership in Cairo proved unwilling to negotiate what it would take to preserve a livable city. If Atlanta could at least plausibly market itself as a place "too busy to hate," Cairo increasingly became one too hateful to be productively busy. As soon as it became clear that Jim Crow public schools were ending, white parents who could afford tuition sent their kids to a local all-white academy, extravagantly named Camelot. Its founder, Larry Potts, also minister of the large and well-appointed white Baptist church, was just months away from having avoided prosecution for beating to death an elderly Black man whom he had charged with attacking his wife. When the Cairo pool failed to survive as a Jim Crow space because neither intimidation nor the subterfuge of pretending it was a private club any longer worked to evade the law, city fathers simply allowed it to be abandoned.

According to the reminiscences of local activist Anne Winters, reporting in Newsweek on the pool closure caused the sale of that magazine to end in Cairo. The offending line read: "White people swim in the pool and the colored people die in the river." When integration "threatened" the Little League in the late sixties, leaders suspended the games.

My mother's reaction to the closing of the pool spoke to the complicated ways in which what the sociologist W.E.B. Du Bois called a "blindspot" about race operated among whites and especially among poorer ones. "Now," she said of the closing of a pool built in her teens, "kids will start drowning again." That is, given low-lying Cairo's long hot summers, the rivers and their overflows would tempt children irresistibly. Without a pool, swimming would again be poorly taught and unsupervised, often in dangerous currents. It was a humane comment and even a class-conscious one. She knew that her richer distant relatives had access to swimming at the country club to the north. Nevertheless, it did not move her to register the fact that during the three decades the pool existed, only for whites, Black parents had to worry over all those fatal attractions of the rivers. They were always without any place for their families to safely learn to swim. Like many whites in Cairo, my mother did not so much disregard Black miseries as fail to regard them at all, until she changed her views in later life. My own understanding—I was ten—stopped at just the same point. I saw the closing of the pool as a tragedy, for me.

In many ways my mother's life in Cairo illustrated why Du Bois insisted that the behavior of ordinary whites who failed to challenge a system that gave them little required explanations that were material—but also more than that. Whites received, he said, a "public and psychological wage." That is, in addition to higher wages, better jobs, and greater wealth than African Americans, whites all knew that the best parks, pools, and schools were theirs, and could at least hope that police power would not systematically make them victims. To the extent that whites regarded these as their natural rights—even, as the legal scholar Cheryl Harris puts it, as their property—they scarcely acknowledged advantages, perhaps especially if their lives held challenges even with the advantages.

My mother, born in Cairo in 1922, became an orphan by age five. She lost her mom at two as a result of complications from the births of her twin brothers. Her dad, a skilled worker in a railway brotherhood that reserved jobs for whites, acquired three small houses as a young worker but died in a work accident as she started school. The family retained one house with her widowed grandmother raising my mother and the twins there. The white advantage of my grandad's access to a skilled but dangerous Jim Crow job sustained a very disadvantaged family. A polio epidemic left one of the twins, James Lind, with a serious limp. He intimated later in life that he was a runner in Cairo's underworld in his teens. Accumulating enough cash to buy a fast car on credit, his white skin did not protect absolutely. He was left for dead in the Ohio River bottoms in a combination gay-bashing hate crime and auto theft.

My mother—much more on her life comes in a later chapter—and the twins benefitted from excellent Catholic school education, first at the grade school associated with the Irish parish three blocks from their house, and then at the high school associated with the German parish further uptown. Catholicism likewise practiced Jim Crow. At least in reminiscences, my mother's map of social difference in her youth did not include African Americans at all. Her nemeses in growing up years were "publicans"—the white public schoolkids—who derided her and her parochial school peers as "cat-lickers." Her aspirational peers were whites living still further uptown, past the pool, and often around the magnificent park, both of which welcomed her and excluded African Americans.

From its 1928 founding until its closure in 1963, students at the small all-Black St. Columba parish had access to a Catholic grade school. At times it had 125 students, those in every grade studying together, and only two teachers, both nuns. One of the dedicated teachers there after World War II recalled very positive experiences but also spoke of students having to miss classes to pick cotton part of the year. School began only in late September, and ended in early May, to accommodate agricultural labor needs. The proximity of the segregated white Catholic school and church to my mother's home solidified her idea that the neighborhood was white and perhaps even that it was Irish. The long block of mixed modest—ours—and better houses on which the family lived was white. However, the damp and mosquito-ridden older part of Cairo near the Mississippi levee where she lived was anything but strictly segregated beyond the block level, making segregated institutions crucial in defining how neighborhoods were imagined and policed.

If the church provided one such institution defining how neighborhoods were seen and saw themselves, the state furnished another. The house that my mother's family owned stood one lot from where 10th Street ended at Cedar. Across Cedar lay the levee but before that, during my mother's childhood, was a stately US Marine Hospital in lush grounds. The facility, one of many such federal ventures scattered across the country, served sick and disabled workers in the Merchant Marine, a federal fleet transporting goods and performing infrastructural work on and around waterways. Built in 1886, the Cairo hospital was probably never anything but Jim Crow, but the Woodrow Wilson administration removed all doubt, making the Marine Hospitals segregated places before suspending operation of the Cairo one in 1919, sending its patients elsewhere.

In 1933 the New Deal's Civil Works Administration's Federal Project F-26 began rehabilitation of the hospital as part of a program for "improving facilities for sheltering transients." It was to become "a shelter for whites" with a smaller structure outfitted "to care for colored transients." Those buildings eventually fell into disuse. However, when sites were chosen for public housing initiated in Cairo after World War II, adjacent land between 12th and 14th Streets and just west of Cedar became the site of Pyramid Courts, the all-Black projects and, by the late sixties, the beating heart of the Black Freedom Movement in town.

Characteristically, the plan for the projects centered on segregation, with the more well-constructed, brick Elmwood projects sited further uptown. The planning probably reflected a sense of history, with the Pyramid Courts projects occupying the same chronically damp land as the Cairo Contraband Camp had in the Civil War. It was a short walk from my aunts' house to the complex where up to a third of the Black population in Cairo lived. Between our house and the projects, a small grocery with a worker-owner from the Middle East—Cairo then had several such stores—did business. Even as a little kid I could walk there to redeem empty soda bottles and use the pennies paid to buy candy. This freedom involved no expression of liberalism; I certainly was not allowed to walk a further bit to play at Pyramid Courts. My Cairo family still, however improbably, imagined themselves as living in a white neighborhood.

Income in my mom's family came from two tough and giving aunts, with the work of feeding and inspiring the household done by a lovely grandmother—for me great-grandmother—who lived well into my lifetime. The older of the aunts never married and the younger separated quickly from a mostly absent husband, who worked on the Mississippi as a boat pilot. The former kept books in a coal delivery company near the site of the James lynching. The latter, Anna Mae Lucas, worked for Southwestern Bell as a telephone operator. Her job required skill and locution that identified it as middle class but it was closely supervised work at a brutal pace. Much of her working life centered on split shifts because sustaining eight consecutive hours was so difficult. Simultaneously, her meager pay stretched to hire a part-time Black domestic worker two afternoons a week, though only because the "maid" had such scant labor market choices. This neglected pattern of white, working-class families and individuals hiring Black "help" strengthened the idea that even poor whites were middle class, uniting their interests in cheap Black labor with those of employers on the river, in factories, in the cotton fields, and in the mansions on Millionaires Row.

The phone company preserved a color bar that restricted its union jobs to white workers for so long that by time the discrimination was relaxed the jobs themselves were disappearing in the face of new technologies. In Cairo, Clydia Koen, a Black United Front activist married to the organization's leader, Charles Koen, helped break the telephone operator color bar, with white workers dogging her efforts. In a recent interview with Barack Obama in which he tried to draw optimistic lessons from Cairo to keep the hope of racial progress alive, he recalled a campaign visit there with Illinois Democratic Senator Dick Durbin in 2004 when Obama ran for Senate. As they drove south, Durbin recalled for Obama his own first visit to Cairo, investigating racial tensions for the lieutenant-governor's office. Just out of law school, Durbin took the bus. A local resident drove him from the station to his hotel and offered advice: "Don't use the telephone in your motel room." The driver added that "the local switchboard operator is a member of the White Citizens Council and is going to report on everything that you say." (I don't think this was Anna Mae, if only because there would have been no constraint barring her bragging about it within the family in 1969, when Durbin had arrived.)

However, Durbin's story does suggest the extent to which the support of white workers for white racism mattered in Cairo. Black workers' class-conscious militancy constituted by far the city's most vital tradition of resistance. African Americans initiated the large 1937 welfare rights protests that ended in a food riot and battles with police. Two years later Charles Hayes, just out of Cairo's Sumner High School, led the organizing of 300 workers at the Bruce Company, makers of hardwood flooring, into the Carpenters Union. Hayes, later a Chicago Congressman and left leader of the packinghouse union, became the

Bruce carpenters local union president, representing both Black and white members. Black-led, integrated labor organizing in thirties-era Cairo was a sufficient threat to make the city reject funding for a US Treasury Department-sponsored mural because it was to depict workers cooperating interracially to place sandbags on the rising river, saving the city from the prior decade's flooding.

The city's largest and long-enduring factory, Burkart Foam, had an interracial local in the Machinists' Union when I grew up. The plant generated abundant charges of both unfair labor practices, initiated by the union, and racial discrimination, initiated by Lawyers Committee on Civil Rights Under Law. Evidence from the latter group in grievances proceedings suggests how white workers benefitted from discrimination and could be encouraged to aspire to management jobs. A Black machine operator at Burkart testified, "They would bring in a white person to me and, tell me to teach him what I know, and he would become my foreman." In 1972 about a third of the factory's laborers were Black. Among foremen however, 36 of 38 were white, among officials and managers again 36 of 38 were white, and among clericals, 24 of 26. In answering such powerful evidence of discrimination, the company noted that three Black workers had declined promotion to foreman, preferring to be in the union. While this hardly accounted for the stark patterns of discrimination, it does speak to class consciousness in important ways. Nevertheless, white workers often dismissed Black working-class demands as self-serving and regarded Black activism as a threat.

As of 2022, Cairo had 1,513 residents, a tenth of its peak and a sixth of where it stood when massive resistance to civil rights began there seventy-five years ago. About 400 whites remain, less than a twentieth of the total of a century ago. Cairo's school system endures under threat of closure. You can't buy vegetables in the city. The last grocery store closed in 2015. The Trump administration shuttered both public housing venues, finally integrated in the seventies, promising only to relocate residents to cities in the region. Online forums make a case for redevelopment as a site of maritime commerce but without planning for renewed local jobs or rebuilding the community. A variant sees a future based on moving *everyone* out of Cairo, leaving only a tourist district consisting of the library, custom house, park, and restored Southern mansions.

Columbia: Social Divisions, Family Strife, and Evasions of Race in a Sundown Town

Columbia, my sure-enough hometown most of each year of my youth, sleeps a dozen miles south of East St. Louis and 130 miles north of Cairo. A key moment in its economic development came in 1875 when a spur connecting it to the railroad from St. Louis to Cairo became operational. The town's history proceeds from Illinois' two founding exclusions: the ethnic cleansing of Indigenous peoples and the banning of Black settlement by early state constitution makers. Built around a grain mill and a limestone quarry and perched on the bluffs overlooking rich Mississippi River Bottoms farmland, the town I remember sported a sign at its city limits putting its population at 3,200. The prior census, closest to my birth, did not count even 2,200 inhabitants. Today a suburb of St. Louis, Columbia's population reaches 11,257. As East St. Louis and Cairo lost 80 percent of their residents, Columbia's numbers quintupled. Its almost all-white population stood as a selling point, with some white flight from East St. Louis ending in Columbia, replenishing the stale stock of lore about African Americans circulating in the town. Columbia currently enjoys a reputation as a hot spot in the metropolitan St. Louis real estate market. It has three Black residents.

Such thorough and longstanding exclusionary practice needed deep roots. The ethnic cleansing practiced in the making of Illinois as a state helped model and sustain it. I knew little of this as a child, though we'd find an occasional arrowhead crawfishing in the creek. Historic preservation regarding the violence of settlement took place mainly in restored forts dating from the period of French settlement before 1765, displacing the carnage to another group of white settlers. The memorials of Illinois' brutal Black Hawk War, which capped the Indian removals from Illinois in 1832, sat further north, where the fighting occurred. Those for the Trail of Tears, the brutal and massive removal of Cherokees from the US Southeast to Oklahoma, but improbably passing through southern Illinois, are closer to Cairo.

A little distance from Columbia, Moredock Lake nestles in the Mississippi River's bottomlands. I passed it often on a bike or being transported to play baseball. Local pronunciation drawled the lake's name, which was said often but appeared only rarely on signs. I heard it as "Modoc Lake," which gave it what sounded like an Indigenous origin, but any Modoc were thousands of miles away.

The truth of the lake's name turned out to be grimmer. I ran across it while teaching Melville's *The Confidence Man* in an American Studies course. Near the 1857 novel's center, readers encounter the story of "Colonel John Moredock, of Illinois," mischievously related second- or third-hand from a then-popular account, loosely plagiarized and tellingly repurposed. Colonel Moredock, a shady character the novel tells us, stopped short of being the "Indian hater par excellence" but only just. Moredock—having repeatedly lost family in clashes with Indians and devoting his life to revenge—is offered by the novel as an example of what Melville memorably calls "the metaphysics of Indian-hating." Moredock, who had quickly risen to power in the Illinois legislature on a path toward a shiny political career, sacrificed it, in Melville's account, to be always ready to attack those whom he so hated.

Was the Moredock Lake of my childhood named for this "Indian hater"? I found the answer in a local history book: "One of the most remarkable persons who ever lived in this part of the country, was John Moredock. In his honor this precinct received its name. His house was on the south side of Moredock Lake." What Melville describes as Moredock's "vacations" from genocide and his respites in the "soft enticements of domestic life" took place on the shore of that familiar little lake. His grave is in a settler cemetery on a high bluff overlooking the lake, one popular in my youth as a spot to get high. Had I been born fifty years before, I could have read of the Colonel in my town paper, learning of his ennobling "eternal enmity against the savage race." By 1959, as I started school and the town published a centennial history, "military history and trailblazing" received praise, but Moredock disappeared.

Whatever the desire to forget, Indigenous presence structured Columbia's history. Kaskaskia Trail, an Indigenous route, was the "deciding factor" in the location of the town, as the centennial history allows. The early US settlements of 1786 to 1790 faced such strong Kickapoo opposition that the form of settlement first featured block houses designed for defense. Only with the end of the War of 1812 could this threat of Indigenous resistance be allayed in the county. Distribution of Indian land became the key to development in the county and the state, with bounties and head rights granting access to land to Revolutionary War veterans and anti-Indian militia members.

Columbia described itself as a "sundown" town. The term describes a dominant urban form, especially in the Midwest, one taking its name from the practice of barring Black people from being present after dark. I grew up knowing that my town was such a place, even believing that there was a law saying as much. Such an ordinance may have existed, but it would have run afoul of Fourteenth Amendment civil rights protections. Police practice and folk belief remained other matters.

The superb historian and sociologist of sundown towns, the late James Loewen, knew of my background. When he based his fieldwork interviewing sundown town residents in Champaign, Illinois, and I taught at University of Illinois, we would sometimes get together after he returned from an outlying village. One day he described a visit to a nearby small railroad town in which residents told of their "sundown whistle" going off at 6 p.m. every day to warn against Black presence after dark. "Sundown whistle?" I asked, adding that Columbia had such a nightly whistle but that it was unconnected to the town's exclusionary practices. I'd heard it almost every day for eighteen years without a second thought. If pressed I would have said it was designed to remind me to come home for dinner after baseball or basketball practice. Jim did not say I was wrong but did urge, "Ask around." The next visit home I did question my mother. "Oh sure," she replied. "When I moved to Columbia the chief of police visited to say I'd be safe" because of the six o'clock warning whistle. The chief, nicknamed "Mr. Dips" and a figure in my own childhood, then explained to her the exclusionary purpose of the alarm.

For all of the efforts enforcing racial homogeneity, Columbia's history was marked by sharp social divisions among whites. Settlers in the period after the US became a nation claimed land based on titles from the period of French occupation, from times of British control, and from competing

claims of Revolutionary War veterans, often from the upper South, some
of whom had fought in the area and returned to settle. Some Virginia
planters bought large estates, brought slaves despite the free status of the
territory, and built lavish houses. Squatters who cleared land and spec-
ulators scrapped, sometimes right in land offices. In the 1830s German
immigrants joined the mix, largely farm laborers but willing to work
for land rather than wages. "Clashes of the two personalities"—Scots-
Irish migrants from Virginia and Maryland, on the one hand, and the
German newcomers on the other—came "in plenty" and were "bloody,"
according to the centennial history of Columbia. Eventually though, readers were reassured, the Germans learned to pattern their lives after the
grace of upper South planters and the latter came to imitate the "thrifty
hardworking Germans" in "this melting pot of America."

Cheery as that thought may have been, the German immigrants clearly
prevailed both in their share of the population and in cultural influence.
No enduring variant of southern US Protestant religion took hold in
Columbia, although a Baptist congregation began what became a very
successful church in the fifties. The Germans split along religious lines.
By the late fifties, as I entered grade school, Columbia had three dominant churches, all founded by German congregations. Two reflected
doctrinal differences among German Protestants. The largest were the
relatively liberal Evangelical Reformed Church with 1,400 members and
the Catholic Immaculate Conception Church, reporting 450 "families" in
its parish. The smaller Missouri Synod Lutheran St. Paul's Church, with
just over 300 members, preached a biblical literalism sometimes ready
to brand even its Protestant co-religionists as being in the service of the
Anti-Christ. The German Turners Gymnastic Association had, from just
after the Civil War, the largest hall for weddings and eventually rock
concerts and sports—and exerted great influence in what was sung and
danced. Elsewhere, the Turners sometimes embraced socialism and free-
thought ideas questioning religion. If those emphases graced the Columbia Turners they seem lost to the historical record and popular memory.

Making It Personal

"Nobody," the critic and theorist Edward Said used to say in a line
expressing with simple eloquence what academics mean when they

say that identities are "intersectional," is "only one thing." My parents and their families surely weren't. Within a common whiteness, and living mostly in a fiercely monoracial sundown town, their differences and similarities shaped my childhood and adult life. Both sides—and everybody took sides—of my family were suffering working-class people who benefitted from white advantage. Both my mother and father tried their hands at being middle class. None of this helped them to be able live out the love story they began in World War II. Their division reflected deeply personal, all-too-human problems, but they also mapped those problems onto the ethno-religious fissures Columbia featured and the class tensions it hid.

In different ways both my mother's family and my father's displayed an alarming interest in whose side brought what to the marriage, whether resources, stellar qualities, or failures. Ear canals too flat and lots of infections? Baldness? Weight issues? Not from our side, each set of relatives insisted, but from the other side. I think a German peasant background, probably on both sides but definitely on the Roediger one, pushed in the direction of thinking about who brought what assets and liabilities, very broadly considered. My mother's teacher training also involved learning lots of eugenics, especially so-called positive eugenics, which involved wise choices of partners, avoiding the alcoholic, the weak, the nervous, the southern Italian, etc. My years, till age eleven or so, of tagging along to lectures at regional teachers' meetings had me passively learning eugenics too.

My mother believed for a long time that IQ scores were destiny. From the start of grade school I always scored off the charts, by southern Illinois standards. This buttressed my mother's faith in the magic of the IQ score but it burdened me with expectations. I eventually learned to bracket all that by figuring out that if musical and artistic intelligence went into IQ I'd have been average at best, worse if had emotional intelligence figured in. Eventually the work of the great paleontologist Stephen Jay Gould debunked IQ more systematically for me, especially by showing its connections to the making of racial hierarchies. For some time though I benefitted and suffered from teachers' expectations based on standardized tests.

One certainty of my mother's "eugenics for schoolteachers" knowledge of IQ was that those with an IQ below 50 were "trainable" handicapped people and those just above 50 were "educable." The former group's destiny was to be cared for; the latter could work independently. When I turned nine, we met a family in Cairo with a child whose IQ my mother ominously reported to be in the 40s. This came at high tide of my taking Catholic catechism classes seriously and I prayed to give ten IQ points to him, thinking it would change his life. In truth, I probably also wanted to shed IQ myself. For someone growing up in rural isolation as I did, the relationship between standardized tests and white advantage far exceeded the plain fact that the tests measured ability in a racially discriminatory way. They also gave the imprimatur of science to elite institutions as they decided which few students from nondescript high schools, where grades were suspect, to admit and anoint.

More German than Irish in lineage and more Irish than German in cultural and political identifications, my mother's family lived two blocks from St. Patrick's Catholic parish, a center of their lives and of Irish American Cairo. By high school, however, mom came under the tutelage of nuns associated with the distinctly German-American St. Joseph's parish. They, like her relatives at home, provided models of female planning and authority decisive in everyday matters, if not in larger hierarchies. For many working-class Irish Americans, sending a daughter to college symbolized social ascent, and credentials as a schoolteacher concretely guarded against a widowhood without resources. The nuns recognized Mary Ann, my mother, as a talented, competitive student, allowing her to skip grades and encouraging plans for college in a family that considered itself "as poor as Job's turkey." Her aunts' sacrifices joined scholarships, her savings from a longstanding job at the Kress store in Cairo, and state support, keeping higher education relatively inexpensive and making it possible for such plans to materialize as the Great Depression gave way to world war. The dime store job again surfaced relative white advantage, as breaking the color line on jobs at "downtown" establishments remained an unrealized goal of the civil rights movement in Cairo through the sixties.

College in this case meant the accessible Southern Illinois Normal College in Carbondale, fifty-three miles up the road. The "normal" identified the school as one devoted to teacher training, with my mother choosing to emphasize elementary education. The school's populist accessibility barely extended to Black students, although from its founding it admitted a few African Americans. In the two years that my mother attended, Madlyn Stalls' 1991 dissertation tells us, Black enrollment remained tiny and Black faculty and administrators apparently non-existent.

Two years of college sufficed in the late-thirties Illinois to certify a teacher. That's how long my mother stayed. By the time that she pieced together enough courses in summer, by mail, or at night to graduate twenty-five years later, the normal school had become Southern Illinois University (SIU), having grown about ten-fold, with undergraduate enrollment reaching towards above 20,000. In 1997, I took her along when speaking at SIU, and she found Carbondale utterly transformed and still warmly familiar. She remembered young loves, spectacularly good grades, and the name of every kind of tree on campus, having learned them in a biology class. But she also remembered hunger, pointing out all the places where free food had been on offer—sometimes just popcorn, but lots of it.

I think my mother chose Columbia because that it was the first job offer that she received. No longer burdening the budgets of her aunts mattered in her decision. No expectation that she pay them back would have obtained, but rather one to pay things forward, as she did in supporting college expenses of her niece, son, grandsons, and a host of others. She never lost track of Cairo but never made any effort to return there to work. Meeting and quickly marrying my dad were the initial reasons for unequivocally relocating, and my birth some years later provided another. They courted quickly as a world war began.

My dad, I was told, wolfed down bananas at that time as his weight was just short of the minimum for his height according to Navy requirements. He joined early and stayed long, seeing the Atlantic and then Pacific Ocean from the decks of the USS Iowa, especially in support of American operations in the Marshall Islands and the bombing of Japan in 1944 and 1945. After briefly participating in the occupation

of Japan and witnessing the damage inflicted there, the ship's crew and
other homeward bound servicemen gathered for a festive return to the
US. At his lowest moments later in life, my dad sometimes wished he
had stayed in the Navy. The exuberant homosocial pictures he kept of
victory celebrations in California suggest some of the reasons why. But
much of the experience of being under threat, around smoke, noise,
and fire, and surrounded—as a non-swimmer terrified of water—by
the ocean surely cut the other way. Whether his later alcoholism mixed
with PTSD in some combination stays an open question.

White advantages and the hidden injuries of class coexisted in the
life of my paternal grandfather, Otto Roediger. His wages as a skilled
mechanic—the 1940 census said "Repairer"—at Columbia Quarry
Company sufficed to support a large family, though he was educated
only through sixth grade. The job held dangers—three fires in the
company's first fifty years with my grandfather very much around for
the 1947 one. My grandmother listened to the limestone quarry both
for the sounds of the dynamite that loosened rock and for the possibility
of a fire whistle. Nevertheless the job counted as a relatively good one.

While the sundown town form of discrimination is sometimes
seen as victimizing African Americans by affronting dignity, limiting
housing choices, impeding travel, and creating terror—all true—it also
functioned in much of central and southern Illinois to literally distance
Black workers from good, sometimes union, working-class jobs. Nor
were sundown towns all small. The sundown twin cities of Lasalle
and Peru on the Illinois River sometimes approached a population of
25,000 people and had a varied industrial base and nearby mines. The
quarry where my grandfather worked employed 125 workers, as the
largest limestone producer in southern Illinois. Other sundown towns
likewise fed workers to the competing quarries that dotted the region.

My dad's family of nine purchased a modest house in town, one
within shouting distance of the median US home value in 1940. His
father and mother joined three sons and five daughters. All but one
of the children had left by the time I was born and it still seemed
crowded, especially when my father returned after his divorce. In size
it approximated my mom's family house in Cairo, but it was a little
better constructed and far better situated on the land. What surrounded

and sat under it held more fascination than the house itself—a cistern, a cellar, a pump, a goldfish pond, and fruit trees, all backing onto a forest, complete with rabbit traps, blackberries and, in the spring, morel mushrooms. Quarry wages kept the family supplied with guns for hunting, fishing gear, and excellent tools.

As my birth approached, my father and grandfather used those tools to help my uncle build a solid house in a new development, enjoying the post-World War II subsidies that went typically to white home-owners. They then turned to building the house in which I grew up, similarly subsidized, one lot up the hill. Otto died in an accident shortly after that house was finished and I was born. Our house cost $9,000, about $101,000 adjusted for inflation in 2022. My mother lived in it for 70 years before her death in that year. It sold for about $200,000 when her estate settled in 2023. It has remained practically unheard of for families in the abandoned cities of Cairo and East St. Louis to transfer wealth intergenerationally through home ownership over the past fifty years.

Selma, my grandmother, labored constantly, largely without recompense. Exceptions included the money that my father gave her after moving back home post-divorce and similar contributions by one of my aunts who lived at home while working in St. Louis. My grandmother fed toddlers in the extended family by easing a spoonful of food to the mouth and insisting "Put it in the crusher," alluding to the quarry's machine for making smaller stones out of bigger ones. Selma's work kept the household fed, well, and at least a little German. She spoke snippets of German around the house, with the answers coming in English. Five of her children took jobs in St. Louis, with four moving there but three later returning.

Every Sunday was a homecoming and a feast. I later learned from the historian Dorothee Schneider that some German American immigrants regarded their ability to have meat for breakfast as critical in judging whether or not migration to the US had been a good choice. My grandmother surely agreed. Sunday dinner likewise featured meaty dishes, often from German recipes. The family presented a triple threat to rabbits, trapping, shooting, and raising them to marinate into the German stew *Hasenpfeffer*. The rabbit I kept carried the perilous name

Hasenpfeffer. Sundays turned then to the playing of pinochle and drinking rivers of lager beer.

Even within a very German American town, my dad's family members thought of themselves as especially so. Selma raised me when my mother had to work after school both before and after my parents divorced. Her English stayed relentlessly accented with "w" and "v" sounds inverted, "j" rendered as "ch" and "gr" becoming "cr." Baseball contributed to English and much of our time was very much devoted to listening to Harry Caray announce St. Louis Cardinals games. I learned to keep the box score of games, strangely enough, on her kitchen table. Her habit of briefly turning off broadcasts of games going dismally to "change the luck" of the team became my superstition too, transferred ultimately to all radio and television sports watching.

The Roedigers practiced that brand of Lutheranism associated with the Missouri Synod, a conservative body politically and theologically. My parents very much considered themselves to be in a "mixed marriage," religiously rather than racially. They married in a civil ceremony and postponed figuring out how they would later live, let alone raise a child, while the war raged. Perhaps my mother miscalculated in thinking that she could do without Catholicism and knew she did not want to live without my dad. For a dozen years no baby came. When I did, in 1952, they mutually repackaged the arguments raging between them as religious, or more precisely about my religion. My mother spirited me away to Cairo for a Catholic baptism.

Even my name, and subsequent confusions regarding it, reflected religious belief. My parents always intended to raise me as Randy, but my mother reckoned that a Catholic saint's name was needed too— apparently no Randy had ever risen to status of Catholic sainthood— and David was added. For the sake of flow, the order became David Randall. I responded only to Randy until I was 22 but was too shy to make corrections in graduate school and ended publishing only as David, eventually sliding into being called Dave in private life, except in Columbia, Illinois or among family and some old undergraduate and New Left friends.

My dad was not in the least a churchgoer, as the Lutheran preacher menacingly pointed out at his funeral. Nevertheless he accepted his sisters dragging me to Lutheran Sunday school. One resulting blowup concerned my coloring Mary's clothes green in a manger scene. Here my mother's family took the offensive, deeming any deviation from blue in Mary's clothing an attack on the whole idea of a virgin birth. It could have been about anything. My mom, for example, swore I shared her hatred of coconut and my father equally maintained I shared his taste for it. I situationally wolfed down or refused Mounds bars. But usually the troubles got couched as religious wars with high stakes.

Ultimately, with my mother having custody of me in the divorce, the fact of my being raised Catholic came to be a little less fraught, although I tended to get sick and miss milestones like first communion and confirmation. A curious rule of my mom's employment, one that speaks to divisions in the town, kept the explosive issue of my going to Catholic school from arising. No public school teacher could send a child to Catholic school! I therefore went only to Sunday school, mostly memorizing the catechism, which seemed reassuring at the time.

My first childhood memories are of two sorts. One set has me going to bars with my dad, Art Roediger, and becoming a pretty good player of coin-operated bowling games and pinball machines, for a five-year-old. My father excelled in bars, especially early in the evenings, the time when I was most likely to be allowed to come along. He smoked stylishly, like a movie star, both he and I thought. He kept up his end of the banter during dice games, which were less about who'd pay for the next round than about extending the total number of rounds. You could joke with him, even at his expense. One local bar had a duck decoy—used by hunters to attract birds—with a sign earnestly crediting my father with bagging it. Local strictures against shooting a sitting duck were pretty severe, for sporting reasons, so the display came at his expense. But he rolled with it. His routines provided a certain regularity and economy: a shot of Ten High with a beer back. The grimace he allowed himself after the shot seemed worth learning until its costs became apparent.

As the nights went on, the fun ebbed. Late nights could see him catatonic in a corner at home, nevertheless determined to try to smoke. The years also took a toll. His balance failed, his driving became erratic, then reckless, occasionally suicidal, and finally preternaturally slow.

He had trouble being anywhere but at a bar or at work and eventually began to drink at work. He attended only one of my many baseball and basketball games and our one attempt to play catch—he'd been a good high school third baseman—ended with him getting hurt. My parents divorced when I was seven. In the aftermath his sisters came to fetch the hunting rifle and shotgun he kept in the hall closet. This delighted me not so much because I was scared of getting shot but because my father had shot a family dog chained in the backyard for barking. In the aftermath of the divorce an Alcoholics Anonymous Big Book sat at the ready on the nightstand in his room in his mother's upstairs, without result.

My father died, of liver disease and heartbreak, in the St. Louis Veterans Hospital when I was 15. He had just turned 46. So much of his troubles with my mother got couched as being about me and my soul that I was long tempted to imagine that those troubles were caused by my coming along. Perhaps my parents could have coexisted in the same house without a child. During the longer stretches of better days each parent convinced me I was loved, but the blowups put that in doubt.

Dad's death particularly gutted me because it offered a last chance for me to feel responsible. No longer able to work at the quarry, he had taken severance pay and moved to St. Louis. I could not yet drive and saw him only once, in a hotel room full of Ten High bottles. He then moved in with family in the city and talked of using his severance money from the quarry to join two of his sisters in a dry-cleaning business. He was right in thinking that a corner of his problems lay in working for insufferable bosses. I thought things were looking up, but he declined quickly. His brothers and sisters, desperately sad, blamed me—and through that my mother—for having abandoned him. I'd lost interest in most of the family by then and seldom saw them, except for my next-door cousins. But the fallout from the death did cost me seeing my grandmother, whom I still treasured.

The other set of my early childhood memories registers anxieties concerning my dad's aggressive upset at my mother's trying to take me to see her Cairo family. In one incident he tried to prevent us from boarding a southbound train. In the other, he confronted my kindergarten teacher, whose family lived near Cairo, for giving us a ride there in her car. While my baptism in Cairo puts such hostility in a religious frame, the drama over going to Cairo, like so much else in my parents' relationship, was not just, or even mainly, about religion. To have a career after becoming a wife was rare in the forties and fifties, though changes were afoot. At the start of World War II, and thus of my mother's career, 87 percent of school boards refused to hire a married woman; 70 percent would not keep in employment a teacher who then married. By 1951, less than a fifth of school boards barred hiring a married teacher and just a tenth refused to retain a newly married teacher.

Working after becoming a mother was rare in the larger society. My mother took the first year of my life off but then worked steadily for another 37 years. The ideal in the Roediger family remained a male breadwinner and a non-working wife. Those marrying in, male and female, were strongly encouraged to organize their Sundays around a family dinner that was not for their biological family. My parents were inventing, or rather failing to invent, a new form in which the working wife and mother would exist far beyond the ranks of the racialized working poor. The change simultaneously empowered and endangered my mother.

While his brothers followed their father into skilled blue-collar jobs, one a printer and union leader and the other a pipefitter, my dad bucked that trend. Clever and good with numbers, he took a white-collar job at the quarry after World War II. Being employed in the office meant he was not in the union. He kept the books in the company's headquarters, right next to where limestone was crushed. He shared office space with the quarry's owner and his wayward son, the company's heir apparent. In the next room several other clerks and technical workers toiled. The owners came and went at will; my dad clocked in and out. The owners showily kept copies of Playboy on their desks.

My dad increasingly smuggled in whiskey bottles, having just enough unsupervised time, and for a while enough wits, to drink while doing a thankless, demanding job scrutinized by two bosses, their desks each not fifteen yards away. That setup helped to kill him before age fifty. The owners dressed expensively in what would later be called business casual attire. My dad literally wore white collars, spending a fair amount to signal success. He was allegedly upwardly mobile. Nevertheless, materially and spiritually, he fared far less well than his relatives in the skilled trades. A particularly painful memory from my early life concerns an extended and wildly drunken family fishing trip designed, I now realize, to distract my dad from the fact that if he'd not taken vacation, he would have been expected to work during a labor dispute at the quarry. He held a working-class job that required a middle-class costume and carried with it specific sets of sadnesses.

My first teenage jobs catered to the baronial properties the owners maintained near the quarry: a disastrous effort to stain a porch and the removal of mussels taking over a pond. The latter taught how little we really can know in muddy water about the difference between a snapping turtle and a shellfish. As I became higher ranked as a tennis player—the quarry owners had a court and a three-hole golf course—I briefly gave lessons to the grandson of the quarry owner. Attempts of my father's family to live a rural German life of hunting, gathering, and fishing depended in large part on quarry lands and on the sharing of access to a well-stocked lake by a munificent bar owner. We were meant to feel grateful. My dad hated, disdained, and sought to emulate his employers in about equal measures.

My mother long made less money than my dad. The professional organization that she joined saw teaching as a respectable middle-class profession. It arrayed itself against unions and strikes, until nearby work stoppages by militant unions attracted raises and set a good example. By mid-career—she taught forty-nine years—my mother was a local union and strike leader. It was only then that she secured something like what was considered a middle-class income. She rarely had a superintendent—save one whom she briefly married—whom she found a reason to respect in either intellectual or practical terms, let alone a principal.

But the alienation of her job cut less into her spirit than in my father's case perhaps. Administrators rarely roused themselves to visit classrooms, and her teaching could be something of an experiment in workers' control, including a firm, strictly personal no-homework policy responding in part to class differences among students regarding having a home environment congenial to working. She taught generation after generation of families and knew that she was extremely well-loved for her work. Even in her 90s a trip to the doctor invariably involved running into someone she'd taught, or whose children she'd taught, whose parents she taught or grandparents.

Whatever they shared in terms of white identity and even class position, my mom and dad could hardly have been more mismatched in other realms. He could not stop drinking, and she professed, eventually convincing me, to never have had a drink in her life. He lit a cigarette before breakfast and kept smoking till he dozed off precariously at night. She smoked once at about age 12 when the cigarmaker father of a Lebanese American friend gave both girls a very potent free sample designed to make them sick in the short run and nonsmokers in the long. It worked, in my mom's case.

My father supported the baseball Cardinals, but not the Catholic Stan Musial. She cheered, almost alone in Columbia, for the Chicago Cubs, hating the St. Louis team but making an exception for Musial. I cheered for, and still support, the Cubs until they invariably fell out of contention, and only then rooted for the Cardinals. By most reckonings that made me neither a "real" Cubs fan nor a diehard Cardinals one. My mother most enthusiastically voted, before their disappearance, for New Deal Democrats. Dad and his family called Franklin Roosevelt the "Great Destroyer" and even denounced Roosevelt dimes. I have voted seldom and then for small, left parties.

Very occasionally these political differences bled into discussions of race, overwhelmingly when my father drank heavily. He had picked up a fair bit of anti-Catholic conspiracy theories—nuns, priests, and sex plus the Knights of Columbus as paramilitary plotters—in Columbia it appears. At least he treated those tales as common Protestant local knowledge—things that everybody knew. But when he spoke with a certain reverence for the Ku Klux Klan or claimed to know about "the Jews," Blacks, and even the allegedly mixed-race origins of the "Black Irish," the Navy and knowledge he imagined he had gained from seeing the world invariably came up. He did not read beyond hunting and men's magazines at that time in his life and was in no way a student of right-wing ideas, nor organized enough to be politically active. But he did have his store of supposed racial knowledge, repeatedly rehearsed.

Reflecting on those performances has raised for me the question of where alleged racial knowledge comes from in all-white and all-gentile towns. Columbia had only one Jewish family, I think, in all my years there. They left quickly.

The association of the middle-class job with some misery and working-class struggles with some forward motion came early to me, certainly before I knew anything of the relevant languages of class. Other habits of mind also came in childhood. One hard-won lesson was that when two painful choices stood on offer it was better to pick neither. I avoided being either pro- or anti-coconut, advocated neither green nor blue for the Virgin Mary's clothing, and soon enough was neither Catholic nor Lutheran. It later troubled me little, critics say too little, to reject both sides in the Cold War and both major political parties. But I had my reasons, or habits anyhow.

2

SAVED

Strands of my childhood predisposed me to think about social difference and to feel my own miseries. But it took social movements
and getting out of Columbia to braid those strands into a fathomable
sense that the world had to change. Just about all of my high school
classmates got out of town quickly. We overwhelmingly left for good.
During my senior year a hundred of us were in the class, so it would
be easy to work out percentages. College, war, and jobs in St. Louis
provided early destinations. I had only one close friend who stayed.
Most of us did not even talk about the possibility of staying. After 1970
we found ways into a beckoning and threatening world. Even as it
quintupled in size, Columbia thus lost a huge number of its daughters
and sons. Both the tremendous in-migration and the outflow made
it lose its character as a German American small town and gain one
approximating a typical St. Louis suburb, though still with sundown
town patterns of racial exclusion.

I'm not concerned with recounting the drama of getting out of a
small town. There wasn't any. I was delivered in a set of lucky hap-
penstances and concerted efforts from ideas supporting the sundown
town and the abandonment of integrated cities. Fathomably enough,
it happened to many friends, on different wavelengths. I was "saved,"
if you will, as the Catholic left and religiously based Black Freedom
Movement in Cairo transformed me.

My initial political act and first sustained reading both came from
baseball. In Columbia, it mattered more than any other sport. The town
remained too small, and with too many of the best athletes doing agricultural labor on family farms after school, to field a football team.
Although St. Louis was a great center of US soccer, we in southern

Illinois small towns did not even know the rules. We played fall baseball instead of football. Then we played baseball again in spring when
the bigger schools did, and of course a full slate of summer ball from
the Khoury League through the American Legion games. A short walk
up the hill took me to the high school ball diamond. I attended almost
every local high school ballgame from first grade on. I scrounged out-
sized broken bats from the field and nailed them together for reuse. The
level of baseball was excellent, but I wasn't. For two summers, at ages
seven and eight, I did not so much as hit a loud foul—no tee ball back
then alas—although I could field adequately and pitched well enough.

The happy result of my two-year slump was that my dad's little
brother tried to sustain my interest in baseball by buying me a sub-
scription to *The Sporting News*. Billed as baseball's "bible," that weekly
newspaper covered everything from the major leagues to the lowest
minors and became a place where I could submerge myself in statistics.
I awaited its arrival in the mail eagerly. It worked to keep me playing
and made me for the first time an enthusiastic, self-motivated reader. In
The Sporting News I happened as a grade schooler on the announcement of
an initiative to make the matchless Negro League pitcher Satchel Paige
a member of the Baseball Hall of Fame. I signed up.

The years I most played schoolboy baseball coincided with the star-
dom of many Black and Latino Cardinal players: Lou Brock, Bob Gibson,
Curt Flood, Bill White, Julián Javier, and Orlando Cepeda. We loved
those players because they brought pennants and World Series wins and
because many brought a freewheeling style and elegance to the game.
For many years my internet passwords stemmed from either curtflood
or loubrock. The late music critic Greg Tate once charged that such
adulation of Black style and excellence often involved whites wanting
to bask in "everything but the burden" of Blackness. Tate stated a fair
point, in our case where sports stars were concerned, and it could
easily extend to the attraction to soul music, Jimi Hendrix, and local
heroine Tina Turner among some of the more voluble racists I knew.
When the sports establishment turned on African American stars, for
example Cleo Hill, the creative basketball guard, a sensation for the St.
Louis Hawks in 1961, who was then run out of the league for his style,
we saw no political stakes involved.

Nevertheless even my immature sensibilities regarding Black athletes contributed to my being ready for antiracist politics, especially when combined with relationships with African American sports competitors. I came to play tournament tennis competitively after age 15, catching a bus most winter afternoons to play and, ultimately, to take lessons, on the wooden courts of a disused armory where Jimmy Connors' mom sometimes taught. I improved fast on shaky foundations, deploying tools from other sports, and soon came to be near the top of the junior rankings in the St. Louis metro area. Tournaments took me to a variety of clubs, suburban schools, and tennis complexes where I did not much fit in, either in class terms or among a group of players who had mostly known each other through years of lessons and play. Apart from my coach, an ex-boxer differently out of place, it was Dr. Richard Hudlin who most welcomed me into this world. Everyone knew Dr. Hudlin as a renowned educator in the city and especially as the coach who hosted and trained the great Arthur Ashe when he spent decisive time in St. Louis.

In the late twenties, Dr. Hudlin had captained the University of Chicago tennis team, the first African American to do so. As World War II ended, his lawsuit moved the intricate process of integrating tennis St. Louis forward. By the time Ashe arrived, he faced barriers but not the Jim Crow prohibitions that he had experienced in Richmond. Because of Dr. Hudlin, I came to know several young Black players, especially from the Blount and Foxworth families, juniors on a path to be better players than I, but with whom I matched up well at the time.

Tennis integrated very late in St. Louis, with Dr. Hudlin playing a persistent, insistent role. There were separate Black tournaments sponsored by the American Tennis Association, but not the US Tennis Association. In 1969, a tournament with a strong field from out of town took place in Fairgrounds Park, where in 1949 a giant local public pool closed after 5,000 whites rioted on the first day that the facility integrated. Shortly thereafter the glorious pool closed forever. By the sixties the neighborhood around the park housed African American families, and the park hosted the tournament. Dr. Hudlin asked me and one other white player to enter and I did not lose until the semifinals. It became harder to believe the whitelore of Cairo and Columbia in such circumstances.

Knowing Dr. Hudlin only increased my love of Ashe's game, grace, and style. As powerfully as he hit, Ashe was relatively slight, though rangy. Me too, minus the power. Truth is, we all wanted to be like Ashe, though relationships with those in his St. Louis milieu made me hope that mine was more grounded admiration. Even though Ashe entered the army and was assigned to West Point, as I joined struggles against the attacks of the US on Vietnam, he stayed my favorite tennis athlete. I found him funny too, in a deadpan way. In perhaps 1969 a downtown St. Louis luxury hotel—more recently famous as an urban ruin two minutes from the Cardinals' stadium—publicized its addition of a single outdoor tennis court by hiring Ashe and three other pros for a casual exhibition match. He'd just contracted to play with a space-age metal racket that looked like a snowshoe and stared at it disdainfully every time he missed a shot, as if it had just landed in his hand from the outer limits of the universe. It delighted me to watch his subsequent political evolution, especially around opposition to apartheid in South Africa. Later in life I got to work with the civil rights minister Jefferson Rogers, whose church Ashe attended, and to hear just how much effort and education went into supporting Ashe's political development. By 1968 my reactions to athletes raising Black Power fists in protests at the Olympics in Mexico City made me think for the very first time that my politics might be radical rather than liberal. But that's part of broader stories involving what I learned in Indiana, Georgia, and back in Cairo.

Finding an Antiwar Movement

I come from a town so backwards that I had to go to Georgia to learn about opposition to the Vietnam War. At least that's what I told friends I met in college. It was even worse than that. I had to go first to rural Indiana and then to Georgia. Both experiences contained juicy irony. The summer I turned sixteen, just after my father's death, I desperately wanted out of both Columbia and Cairo. A brochure at school advertised a National Science Foundation summer program that paid travel and expenses for high schoolers to study science on college campuses. Months later, after I'd forgotten that I'd applied, Manchester College offered me a place in chemistry. Ironically, the initiative reflected a Cold War effort to "catch up" with the Soviet Union in the sciences, though this particular program involved no preparation for military confrontation. Instead, it taught me how to reject the Cold War.

North Manchester, Indiana, home of the college, looked a lot like Columbia. Indiana being a Ku Klux Klan stronghold, the town had an equally troubling past. Its sundown practices clashed with the presence of some diversity at the college. The census before my stay there counted almost 4,500 residents, two of them African American, while local residents later told historian and sociologist of sundown towns James Loewen that exceptions had long been made for tiny numbers of "our Blacks." Lore held that the local Klan, acting on rumor that the Pope's plotting in the US had brought him personally to the Indiana countryside, had once pulled some unfortunate soul from a passenger train in the middle of the night in North Manchester and made him prove that he wasn't the Pope.

Though the town seemed all too familiar, I loved the other students and faculty, if not chemistry. The Church of the Brethren, a small pacifist denomination, ran Manchester College. One English class, with "justice" in its title, supplemented the program's chemistry curriculum. The college kept a well-stocked reading room of materials calling into question what the US was doing in Vietnam. Reading Alaska Senator Ernest Gruening made me think deeply about the war. Gruening cast one of only two votes against the Gulf of Tonkin Resolution authorizing the wider war. He wrote against the war in a very matter-of-fact way that could reach me at that moment. Just as I became excited about this newfound knowledge, I broke my right radius in half in a bad fall playing tennis—a groundskeeper wedging weeds out of the crack separating courts had left his tool sticking up to mark his place while on break and, chasing a wide ball, my foot found it—and had to return home.

The next summer, I hit the NSF jackpot, finding a place at the University of Georgia that was not in the hard sciences but rather in political science. The work I did involved data entry for computer research, complete with punch cards and a computer the size of a boat. The summer went swimmingly in a big program in which high school researchers argued about ideas. A couple of them played tennis at a high level and we met on the university's beautiful clay courts. Best of all, a Students for a Democratic Society chapter thrived in Athens, Georgia, home to the university. The South, which I identified with the postures of white Cairo and lots of horrific television images from the attacks on the Freedom Riders—with Selma and the murder of Medgar Evers—had also produced something else. Several underground papers circulated but my favorite was Atlanta's *The Great Speckled Bird*, an image that I knew not from the Bible but from country music. At least in my head—things were too chaotic to formalize matters—I joined SDS in July 1969 in Georgia. But I then went back to a month in Cairo and sundown town life in Columbia.

All of this happened very fast, as it did for much of my generation. In my sophomore year of high school, I argued in class that non-tax-payers—as Republicans in Columbia and white Democrats in Cairo ridiculously imagined Black people to be—ought not to be able to vote. It was what I'd constantly heard. A delightful young English teacher urged me to remember to revisit those comments after living a little more. In my senior year, radicalized, I wrote a paper on *Macbeth* that argued that the play was OK but was assigned mostly to warn young people of the bad consequences of shaking things up. The same teacher wisely had the same response.

I would probably have gotten to opposition to the war on my own, without help from Cairo, Indiana, and Georgia. Vietnam, and even strains of the antiwar movement, were making their ways to little Columbia as life-and-death issues. The town lost Staff Sargent Robert Holden in battle in Gia Dinh Province of South Vietnam on May 7, 1968, just days before his twenty-third birthday. I'd watched him play ball on the field near our house. At about the same time, one of the most charismatic and athletic of the older students in the school took off for Canada to avoid being drafted to serve in a war that he opposed. That direct action from a seemingly apolitical friend made lots of us realize that our lives were not foreordained to be in the service of the state.

By 1969, after massive antiwar demonstrations and US defeats on the battlefield, the Nixon administration instituted an annual draft lottery, drawing birthdates to determine who would serve. The high number I ended with all but ensured I'd not fight. Nevertheless, in solidarity with friends with low numbers and with the Vietnamese I applied for Conscientious Objector (CO) status, forcing a hearing before the selective service board in Waterloo, the county seat. I lost and probably should have, given that the Catholic Worker pacifist traditions I had picked up secondhand from priests swirled with lots else amidst my flailing for political positions. Indeed, even when I came to identify with surrealism, perhaps the most thoroughgoingly anti-religious location on the left, I thought fondly of the Catholic Workers, especially Dorothy Day and Ammon Hennacy. (St. Paul, Minnesota where I lived years later, was a center of Catholic Worker agitation and charity and even in my 50s I organized an effort along with the Newman Center at the University of Illinois to honor Day, a former student radical there in her pre-conversion days. I loved it when Utah Phillips, the wonderful Industrial Workers of the World folksinger and personality whom I came to know, recalled so warmly learning from Hennacy.)

A draft board member said, not unfairly, that while I professed to be blanketly antiwar I seemed to have more sympathy for the enemies of the US than for my country. My spontaneous response drew on sports, and the magnificent boxer Muhammad Ali, then suffering mightily for "draft evasion"—though his declaration that he "had no quarrel with them Viet Cong" was hardly evasive. My answer at the draft board hearing pointed out that I opposed the brutality that was boxing, but supported Ali against his opponents, political and sporting.

The other memorable aspect of the hearing occurred when I realized who did the clerical work for the board. A family friend, she had just lost her own son who was about my age, to a traffic accident while he served in the armed forces. Her sadness and inner conflict showed on her face throughout the hearing and ended up becoming my main emotional response to the drama. She gave me a first sense of how necessary it was for ordinary people opposing the war to care for ordinary people supporting it. I had been both, and I emphasize this point because of the considerable nonsense that has been written and spoken concerning the supposed animus of the peace movement to soldiers—what the sociologist Jerry Lembke calls the myths of the "spat-upon veteran" and of the "spitting antiwar protester."

In Columbia itself there never was an antiwar demonstration. However, the parents of two of my best friends, along with a young minister in town, began to participate in Senator Eugene McCarthy's 1968 peace campaign in the Democratic presidential primaries. I never caught the "Clean for Gene" fever, nor that brought by the later, tragic Bobby Kennedy campaign. However, to see that support for the war and for police violence at the 1968 Democratic nominating convention stopped short of unanimity even in Columbia impacted me greatly. Moreover, going to out-of-town rallies became imaginable. The St. Louis area peace movement featured the contradictory Teamsters' Union leader Harold Gibbons, whose militancy and corruption reached legendary proportions, and whose tough-talking style at first impressed me.

We also began to seek out speakers offering more far-reaching critiques of US empire. Those included the remarkable St. Louis-raised comedian Dick Gregory, running for president on the Freedom and Peace ticket in 1968, the Peace and Freedom Party seeming to him insufficiently radical. The freedom movement leader Julian Bond spoke in a town about as small as mine, but integrated, twenty miles away and gave me a first sense of how learning history could support emancipation. In May 1968 Catholic radicals who came to be known as the Catonsville Nine seized and burned draft board records in Maryland, and we soon heard about their defense campaign in St. Louis. About this time a dynamic early-career priest rotating through the local parish wondered aloud in a sermon why professedly agnostic young people whom he encountered in the peace, civil rights, and anti-poverty movements seemed to embody humane and Christian values in ways orthodox Christians often did not. I heard this as a call to be a good and serious person beyond being Catholic or Lutheran.

Saved by a Shorter Church Service

Through the time I attended school and lived at home, attending Sunday Mass was an obligation. The ritual seemed tolerable, and I did not resist churchgoing, trying instead to minimize it. I eventually found late afternoon Sunday services in nearby cities, combining late attendance with use of the car. In Cairo, only the long ornate morning services at St. Patrick's seemed on offer until I noticed that sometimes my aunt attended St. Columba Mission. That small Black congregation worshipped just doors from the telephone company where she worked and six blocks from my extended family's house, once again underlining how unevenly segregated the city was geographically. The Black mission church, a cooperative venture of the dioceses and the African Mission Society, remained worlds apart from St. Patrick's where I had attended. I walked to the mission church more and more, attracted at first mostly by the incredibly short duration of its masses. I was allowed to go there by my family after age nine or so. While Black parishioners were made decidedly unwelcome at St. Patrick's, I attended the Black church without incident. That ended in 1963 when the diocese closed both the school and church at St. Columba.

The closures actually reflected a hopeful moment and what seemed a victory for the civil rights movement. After the demonstrations around the integration of the pool and the madness of the white response, the city briefly seemed capable of pulling back from the precipice. An avowedly moderate city government won election and some white ministers joined interracial efforts at reconciliation. A Student Nonviolent Coordinating Committee team challenging Jim Crow began direct actions aimed against restaurant and hotel segregation, with lots of failures but some successes, for example at the big downtown Cairo Hotel. The city known, as the *Chicago Defender* reported, as "Little Mississippi" showed signs of opening up. Closing St. Columba seemed then to presage integrating the white Catholic schools, as planning for integrating the public schools also appeared to be proceeding apace. To me the closure seemed to be just another shutting down of my options in Cairo.

When the diocese reopened St. Columba five years later, that too represented a victory for the civil rights movement, one now interlaced with Black Power ideas. When the young white priest Father Gerald Montroy came to Cairo in August 1968 after an earlier assignment to East St. Louis, it was unclear if the church would reopen or the structure would simply be used for church-to-community outreach. It ended up being both, with Montroy deciding to offer Mass again in response to all he heard regarding how ill-received Black churchgoers were at St. Patrick's.

By the time that I returned to services at the mission church its status in my world changed from convenient to deeply meaningful. The

Black United Front, the central organization of struggle and self-defense against what were now armed attacks on Pyramid Courts and on the church itself, moved its offices to St. Columba. An arresting graphic of a gun and the Bible was on prominent display. The congregation went from accepting a white presence to being downright friendly, in part because the church also hosted Saturday night protest meetings where whites, often from out of town, attended to support the United Front. Impressive leaders, including Charles Koen, Preston Ewing, and Hattie Kendrick, vilified in the local press and in family conversations, now could be seen and heard on a human scale. Koen, only seven years older than I, particularly engaged me. Raised in the segregated projects near where I stayed, he played a central role in the 1962 swimming pool protests as a high school student, receiving a brutal beating for his heroism. The church service at the reopened St. Columba remained short.

Part of the change came from within me. I had learned enough from the beginnings of antiwar activity to want to be on the side of motion toward peace and freedom. Moreover, my wealthier distant relatives and family acquaintances in Cairo had armed themselves against the protesters. One "uncle," very expansively figured, showed off a gun at his clothing store, to make us all feel safe. When the farthest right forces in Cairo took fuller control of local politics he became mayor and the defendant in a series of lawsuits, pressed by Koen, Kendrick, and Ewing, that cracked the near-monopoly of whites on local government positions, power, and patronage. Coming to Cairo by then only once a year for an extended stay and every couple months on a weekend, what I saw challenged not just the morality of the intransigent white leaders in Cairo but also their grasp of reality. The effectiveness of movement boycotts of downtown business, sometimes with mass picketing, could not be denied.

Moreover, the eyes of the nation came to be on Cairo and the reporting could not have harmed the city's reputation more, especially when uniformed Nazis descended on Cairo's downtown to support local whites. Nevertheless leaders of the paramilitary white groups, and then of local government, convinced themselves that a corner was about to be turned, that there was light at the end of the tunnel. Almost no local whites found an ongoing way to support the freedom movement or reign in extremists. By the beginning of my senior year in high school, I was a supporter of the United Front. Lessons learned from that period in Cairo included the fact that while following the money and the needs of rulers explained much about racism, a deeply irrational, hyper-masculine, and tortured psychological dimension also required attention.

Cairo Comes to Columbia

The high school that I returned to that fall remained so small that one could do lots of things. I was the incoming student council president—the prior year one of the candidates had made racist jokes, complete with the N-word, in his nomination speech—and had a column in the high school paper, which I co-edited. In my column I wrote about the peace movement, labor, and civil rights in general, without incident. But then I wrote about Cairo and successfully proposed that the student council annual project should be to raise funds for the United Front there. Suddenly my columns required administrative approval. The principal forbade any money going to Cairo. The compromise on the money-raising issue involved distributing holiday food and gifts in Kinloch, a Black town that had become a suburb of St. Louis. A home economics teacher who also made available to students her cache of popular books on educational inequality, coordinated the distribution. A big success and an education for students who had only experienced Black poverty by driving past it, the drive remained a poor substitute for what might have been learned by going to Cairo.

We took our lessons on the history of racism where we could get them. The only concerted effort to impart knowledge came in my early teens from a young teacher perhaps emboldened because her appointment was temporary. A recent sociology graduate, she clearly had kept her lecture notes on race and inequality. Her class featured the demolishing of one anti-Black stereotype after another. Many of us learned eagerly. However, she surrendered much moral force and seeming expertise the last week of class. In discussing her Texas roots, she allowed that anti-Mexican stereotypes remained supportable, especially regarding bad driving. Our high school sat twenty-three miles from the glorious Cahokia Mounds, a site reflecting a high point of pre-Columbian Indigenous urban life. None of our many field trips ventured there nor did our classes consider Native American history. All of my teachers, K-12, were white.

The issues of free speech and the censorship of the school paper remained hot. It was the era of underground newspapers and the excellent St. Louis *Outlaw* had come to influence us. The two friends whose parents had taken us to rallies and talks and a few others batted around the idea of trying our hand at producing one. Producing even one issue to show we'd not back down from printing what couldn't freely go in the school paper seemed worthwhile. We came up with an inspired, rowdy name, *Huggermugger*, which to us meant disorder. It can also mean anarchy. The local press called it "Huggermugga," the spin I kind of prefer. We wrote about racism and war, in articles and irreverent one-liners, some of which landed while others didn't. The content owed as much to *Mad Magazine* and *National Lampoon* as to the political left. Kindly adults at the Peace Information Center near St. Louis' Washington University and local allies in Columbia helped teach us how to put the double-sided legal-sized sheet onto a stencil and make copies on a Gestetner duplicating machine. We proudly handed it out at school and thought ourselves done, having made a point.

Instead we soon received further lessons in how power works, out in the cornfields anyhow. The very mild and kind of funny paper seemed to the principal and superintendent to require a response. We were hauled into their offices and placed on probation for distributing "questionable" material. The penalty lacked teeth and the local paper did not even publish our names as offenders, but the threat was meant to be serious. The superintendent, my mother's boss, called her in for a firm talking to about bringing me into line. Initially scared, jobwise, she soon had second thoughts that saw the threats as offensive. The school's only guidance counselor, an affable guy who could not get far into any conversation without bringing up his evangelical faith, knew I had been admitted to Yale. He reported that it was his duty to report my trespasses to the college and gave me time to reflect. Getting no response, presumably he sent his letter to some puzzled person in New Haven. We thought that the right to publish had to be defended, which meant producing a second issue. The school officials convinced us that they would move against distribution on school grounds, and we therefore passed them out across the street. Not wanting to be risk being arrested, we tried do so quickly. Help with distribution materialized without our asking from classmates who had long rebelled against school discipline and identified with our defiance. We could then declare victory, and I was done with radical publishing—I thought.

I slowly learned to not always speak truth to power. One teachable moment in this regard came as I was entering my junior year during a meeting in which administrators convened a meeting of the local National Honor Society's members and presumably incoming members like me. We were shown a movie, or perhaps a filmstrip, on the dangers of drugs. The go-to choice in this genre at my school, an anti-LSD vehicle, achieved the just-the-facts vibe of the TV show *Dragnet* while conveying wild misinformation.

As it happened anti-drug films had made it to southern Illinois schools pretty far in advance of the drugs. Some marijuana had showed up and of course students drank when they could get alcohol. I did neither, not being plugged in enough to get pot and warned off of drinking by my father's death. After the film, those who had watched heard school authorities and a policeman address them as student leaders with a grave responsibility to turn in friends in possession of drugs. They asked if anyone were not on board, and I somehow took it as a serious question and volunteered that I probably would not be doing that. My National Honor Society membership was then withheld for a year. The whole truth-to-power thing, it became clear, should include picking of spots.

Changing Plans

Once admitted, going to Yale seemed a foregone conclusion. I'd made it through an interview process, wildly nervous, with a Yale alum lawyer at a big St. Louis firm. Politically New Haven offered a great fit. The celebrated trials of Black Panthers in that city—they would lead to interruptions of a Harvard-Yale football game with chants of "Fuck Harvard; Fuck Yale/Let the Panthers out of jail"—occurred as I decided on schools. Lavish tennis facilities beckoned. Nevertheless a few things kept me delaying the decision. The first stemmed from not knowing that going to Yale was a big deal. Graduates from my high school, if they went to college, went mostly to Southern Illinois University, sometimes to Eastern Illinois University or to Illinois State University and, if wealthy and/or high-achieving, to University of Illinois. If there were college rankings then, I did not know about them. The process of finalizing aid took a long time and the Yale expenses, much as they seem a bargain by today's standards, beggared imagination; a year's cost roughly equaled the value of the full mortgage on our house.

Finally, I was taken with the invitations that continued to come from tennis coaches and academic recruiters. One of those, I think merely based on standardized test scores of Illinois seniors, came from Northern Illinois University. I stayed in the process and before I had to decide on Yale an offer to interview on-campus for a full ride, four-year academic scholarship came. The dynamic young tennis coach at NIU, who had recently recruited Tim and Tom Gullikson, the Wisconsin twins who would go on to impressive professional careers and in Tim's case to fame as Pete Sampras' coach, was in touch. When the offer from NIU came, I started to weigh the tennis possibilities versus Yale and to appreciate that I could either go into what then seemed like steep debt or have college fully paid for and save the government benefits supporting me after my father's death plus the money my mother had put aside for my education. The tennis coach tipped the balance in favor of NIU.

In fall of 1970 as I arrived in Dekalb, home of NIU, the tennis coach announced his departure for Notre Dame. The new coach, recently replaced in a job coaching football, could hardly have been more different than the one who left in terms of a specific commitment to and knowledge of tennis. Dekalb itself seemed woeful compared to my only comparison for a college city: Athens, Georgia. I soon learned that northern Illinois got cold three weeks earlier than my part of the state and warm three weeks later. Nothing blocked what the weather forecasters called "cold Canadian air." What was I doing there? What was I thinking in not going to Yale?

3

HIGHER EDUCATED
Coming of Age on the Left

The process of radicalization, or as the historian Robin Kelley calls it, "catching the Holy Ghost," remains deeply mysterious. Left historians studying the process can rarely describe its workings convincingly at the level of individual transformation. We radicals, despite a century and more of "How I Became a Socialist" stories, have hardly been convincing. Attuned to broad social forces, our accounts are often extremely reticent about all that is personal.

Let me begin—back to Northern Illinois University shortly—with a point peculiar to the mindset of an historian and not available to me at the time. It re-emphasizes that to join the university-based New Left in 1970 involved arriving when the movement was at death's door. The timing—what I have elsewhere called "coming in late" to the movement—mattered greatly. Many of my later closest political associates, and academic radicals with whom I would teach, were but five or ten years older than I. However, if they had come into the New Left in 1965, for example, they had sets of experiences and skills vastly different from mine. If they were around for the 1962 beginnings of Students for a Democratic Society, a central organizing success and tragedy of the campus left in the sixties, they would have attended an initial meeting of less than 100. By 1969 SDS had perhaps 60,000 members, by some estimates 100,000. That year it imploded and quickly became nonexistent according to most of its former leaders and members. I experienced neither the highs nor the lows. Never for a moment did I imagine that revolution loomed around the corner. My passion focused on lasting left institutions we might realistically hope

to build. Conversations that began with "Comes the Revolution . . ."
bored and worried me a little.

Those of my slightly older brothers and sisters in the New Left who
had participated in the Southern civil rights movement had experienced a "beloved community" that was interracial. With the rise of
Black Power struggles, that changed in some ways. Some white New
Leftists I followed into the movement talked with disappointment and
even bitterness about the change, feeling excluded from a Black-cen-
tered movement. My own experience mostly focused on working with
post-Black Power movements, although from Cairo forward those that
encouraged white participation. State repression of Black liberation itself created space for white allies in defense campaigns. My first small
direct act of political resistance was back home on a school break when
I swiped the most wanted poster that the FBI displayed in post offices
while pursuing Angela Davis in 1970.

Similarly, the women's liberation movement and gay liberation had
become a reality during the five years before I entered college. The
"second wave" women's movement blossomed first in Chicago and very
much influenced those on the left who lived an hour away in Dekalb. It
grew in part out of sexism within freedom movements. Learning that
history was important to me even before I decided to study history.
The Stonewall Rebellion and the Compton's Cafeteria Riot, signaling
the emergence of gay and trans liberation movements, had likewise
occurred before I had daily experiences with the left. I felt from the
start that the movement I signed up for was itself a women's liberation
and gay liberation movement.

Nor was I in a position to regard the New Left and a counterculture
featuring drug use and sexual freedom (or, more superficially, bell-bot-
tom pants and tie-dyed shirts) as being in opposition to each other, with
one to be chosen over the other. I was equally a latecomer to both. None
of the small-group revolutionary left, much of which tried to insist on
abstinence from drugs, had a recruiting presence at Northern Illinois.
I still feared drinking alcohol and remained abstemious in that regard.
But I'd made, with friends, a kind of intellectual decision—marijuana
was still scarce at least in our circles in Columbia—to smoke pot. At

college, it was not scarce, but it took me a few weeks to try it, mostly because I did not know how to smoke anything.

The first and only cigarettes I ever bought were to practice so I'd not embarrass myself smoking joints, which I imagined would be social, perhaps because I lived in a dorm where getting high surely was that. I later took up smoking tobacco from a pipe, first as a prop to fool with while waiting for students' responses in my early years of teaching— it used to be fine to smoke in classrooms—and then as what seemed a necessary part of the ritual of writing. I approached such smoking with the emphasis on inhaling appropriate to pot-smoking, managing to produce the sort of moderate lung damage in the ten years before quitting that it takes some smokers a lifetime to inflict.

My belief that being a sex radical was part and parcel of being a political radical was hardly peculiar, and it surely had self-serving dimensions. Whether because of social awkwardness, sadness regarding my dad's death, or too much Catholic dogma, I dated seldom and uncomfortably in high school and not until my senior year. Left literature on sexual emancipation—from Alexandra Kollontai's *Autobiography of a Sexually Emancipated Communist Woman* to Wilhelm Reich's early writings on the "sexual housing problem of youth" to Herbert Marcuse's *Eros and Civilization*—impressed me greatly. The political left on campus was hardly a hotbed of sexual experimentation but it was a place where questions of consent could be openly broached and women's pleasure emphasized, at least in the abstract and with plenty of room for male dominance to insinuate itself. I tended to be in monogamous relationships, sometimes in northern Illinois and sometimes back home with partners who were, as some put it, "leftward moving" young people. The least directly political partners, a student from suburban Chicago engaged to marry but in an open relationship, an Italian American Catholic school graduate, and a woman I'd met hitchhiking in the South, were perhaps the most able to think through the meanings of sexual freedom.

At NIU, architecture and policy haltingly addressed the sexual housing problem of youth. My assigned dormitory was Stevenson Towers, on the west end of campus: a massive outcropping of four linked 12-story buildings literally abutting endless cornfields. Opened only three years before I arrived, the complex housed perhaps 2,500 students. Its scale reflected the state's plan to massively expand NIU, which had been a small teacher's college until 1957. By some accounts the university was slated to grow to 40,000 students by the eighties, and it did rise to 26,000. My stay in Stevenson saw an abandonment, lurch by lurch, of the university's in loco parentis policies designed to keep men and women separated, especially at night. Roommates were of the same gender, as sometimes were floors, and for a time towers. Curfews, about as easily evaded as rules and laws against getting high in dorm rooms, regulated when a man might enter mostly women's spaces, and vice versa.

Contraception was widely available and abortion less so but accessible. Oral contraception had reached the market about a decade before I started college. By the time I left Northern Illinois, Loretta Lynn's "The Pill," an homage to reproductive freedom and women's pleasure, reached fifth place on the country charts despite fierce efforts to cancel it. Sex, drugs, and rock and roll were at that moment both part of our creation of a counterculture and a marketed dimension of the college experience. The culturally transgressive still had its attractions but I also wished for a counterculture with more direct political meaning.

Avenge Jimi Hendrix

Since what comes here describes how I became a self-styled "serious Marxist" in my junior and senior years at NIU, it seems apt to linger for a moment to think about how important cultural radicalism was to my political life—and with what limits. A little graffiti-based history points to how the political and cultural did and didn't quite intersect. Some weeks after I started college, a young woman in the dorm and I caught a ride into Chicago and then took the City of New Orleans train as far south as Carbondale, Illinois. Near the train station when we boarded, we saw very stylish graffiti reading, AVENGE FRED HAMP-TON, the great young Chicago Black Panther leader assassinated by law enforcement not quite a year before.

When we disembarked in Carbondale, graffiti near the college town train station proclaimed AVENGE JIMI HENDRIX, mourning the fabulous rock guitarist who had died in an accidental drug overdose only weeks earlier. The gravity of calling for a response to a political assassination like Hampton's jarred against the seeming frivolity of imagining that what the guitarist John Mayall called an "accidental suicide" of a cultural icon like Hendrix could be avenged. The way that both bits of graffiti moved me probably alarmed my companion.

I'm incapable now of the same mixture of naivete and anguish that led me to connect Hampton and Hendrix as something like co-thinkers. But I wouldn't renounce that connection completely either as emotion or as analysis. The desperation of the late sixties and the callousness of those who ruled lent urgency to calls for an end to misery in the US and 10,000 miles away. We urgently needed delivery from that misery as a political project and as a cultural breakthrough. I would have added revolution to sex, drugs, and rock and roll. I eventually would drop the drugs part and rock never quite covered the music, as country music, soul, blues, and folk also mattered. Still, I got the thrust of avenging Jimi.

Drugs had less staying power in my imagination of how to combat misery. For a few years marijuana relaxed me, especially in social situations. Some old friends moved a bit south and began to farm pot to some extent so that I could pass on some small bags without profit in the dorm. I associated getting high with interracial settings. Pot smoking also lubricated social relationships—and maybe political relationships—with Vietnam veterans. My mind never wanted to be sped up—it erred on that side without chemicals. NoDoz caffeine pills pushed my comfort level and I did not drink coffee until graduate school. Friends on cocaine did not impress me as having a good time nor helping me have one. Even less did being downed out appeal. I took one Quaalude, then the downer of choice, in my life, trying to sleep while on a bus to the march against Nixon's inauguration in 1973. LSD's reputation as a liberatory substance made me try it a half-dozen times but I liked to brag about how little it influenced me, not how much. My last try at taking it came at about age 21 and included reading and taking notes on Lenin's *Development of Capitalism in Russia*. Mescaline, about likewise. In all my years in Dekalb, I never had a fake ID and did not go to bars except to hear music and talk to graduate students.

By the end of my undergraduate years, I was about done with drugs, smoking marijuana rarely, usually in moments of reconnecting with old friends with homegrown pot. On a summertime stay in Boston, after having taught tennis in Maine, I shared with a woman friend a fancy room the hotel-owning dad of students had provided. She had only the slightest experience with drugs but proudly brought a little pot a relative had given her. Laced with something else, the pot produced high anxiety in my friend, and I settled into an experienced user (and guy) role, finishing the joint and talking down her anxiety. Soon I was equally uncomfortable. We walked all over Boston to regain equilibrium. At about the same time, a brush with low-level drug dealing also made me wary. A drug that seems to have been a precursor to Ecstasy came to Dekalb and a friend active in the movement as a veteran suggested we pool money, buy scores of pills, and sell them. I joined in the venture but could not function as the drugs were consumed, worried they might hurt someone.

In retrospect, the experiences I had on the fringes of drug culture reflected white advantage and confidence in it. Back home in early college a deputy sheriff caught us one night trespassing in a nice spot in the bottoms along the Mississippi. I thought I'd kicked the two oversize joints we had under a seat but hadn't. Wrapped in US flag rolling papers, they stood out as the cop's flashlight scanned the car. He simply told us to move on, not even remarking on them. In Dekalb, I lost my wallet while sitting outside on a blanket, listening to music. The wallet contained a joint and a note from a friend about his plan to ship me a box of marijuana he had grown. The campus police called to say they had the wallet. I first thought I'd just not reply. But after waiting a day, I decided to pick it up hoping it would be fine. It was.

Another counter-cultural practice, although it remained also at the time a born-of-necessity working-class one, took me places that taught me much about race. I hitchhiked over 50,000 miles while in college, at (I used to tell my kids) the tail end of the days when getting around that way was safe. That distance stretched around the world, twice. In reality, I mostly just travelled the same routes over and over. About 300 miles separated Columbia and Dekalb. Especially during the two years in which my closest hometown friend also attended NIU, the back-and-forth generally involved hitchhiking. My mother and his parents would sometimes take us to a diner an hour into the trip and then we'd seek rides at a stoplight on Route 66. Returning we'd only have St. Louis as a goal and get picked up there. More fun and warmer were frequent trips South, to New Orleans or the Florida Gulf Coast, with a friend or alone. The experiences, save one brush with a driver armed with a knife and a fair share with drunk or high drivers, affirmed the idea that this was a good way to get around.

Especially in the South we tried to learn what people remembered and thought about the civil rights movement, from Black drivers and more often from white ones. One of the later rides took me and a friend a good distance in a slow car. At first the driver cast himself as a civil rights supporter and then as someone with not-very-guilty knowledge of white terror. We got out hastily in the middle of no-where, somewhere south of Jackson, Mississippi, left the highway a little, unrolled blankets, and unsuccessfully tried for a night's sleep. Mundane exchanges, especially in one-on-one situations, troubled me more and more over time. A ride would start with a white driver trying to generate small talk for a bit. Then I would try. Conversation would soon give way to heavy silences. At that point the driver would fill the void by sharing retrograde racial opinions, sometimes to educate me as a Northerner but more often assuming that as whites we agreed. The important antiracist scholar Vron Ware later shared with me almost the same set of experiences, but hers were in the UK.

Learning to Love Dekalb

I'd put my initial objections to my new home down to the cold and wind, which were not going to change, and the disarray on the tennis team, which I should have been able to process but wasn't. The icy side-walks of a sprawling campus came to symbolize the several problems. Or rather the odd little fences lining them did. Strange little poles maybe two feet high provided suspension for a chain link that drooped slightly as it looped from one pole to the next. We puzzled over the fences, and older students said they had been installed only after the huge student protests of previous years, serving to control how crowds could move across open spaces. At times in the coldest winds (which began in No-vember in my view) I felt so nearly blown away that I was tempted to bend over and grab the chain to avoid Dorothy's fate in the *Wizard of Oz*.

The wind also compounded my problems in tennis, revealing that as much as I could chase down balls, I couldn't really hit through the elements except when serving. I needed coaching badly but had also risen through rankings fast enough that I imagined that I could sort things out on my own. Coaching was not really available from the coach, but the Gullikson twins gave good practical advice, when I listened. I mostly did not seize that opportunity, perhaps in part because they were such great athletes that watching them helped convince me I'd not be a professional tournament player. Nor were there indoor courts at NIU, only lines marked out on a springy indoor track infield available from 10 p.m. till midnight. I did well in the team's hierarchy during fall semester, following on a summer of teaching and playing in St. Louis or in Maine, and declined as the year progressed and activism beckoned. Unfortunately, the matches came in the spring. The exception regarding my poor timing came when I was a junior and played better into the school year. But I was hospitalized with a blood infection right before our spring season.

Even so tennis remained a pleasure. The twins, identical but one left-handed and one a rightie, were a joy to behold, especially in doubles. They and some of the other top players were immersed in fraternity life, but the team also included various interesting characters, including a very talented and well-taught friend more interested in slide guitar than tennis, an unorthodox older player from the Illinois steel town of Granite City, and in my senior year an inspired African American teammate from Ohio. Teaching tennis in Maine offered me a chance to play on clay courts every day with a good staff of talented pros. The experience, an elite camp straddling the line between rustic and luxurious, also sharpened class consciousness.

What had struck me as established institutions and policies at NIU were often instead recent creations born at the juncture of student struggles with relatively flush appropriations to a growing institution. The CHANCE (Counseling, Help, and Assistance Necessary for a College Education) program exemplified this best. When CHANCE began in 1968, less than 300 Black students attended a university where enrollment approached 20,000. Nor did prospects for that to improve look good. The excellent directory of "sundown towns" initiated by James Loewen and hosted by Tougaloo College, lists Dekalb as a "possible" one, with four African Americans among about 12,000 residents in 1950. It lacked effective fair housing policies and did not even have a segregated Black community, though a small one existed in nearby Sycamore.

The tiny numbers of Black NIU students already on campus helped change all that with militant demonstrations after the murder of Dr. Martin Luther King in 1968. One university concession to the protests funded CHANCE to bring in a small group of mostly inner-city students almost immediately and enabled a gearing up to serve 500 more African Americans when I arrived in 1970. Suddenly Northern looked more like Illinois in terms of racial demographics. In the longer run, and despite austere budgets, CHANCE can claim it has aided 15,000 NIU graduates. The student body currently is about sixteen percent Black and Dekalb has over 5,000 Black residents. Although historians of higher education write more about the University of Illinois' recruitment of Black students as part of Project 500, beginning in 1968, NIU's efforts in this regard were more aggressive and enduring. They changed my own university experience enormously.

CHANCE recruited through social networks and the Black students showed impressive cohesiveness. At basketball games, for example, African American fans sat together on one end of the court. They generally did not stand for the national anthem but then rose to sing "Lift Every Voice and Sing," sometimes called the Black national anthem. I had decided at some point to not stand for patriotic songs at public events and this remains the only place in fifty years of sitting where I have been in such good company. As it happened the 1972–73 basketball team went 21–4, the first top-20 ranked team in NIU history, making the presence of inner-city Chicago talent and style ultra-visible, especially in the person of Dunbar High's Billy "The Kid" Harris, later recognized as the best playground player in the history of Chicago basketball. Because tennis had no facility of its own, we shared a fieldhouse locker room with other sports teams, and the two stars with the sharpest ideas critiquing sports and society were Harris and the outstanding hurdler Dan Jacques.

Two of the early places that I put organizing energy spoke to, retrospection tells me, a desire for continuity with my upbringing. Perhaps

I was trying to give my mother, long-suffering regarding my leaps to the left, a break. In going through her things after her death at 100, I found that she'd saved a 1973 envelope delivered to her sundown town home bearing on its back flap: "Agnew's gone and Nixon's shakin' / Today's pig is tomorrow's bacon." The first college activity that she'd have found more congenial involved support of the labor movement, in the form of the grape and especially the wine boycotts of the United Farm Workers. Small contingents of us picketed local liquor stores and supermarkets chanting "You've got to organize / You've got to unionize / You've got to boycott grapes, boycott lettuce, and boycott Gallo wines." Sometimes, in Chicago pickets, we learned to substitute Farah Pants as another boycotted commodity. During the coldest of the thankless liquor store protests—the sometimes-hostile clientele of liquor stores tended to be pretty narrowly goal-oriented—I first made friends with Jenny and Jim Barrett, graduate students in history whose paths would continue to cross with mine for the next fifty years. We had all come to the UFW cause through traditions of Catholic radicalism.

The other activism that registered with my family history, on the maternal side, involved support for Irish nationalism, although at most my mother knew snatches of the songs. For most educational talks and demonstrations I could mobilize at least my old and new friends. They included two other Columbia High graduates who had come to NIU. One, Don Stahlheber, had helped to create *Huggermugger*, which itself included a story on the UFW. Many at Northern joined a fierce struggle against the destruction of a magical central campus arboretum to make way for a dreadful redevelopment project. The pro-Ireland initiatives remained desperately small, however. They centered on myself and one other SDSer learning from a formidable Irish literary scholar newly arrived at NIU and willing to serve as faculty sponsor.

Whether it was the popular connection of Irish nationalism with terror, or fatigue born of so many urgent causes, or the association in Illinois of Irish solidarity work with the stultifying bureaucratic pro-Ireland efforts of the political machine of Chicago Mayor Richard Daley, our educational events remained so poorly attended that we dared not try a demonstration. Nevertheless, in failure I learned more than in many numerically more successful efforts. After reading the powerful work of the young Irish republican socialist Bernadette Devlin connecting African American and Irish freedom struggles and reflecting on the early 1972 Bloody Sunday murders of fourteen unarmed Irish protesters, I called myself a revolutionary socialist for the first time.

I arrived in Dekalb at a very consequential moment in New Left history. As high school ended for me in May 1970, thousands of students at NIU twice shut down the campus, occupying the east-west highway through town. The demonstrations and what the press called "the riots" there unfolded among extraordinary nationwide protests against the Nixon Administration's wholesale bombing of Cambodia. On May 4 Ohio National Guardsmen fired into demonstrators at Kent State University, killing four and wounding nine. Eleven days later police gunfire claimed the lives of two Jackson State students and wounded a dozen. At NIU and nationally such repression sparked courageous demonstrations in response. But deadly force often works to keep people off the streets, or rulers would not so consistently resort to it. As NIU students returned for the fall semester in 1970, student movements stood at a crossroads. At NIU anyway they seemed to stall there, by no means disappearing but without capacity for forward motion.

It took little effort to find the left on campus. The Student Union building featured a variety of tables hawking pamphlets and individuals selling papers. The Militant and Challenge always beckoned, and the Industrial Worker, Workers Vanguard, and many others showed up irregularly. Vietnam Veterans Against the War provided the most theatrical actions, confronting military recruiters with shaving-cream pies and parodies of songs and chants from basic training. Most versatile was "I Wanna Be an Airborne Ranger," dramatically rewritten and delivered in a way that wickedly parodied the recruiters' agenda. A talented graduate student had transformed Leo Huberman's classic history Man's Worldly Goods, a Marxist attempt to narrate and explain the past from feudalism forward, into endless rhyming couplets, and she recited them outside the union. Meeting those sticking around for many rhymes meant meeting some of the left. The performer later taught at the Minnesota high school one of my sons attended.

The right also helped to introduce me to the local left. Smarting from the campus demonstrations in the spring of 1970 and fixated on the ways in which campuses defused the situation by dialoguing with protesters, cancelling school, and flying flags at half-staff, state legislators convened hearings on the "riots" in the fall. The central figure, George William Horsley, a Republican state senator and lawyer, generated a road show, touring college towns including Dekalb. The committee probed networks among faculty who had been debating whether enforcement of loyalty oaths could rein in those faculty who were presumably disloyal because they opposed the bombing of Southeast Asia and the shooting of US students. I both protested outside and listened inside during the public hearings. They made me think my high school guidance counselor was not such a uniquely problematic guy after all. I much later learned that one of Horsley's descendants was and is the great radical cultural critic Eric Lott, who told me when we compared experiences in Illinois. Horsley had for decades been the lawyer for the Progressive Mine Workers of America union in Illinois. Life can be complicated.

The murders at Kent State and Jackson State helped to produce something like a pause in the student movement at NIU. In October 1972 the Nixon administration announced a transition to an all-volunteer military, ending the threat of being drafted for college-age men. That shift also made for recalibration of the possibilities of campus organizing. The national collapse of SDS likewise had repercussions for the whole of the campus left. Certainly the campuses remained poised to respond to escalations of the war. The 1972 bombings of Hanoi and Haiphong produced tremendous campus mobilizations, but those of us who hoped that the momentum of the May 1970 demonstrations would simply grow were to be disappointed.

Nationally, although the splits of 1969 caused most of SDS to take the position that the group was defunct, the faction led by the Maoist Progressive Labor Party (PLP) continued to produce the SDS publication New Left Notes and to sustain activities in the organization's name on some campuses. Prior to the split PLP led a tendency in SDS whose name proclaimed its political line: Worker-Student Alliance (WSA). That tendency then became the leadership of SDS, presiding over its lingering demise, which was only formalized in 1974. The numbers of functioning SDS campus chapters went from 304 in 1969 to 10 in

1970, according to one account by critical PLP ex-members. Whether our chapter at Northern Illinois was functioning was debatable. During the factional fighting, those in the know would have referred to the rump surviving group as SDS-WSA. After the fighting ended, they might simply have said SDS, but there would have been quick dissent by someone pointing out that SDS did not exist anymore. The center of operations of the remaindered SDS moved from Chicago to Boston and the ability of the leadership to support or direct campaigns at Midwestern campuses outside of larger cities outran resources. Still the SDS chapters at such universities existed, at least on paper, and the name SDS retained a certain cachet.

One ironic upshot of this extended moment of hesitation and flux was that young inexperienced activists like me ended up playing leading roles in the SDS chapters that remained on some campuses. Campus SDS reminded me a little of high school in that it was possible to volunteer for a role in an activity and quickly become its leader. One young SDS-WSA activist, soon a friend, found me as a potential recruit. He had some political education from the Progressive Labor Party, little bundles of their paper *Challenge,* and an ability to explain the worker-student alliance strategy. We never progressed much on that at NIU. Tennis practice meant I was not going to be getting a campus job, and my friend's interest in music took him to Chicago often.

There was no pressure on me to join or even learn more about PLP. In some ways national leaders needed people like me if SDS were to be anything more than a front organization enrolling party members under another name. Moreover, even in Chicago enough other ideas existed in what remained of SDS for centralizing attempts to proceed cautiously. My slight experience in SDS did not prevent my being chosen to go a national SDS gathering—the group could still muster a national convention of 1,500 in Cambridge in 1972—as a delegate from Chicago. If anything, it was my lack of affiliation and profile that would have appealed to those pooling money to fund the travel. There is no wish to romanticize here. One of the chants at the demonstration associated with the national gathering began promisingly enough with "Class struggle's gettin' hot" but ended with "Now's the time to off a Trot," meaning to kill a Trotskyist.

The political initiatives of national SDS leadership did not alienate me as much as some PLP members did. The emphasis on building solidarity between workers and students fit with my sense of the centrality of class in my own family. However, PLP's expression of the position imagined students as middle-class allies "colonizing" worksites. About every student I knew also worked and/or came from a working-class home. Northern attracted working-class, later euphemized as "first genera-tion," college students in droves. This particularly applied to veterans, the most thoughtful antiwar activists on campus. Soon enough, SDS made a transition to emphasizing attacks on racist ideas of prominent academics at elite universities, exposing especially Edward Banfield, Richard Herrnstein, and William Shockley. Here again the campaign itself appealed, dovetailing with my own history with the use of IQ scores.

Nevertheless, and not unrelated to the ways that worker-student unity came to be articulated more as class suicide on the part of students than as a materially rooted process involving people in complicated class lo-cations, PLP lacked cultural or political appeal for me. It had come out of the Communist Party, movement veterans told me, as a group with a fair share of rebels, complete with motorcycles. By the early seventies the members I met seemed staid, especially where rigid opposition to drug use was concerned. Moreover, this cultural conservatism got laid at the doorstep of working-class people in a way implausible to me.

To take an extreme example, members putting me up in another city once patiently explained that opposition to whipping children came from middle-class hang-ups and that workers used corporal punish-ment on their kids. This view troubled me for a long time, and on many levels. Surely some of my relatives and childhood neighbors spanked their children, but others didn't. The upper middle-class young people I met through tennis and at college had their own hard stories about parental abuse. Most difficult was to realize that the working class could seem so foreign and simple to those hoping to ally with it. Only as my undergraduate years unfolded did I get enough of a Marxist education to name PLP politics as more generally "Stalinist," but its opposition to the Black Panther Party, and to emphasizing women's liberation in organizing, warned me off before that.

At NIU we in SDS had a few things going for us: recognition as a student organization, access to space, a locker with pamphlets and back issues of New Left Notes, a mailbox, and a name that resonated, at least among those not keeping up with the details. All we lacked was formerly high levels of membership. A few other nearby campuses shared our plight, and like us they marched on, neither under direct PLP leadership nor thinking it necessary to come to grips with all that had happened. We'd sometimes hear from sister chapters at Purdue or from radicals at Southern Illinois University in Carbondale. The latter was a school where lots of my high school classmates ended up and one that had a particularly long-standing New Left that consistently fought with police, often to defend students' right to party, but also had a record of solidarity with Black struggles in Cairo. One occasion for inter-campus communication came when several SDS chapters received in the mail an academic social science survey that seemed hyper-interested in how many members came from "broken homes." A dozen of us who met to discuss it at Northern laughed at its assumptions and then allowed privately that we were all from single-parent or blended families, however unbroken.

We ended up rebuilding a viable SDS chapter around issues other than those that SDS emphasized nationally. Depending on the campaign, a different ten or so undergraduates united and learned. Some initiatives came mostly from us, including a well-researched proposal to keep the university from raising tuition and fees, and fundraising for students to travel to protest Nixon's inauguration in 1973. In others we joined with other organizations, for example in demonstrations against arming campus police, in direct actions to preserve the Montgomery Arboretum on campus, and in supporting huge marches for the reappointment of the Black activist speech professor, Temetra Gronemeier. By far the high point came in May 1972 during a wave of protests against renewed US bombing of Hanoi and Haiphong. After repressive measures and a lull in the campus antiwar movement, our ability to disrupt campus was much in doubt. Those of us from SDS had enough close ties with campus faculty to ensure that they would not urge caution and would help build a mass meeting in that fieldhouse so associated with basketball excitement. The crowd that poured out of the event joined marches, one of which ended in the student occupation of an administration and academic records building.

Serious Marxism

Much in my youth and schooling taught me that it might pay off to be smart and credentialled. Not much spoke to being educated. I read voraciously, but comics, Mad Magazine, the left press (especially the US radical publication The Guardian, for which I soon also wrote) and sports journalism, not literature or history. Sometimes this mix led me to a serious book, for example the boxer-writer José Torres' Sting Like a Bee, a work on Muhammad Ali's personality and craft, or The Autobiography of Malcolm X. Others I took to be profound only for a while: Tom Hayden's The Love of Possession Is a Disease with Them or Eldridge Cleaver's Soul on Ice. Norman Mailer too, although I never made it through a whole Mailer book. Mostly though my goal was to excel in terms of grades while maximizing time for pleasure and organizing. A certain fear of taking myself too seriously persisted. For example, I took a very ambitious art history class early on in college and loved it. Then I took several more, not because I would become educated in art history but because I knew that by attending the first class, plus about half of the rest, I would easily secure credit for all of the courses in the optional pass/fail grading system.

This level of cynicism became harder to maintain as little urges to learn surfaced, first in film classes with little or no reading required. The NIU campus sponsored a series of world cinema films, shown each weekend. At the time one could watch about every canonical film over one's college years. I certainly saw every major Godard film. The shows remained free and students packed them. Sometimes formal discussions followed. Informal ones always did. Between talking and writing about the movies I became confident in defending interpretations, especially political ones, in an academic setting. The absence of film showings on today's campuses must count as one barometer of the impoverishment of student life.

On the other hand, in the one ambitious honors course I took—we read a Shakespeare play a week—I fell completely silent. I wrote a paper using what bits I knew of Herbert Marcuse's work, and challenged the professor to attack the paper politically. He did, expressing sharp disagreement but adding that someday soon I'd need good grades to go to graduate school, and he wouldn't stand in the way. That was the first time that graduate school struck me as a possibility.

Another crack in my reflexive anti-intellectualism came because of movement activities. Some of us in and out of SDS joined a reading group led by a doctoral student, Bill Pelz, specializing in German history. For the first time I voluntarily read things that challenged my ability to comprehend and had me furiously taking notes. The cheapest available classic socialist texts came from China Books and Periodicals in Chicago and featured spartan sand-colored covers. Others came from Chicago's Charles H. Kerr Publishing Company, a big part of my future. We read mostly pamphlets, like Marx's *Wage Labor and Capital* and *Value, Price, and Profit* but some readings stretched to book length, like Engels' *Origins of the Family* and Lenin's *State and Revolution*. Eventually we strayed politically far beyond the confines of the politics of China Books, reading Rosa Luxemburg on the mass strike and on reform and revolution, for example. Because of time constraints, we never touched *Capital*. We rarely ventured beyond European Marxism. However, such study groups gave me the invaluable habit of realizing that the most influential revolutionary theorists wrote to be understood, and reading them in the original texts (or translations of the original texts) ought to be the approach of choice. The ways in which collectivity emerged when discussing works that no one person could master also impressed me. I think of the dynamics of that study group whenever I teach Hegel's "On Lordship and Bondage" to 19-year-olds, throwing them into reliance on each other.

An Interest in History

As much as I thought education should produce some kind of credential leading to a job, I had little idea of what kind of credential. The familiarity of my mother's "teaching certificate" made it attractive, maybe combined with coaching. I did an education degree as much to avoid the five-day-a-week language classes required for a bachelor of arts as to further my career goals. As it became clear that I did not play tennis well enough to make a living at it, I needed a plan. Being a movement lawyer seemed a possibility, although the St. Louis attorney who interviewed me as part of the Yale admissions process remained the only lawyer whom I had ever met.

Deciding on a major represented a first step. The choice resulted from a small scam I was working. My scholarship included full cost of books, and after a semester I figured out that I could first register for classes with expensive books, drop those courses, return the books, and then sign up for classes with cheaper books, pocketing the difference. The classes with the highest number of required books were history ones. They were long and expensive. After a semester or two, nominally concentrating in political science and "pre-law," I began in various off-campus struggles to know radical graduate students from the history department. In raising money to subsidize trips to 1973 anti-inauguration protests, we found that historians were the softest touches for donations. I remembered that the inquisitorial Horsley Committee hearings zealously grilled history professors.

Soon I looked differently at the history books I'd previously bought only with resale in mind. Ten or more of them had come from a madly ambitious class taught by Otto Olsen, a great scholar of dissent in the post-Civil War South. One of those, W.E.B. Du Bois' *Black Reconstruction*, seemed an almost impossible length to be read or even to be made into a paperback whose binding would not break. I decided to try that course, and others. Olsen sang old labor and civil rights songs to punctuate lectures. Marvin Rosen, teaching a European history survey, began the class with hundreds in the audience and any number of knitting needles and balls of yarn on the stage. He coaxed several male students to come up and offered anyone who could invent knitting on the spot an A with no need for further attendance. None succeeded, although they kept trying feverishly as he lectured on the syllabus and on materiality, production, and skill, spinning the topics around the failures to knit. I was hooked.

It turned out that Northern had—along with perhaps Rutgers, Wisconsin, and Rochester—the best Marxist and broadly left history department in the US. Friends and foes called it the Little Red School-house on the Prairie, although the setting was no prairie but instead one of agriculturally engineered corn fields. At some misty point in the past the department decided that it might gain stature by hiring a blacklisted victim of Cold War red scares in academia. Another followed, then more. By the time I arrived the department approached being half Marxists, or at least left historians. Lore had it that the left of the department got every other hire, the more mainstream faculty deferring to them. Collectively the faculty did not so much teach me to like history as to want to be serious about understanding how the world worked and changed.

A clinching event came during a class in which I wasn't even enrolled. The young African American historian John Higginson had come to teach US history even though he was in the process of launching a brilliant career researching African labor history. I had a full schedule but joined his class at times just to hear lectures. At this particular session he was fielding objections to the fact that his class, like many in the history department, required substantial papers to be written, while in other fields multiple-choice tests sufficed. John reflected on his experience at an elite school where writing to defend analyses was frequent. "Why do you think that is?" he asked. Pause and silence. Then he answered himself: "They are learning to rule you." I thought then about not going to Yale and what I needed to get from NIU.

I have since taught and studied at Northwestern, Yale, Missouri, Minnesota, Illinois, and Kansas. None had a department more serious than the "directional" public university of my undergraduate years. In addition to Higginson, Olsen, and Rosen, I took or audited classes from Ben Keen on Latin America, C.H. George on revolutions, Al Resis on the Russian Revolution, and everything I could from Margaret George, whose early research focused on the US but who turned to studying Europe and the world, combining women's and workers' history. Even that roster had me missing the eminent historian of the American Revolution "from the bottom up," Al Young, later a good friend, and the French historian William Beik, as well as Martin Sklar and Carl Parrini, radical historians of the US state. So exciting was NIU as a center of left history and debate at the time that perhaps the greatest historian then writing in English, Edward P. Thompson, was said to be eager to join the faculty if a concrete offer materialized. It didn't, apparently because an increasingly monitored university administration used the fact that Thompson had no doctorate to regard him as unqualified to profess at NIU!

Moreover, the historians considered less on the left came to be in dialogue, or combat, with Marxism. J. Carroll Moody, studying the Steel Workers Organizing Committee, had endless time for me. Steve Kern, a tremendously well-read intellectual historian, made me see the importance of the Freudian tradition and think about syntheses of Marx and Freud. He also pointed out after my presentation to the seminar that I'd gotten the biggest laugh in the course that semester— my speaking did not need to fluctuate between the diffident and the ponderous. The major paper I wrote for Margaret George toward the end of college—she let me hand-write an endless tome—could then attempt to analyze gender and class in a range of Victorian pornography through a now more sophisticated understanding of Marcuse.

As I neared graduation Al Resis returned an exam with a grade but also with the comment: "You know you could do this for a living." I had never thought along those lines at all till then and in fact had already applied to Stanford Law School. But the fact that the New Left lay dying—word had even reached Dekalb by then—leaving very little of institutional consequence behind, struck me as requiring explanation. The idea that I could get paid to read widely, while living in an exciting city, gained appeal. My solution reflected not taking good advice and left me just with the single law school option and one at Northwestern's doctoral program. The latter had in its favor the presence of historians of race and slavery Sterling Stuckey and George Fredrickson, as well as amazing historians of Africa.

Stanford Law replied affirmatively long before any word came from Northwestern. Resis had written to me that I needed a "backup" school for history—he urged NIU—and I supposed he had been proved right. Then Northwestern sent an offer of four years of support with no teaching. Their decision, like Stanford's, doubtless rested on the same use of standardized test results that had gotten me admitted to Yale four years earlier. I had a decision to make. Northwestern, I decided, could be okay to try for a year. I ended up staying four years as a doctoral student and five more as an assistant professor.

4

SCHOOLED BY THE CITY
AND THE LEFT

My explanation, mostly to myself, for choosing to attend graduate school at Northwestern carried a certain high-mindedness. I needed to figure out what had happened to the New Left and could spend a year reading, at the school's expense. Not untrue, the explanation did omit things. I did really enjoy thinking historically, far beyond the history of the New Left. I'd graduated in December and had had a kind of "gap semester" back home in southern Illinois before starting at Northwestern—giving tennis lessons, substitute teaching, and having plenty of time to excitedly "read ahead," especially the writings of George Fredrickson and Sterling Stuckey, knowing I'd soon be with them in classes. Those months also gave me a chance to test, and find wanting, the attractions of returning to small-town southern Illinois as a schoolteacher and coach. When I decided against going to Stanford I did not try to defer but simply declined.

A set of unthinking decisions had me more committed to doctoral study in history than I could admit to myself or to family and friends who found baffling the idea of foregoing a real job search for several more years of student poverty. Paradoxically, coming to appreciate how dodgy a career choice a humanities doctorate was also reassured me that I would not be leaving the working class for a middle-class life. I associated the latter not only with anti-radicalism but also with miseries, and especially my late father's miseries. All of my old friends who took unionized working-class jobs after high school made far more than I did as a graduate student worker and would continue to do so when I was a young college teacher.

Further omissions mattered in keeping me from admitting, or maybe even fully feeling, how thrilled I was about studying the past. To enter a private school for the first time clashed with a commitment to public schools that ran deep in my upbringing. A suspicion of anything smacking of elitism had become central to the very good but not too subtle Marxism-for-beginners education I'd received. Twinned with contempt and suspicion was an unexpressed worry that elite higher education would be too tough, too filled with students far better educated than I. Years of continuing to wonder what I'd missed at Yale fueled such anxieties. During the months I was back in southern Illinois, I took an advanced class at Washington University, the most elite school on offer in St. Louis, succeeding but also weighing the possibility that, being at night, it may not have included top students. I did not want to desire success at Northwestern too much before it was clear that I could have it.

The Right to Cities

Near the end of his long life, I interviewed Sterling Stuckey, my mentor at Northwestern, on what made him such a distinguished US historian and writer on Herman Melville's fiction. Some of the exchange appeared in the *Journal of African American History*. We spoke for perhaps ten hours at a Riverside restaurant and at a recording studio on the University of California campus in that city. In all that time we scarcely said a word about universities, departments, or even books. He talked about cities, about growing up in Memphis, and then in Chicago. He remembered first memorably encountering the "ring shout" (the African-become-African American form of collective and individual movement on which he wrote so brilliantly) as a teenager in a Chicago roller rink. He discussed working in a giant post office setting, one where leading Black intellectuals such as Charles Hamilton and Timuel Black also worked. He recalled cities saturated in jazz, not only in their clubs but also in their high schools.

We remembered his mother, who became the renowned "poet-laureate" of Black history, Elma Stuckey. She'd long before that been a listener to the stories of ex-slaves on Memphis porches and then a writer of rhyming tributes to fellow workers in state government in

Chicago. Stuckey described meeting Paul Robeson through a left-wing uncle and by virtue of having parents brave enough to defy the Red Scare and invite Robeson into their home. He recounted joining the civil rights movement by wandering into a picket line at a Chicago store. As a high school teacher, he took the lead in building the Amistad Society, a group that brought demands for Black studies to public schools quite before they existed in elite universities. Listening to cities taught what universities could not. Or perhaps more hopefully, at their rare best, universities formed a slice of what cities offered. Here, I follow the example of Stuckey in speaking of my becoming an intellectual as deeply tied to living in a city, even if it means delaying getting to Northwestern, and to Stuckey, for a chapter.

The focus of my 1975 excitement for coming life changes centered first on becoming an urban person, coming into possession of the wonders attached to what the French theorist Henri Lefebvre called "the right to the city." I'd never lived in a city of more than 40,000 and mostly in a town less than a tenth that size. With tennis I'd come to spend lots of time in St. Louis and other cities, playing tournaments and practicing, but purposefully and without the meandering that lets us learn an urban area. While living briefly back in Columbia I visited as much as possible with my uncle in St. Louis' Central West End, the city's edgiest and trendiest neighborhood. My uncle stayed there because it put him near the morgue where he was an attendant by day and the Jewish funeral home where he lived and worked nights. The neighborhood hosted centers of the city's queer life and of its Catholic institutions, my uncle's delightfully paired passions. Childhood polio had left him disabled, but mobile and vigorous. We walked everywhere. He seemed the honorary mayor of the CWE, known, along with a succession of very pampered dogs, in every bar, restaurant, and shop.

In truth, even in high school and college, Uncle Gene had been the key to my right to St. Louis and enjoyment of it. Three nights a week much of last two years of high school I would take a mass transit bus from Columbia to downtown St. Louis and stand on a corner awaiting a ride from the person who'd taught me tennis. He'd drive me to a place where we both played and where I got more advanced coaching and then back home. Uncle Gene vouched for the safety of waiting out on the street, in a neighborhood centered on the Greyhound terminal, an area that was also a center of tattooing, petty crime, porn, sex work, and breaches of the color line. He said it was fine, and his word overrode the splashy crime scares retailed in the city's press. In college I almost always took friends to meet my uncle before my mother, the CWE being likely to make a deeper impression. Gene was generous to a fault and code-switched extravagantly between lector at Catholic services and campy female impersonation.

I soon learned that it was possible to live cheaply amid beauty and ideas in a city. The striking St. Louis Art Museum greeted visitors to its hilltop setting in Forest Park with an inscription set in stone above its doors: DEDICATED TO ART AND FREE TO ALL. The adjacent highly ranked zoo did not charge admission either. The city center's main public library, a breathtaking structure, already in the seventies welcomed people experiencing homelessness and academic researchers alike. The city's parks frequently featured free music. Top tennis courts were free or inexpensive.

Left events centered in the CWE and in the University City "Loop" neighborhood, near my university classes. So did bookstores, three of them explicitly radical in their reasons for being. I seldom did more than listen to the conversations of others during those months, but I felt myself entering a word of urban radicalism. St. Louis made a good place to gain that sense. It and Minneapolis, in contrast to larger cities where I have lived on the left—that is, Chicago and London—had a small enough critical mass of socialists and anarchists that there was more hanging out across lines of political difference, debating, and drinking.

Good-natured banter did not mean absence of tension. St. Louis, as I soon learned and came to write about, was home in the 1860s to Karl Marx's most discerning and influential US correspondent and co-thinker, Joseph Weydemeyer. Both an elected official and a Union Army officer, Weydemeyer could plausibly have a local monument devoted to him, as the radical Civil War General Franz Sigel had in the city's Forest Park. One day, drinking coffee, I overheard one local revolutionary describe just such a statue to another revolutionary from a different political tendency, dispatching him with directions. When the latter set off, I approached, saying I'd love to see that statue, and the map-sketcher smiled, saying the statue did not exist but the wild goose chase served the seeker right for his retrograde politics.

The wonderful historian George Rawick lived, I learned, just down the street from my uncle. Both knew another neighbor, Dave Meggyesy, the St. Louis football Cardinals linebacker, who dropped out of that world to write the searing critique *Out of Their League*, and to become an organizer of athletes and of unions. I simply presented myself as needing to know Rawick and to learn how he wrote his classic study of slavery, *From Sundown to Sunup*. It turned out he needed me too, in part because his health was so poor. George described himself as having been, with Herbert Gutman and Warren Susman, the first three openly Jewish graduate students in the University of Wisconsin History Department. All died without living past age 60, and George considered the Madison years to have given them something like an occupational disease.

However, the Wisconsin department also imparted to Rawick a strong sense that "history from below" held the key to how things changed. As much as this characterized Rawick's studies of slavery, it also permeated his research on the whole working class, especially in his insistence that workers in the thirties organized unions rather than unions organizing workers. When his health worsened dramatically, George realized that he'd write only so much more. He signed a contract to edit a three-volume set of the letters of Knights of Labor leader Terence Powderly. His first editorial decision was to include only letters *to* Powderly from ordinary workers. Even in care after a stroke and able to communicate only through a scribe, he held on to that project as a hope.

Rawick taught a certain irreverence towards academia, especially in comparison to "the movement." He had quit a tenured job at Washington University in protest over politically motivated ill-treatment of a colleague whose politics he deplored and ended in a position without security at University of Missouri's St. Louis campus. In 1985, Northern Illinois University held a lavish conference on the "future of labor history." Everybody was invited to speak. Well, everybody except me, despite my having been an undergrad there. Shortly after that conference I met with George and the brilliant "historians from below" Marcus Rediker and Peter Linebaugh in St. Louis. The three discussed what had happened at the Dekalb event. However, George paused every little bit to marvel at the folly of discussing the future of the field during a downturn of working-class dissent, a time in which social movements were not suggesting what the future or the past should look like. Partly he was trying to reassure me that I'd not missed much, but he also meant every word. I co-edited two books in Rawick's honor. The first was published during his final hospitalization, and I got to put it into his hands the day before he died.

Because the leading figure in the Marxist Study Group at Northern Illinois, the German history doctoral student William Pelz, belonged to the tradition of the International Socialists, my contacts in St. Louis mostly led to my meeting with St. Louis activists who shared the view that the Soviet Union was not a socialist society and a practical orientation in the US to building "socialism from below" by organizing in industrial workplaces. The latter especially appealed to me as explicable to family members active in unions. I sold copies of *Workers Power* before class at Washington University. However, the idea of ending school and taking a job in auto or transit held little appeal and Rawick very sternly encouraged me not to join a small socialist group. He had, he argued, at one time or another been a member of many of them. He then joined a last one after warning me off.

If St. Louis seemed a banquet, Chicago proved an ongoing feast. Since visiting with my mother for a teacher's conference in fourth grade I'd had a very soft spot for the city. In that first visit the Prudential Building seemed impossibly tall. When I returned for marches while an undergraduate, the Hancock Building was twice as high. When I came to graduate school the Sears Tower could claim to be the world's tallest building. For years when I approached the city's Loop on the Greyhound or in the 1965 Chevy an aunt gave me, I thought of Carl Sandburg's muscular poetic tributes to the city as "stacker of wheat" and "Player with Railroads and the Nation's Freight Handler" fit images for my materialist and even workerist politics. The subway/elevated train system seemed at first more amusement than transport, wonderfully efficient and endlessly interesting in its parade of riders.

I first lived near the Howard Street El stop, on the city side of the border between Chicago and Evanston, home of Northwestern's campus. If I got to class by walking, I could pass by Lake Michigan's public beaches. The lone beach I'd come to know near home in southern Illinois was Times Beach, a rocky place on the Meramec River south of St. Louis. It soon closed, along with the industrial town bearing its name, after being revealed as the site of a massive spill of dioxin.

If I took the El, halfway up to school at the Chicago-Main stop was (and incredibly still is) a spectacular newsstand with all things popular but also whole sections of left periodicals, literary magazines, and even academic journals. A few doors down, until its sad closure in 1978, the relatively low-cost music venue Amazingrace hosted jazz and folk performances in an intimate setting. The coffeehouse grew out of the 1969 Moratorium to End the War in Vietnam movement. I first saw Odetta, McCoy Tyner, Randy Newman, Ry Cooder, Sonny Rollins, and Sweet Honey in the Rock there. If I got off the train at the most logical stop for the university, I immediately encountered the excellent Great Expectations bookstore, where the Evanston-based Catholic journalist and historian Garry Wills hung out and held forth. We later became friends as colleagues at Northwestern. His prodigious memory produced overheard lines at the bookshop like "As Clausewitz writes on page 337 of On War. . . ." Wills' dad was a boxing official, and the son had a great storehouse of stories of fighters as well as reminiscences of reporting on the civil rights movement.

My first little apartment sat above a tremendous West Indian restaurant, and I soon learned that however expensive big cities were at the top end, the millions of poor people in Chicago loved good food and supported affordable restaurants. Two blocks away sat Biddy Mulligan's, a neighborhood blues bar that attracted fans from all over the world. I'd started to love the Chicago blues, improbably enough, in Iowa City visiting a Louisiana-born girlfriend who ended up at the University of Iowa. The big Chicago blues acts came to Iowa City midweek and the crowds tended to be both small and devoted. I'd never really warmed to bars or drinking much, but blues changed at least the first of those. I seldom missed Hound Dog Taylor and believed that the marvelous Koko Taylor would have recognized me if we met in the street. The historic

Maxwell Street Market south of the Loop convened blues performers on Sunday mornings in free, wildly multicultural, and inspired performances, until a predatory University of Illinois at Chicago redeveloped its home. There were also folksier performances in my neighborhood's atmospheric No Exit Café and, after 1976, food, music, art, and political conversation at Heartland Café, which managed a forty-year run as a haven for Chicago's left and countercultures.

A short El ride in the opposite direction from Evanston lay Wrigley Field. When I arrived in the summer of 1975 the Cubs trailed sufficiently in the pennant race that sellouts never threatened. I could decide to go to a game, hop on the train, get off at the Addison stop, walk three minutes, buy a bleacher ticket, eat and drink, and not spend ten dollars. Such a treat could happen even on the glorious sunny, warm, wind-blows-out days when home runs flew into the bleachers in numbers. In my four years—but parts of five Cubs' seasons—in graduate school the team never won more than half its games, and the need to plan to go to a game remained negligible. The Cubs were on free TV, and I seldom did academic work without them. They were present in almost every North Side bar.

The White Sox games involved a longer train ride and then a longer walk to a much less appealing park. I sometimes went, supporting the team and their renegade owner, Bill Veeck. Too broke to run a franchise, he patched together appealing teams. One morning at Northwestern, having coffee in the student center, I noticed a leaflet saying Veeck was about to speak on campus. Virtually no one came, even from the sponsoring group—business students if memory serves—and he ended up taking me to a long lunch and regaling me with stories of stunts he'd pulled to drum up business on a shoestring.

Veeck's star announcer at the time was Harry Caray who had been the very voice of baseball for me growing up, on the Cardinals' broadcasts. Caray's trademark seventh-inning stretch renditions of "Take Me Out to the Ball Game" began when Veeck forced, or perhaps cajoled, him to lead the crowd in singing it. Caray sometimes broadcast from the Sox bleachers, occasionally shirtless. By the time that I moved back to Chicago after a year at Yale and returned to the bleachers of Cubs' games in the early eighties, Caray had switched to working for that team.

No Enemies on the Left?

One of my favorite undergraduate professors repeated at all opportunities that the slogan "No Enemies on the Left" ought to inform our organizing and our lives. I didn't agree at all. The very way I'd learned Marxism proceeded from political difference: Marx skewering the "poverty" of Proudhon's ideas, his *Critique of the Gotha Programme*, Engels writing *Anti-Dühring*, Lenin on "infantile disorders" and on "the renegade Kautsky," and Trotsky on a revolution betrayed. I liked the combat of ideas, even while enjoying imagining possible syntheses of supposedly adversarial positions. Such was especially the case with Marx and Freud, after I'd read Herbert Marcuse's *Eros and Civilization* and, on Rawick's recommendation, the early work of Wilhelm Reich. But even this passion took the form of an argument, attacking those who denied any possibility of bringing psychoanalysis and historical materialism together.

Within the NIU History Department, a national left group called the New American Movement (NAM), had attracted some support. It was a tendency that later merged with the Democratic Socialist Organizing Committee to become the Democratic Socialists of America, today's largest socialist formation in the US. Increasingly trained in radical traditions that insisted on not voting for Democrats and supporting reforms as steppingstones to revolution not as a social democratic end in themselves, I avoided the group. Moreover, I regarded efforts to rebrand the left as American as non-starters at best. I had no problem seeing NAM as an enemy on the left even if I disdained wasting time attacking them.

My own reflections on the sorry state of US radicalism led me to lament not that we'd failed to lead a revolution—again I'd missed being a radical at that phase of the sixties—but that so few broad left institutions had established lasting foundations. In talking to grown-ups in the history program at Northern Illinois, though, about why they did not speak out more on particular groups and concrete issues, I came to understand that I projected more political agreement between myself and my favorite professors or TAs than was present. Moreover, I admired the radical historians' achievements in producing a department able to fend off attacks from the state government and to continue reproducing a left presence, which *depended* on seldom going to the mat against each other. From that point of view "no enemies on the left" had a certain logic.

My political work in Chicago, beginning in the mid-seventies, radiated from attempts to build two lasting institutions. The first, a bookstore collective, did not survive for five years. The second, the Charles H. Kerr Publishing Company, remains the oldest radical publisher in the English language ever, still working on another of its many lives. It was nearing its hundredth birthday when I joined its collective leadership after moving to Chicago in 1975. Trying to sell books, whether as a store clerk or a publisher, made me materially invested in not recklessly making enemies on the left. To paraphrase the great Chicago thinker Michael Jordan, "Left liberals buy books too."

Bookseller 1.0: Red Rose Collective

My first attempts to sell left publications came in a context that was unusual not only in the world of books but also in the context of radical organizing. Collectively run radical bookstores, hoping to function also as free spaces for reading groups, lectures, socializing, and building protests had popped up broadly enough. They were among my favorite places. Some were projects of left groups. Chicago had a bookshop run by the Socialist Workers Party, and another in Chicago was associated with the Communist Party. Our local model, Chicago's New World Resource Center, which did business a fifteen-minute bike ride away from our store, drew its energy from members identified with the Maoist New York-based *Guardian* newspaper and from around the New Communist Movement groups variously inspired by the Chinese and Albanian revolutions. Anarchist-led collectively run bookstores we knew about and visited included the Lucy Parsons Center in the Boston area from 1969, Seattle's Left Bank Books from 1973, and Philadelphia's captivating Wooden Shoe Books from 1976, which doubled as a great record store.

Red Rose Collective initially gathered members who had known each other at Northern Illinois, including Pelz, the Socialist Party activist Art Kazar, Dolores Portis, and myself. Dolores' daughter, Nora

Portis, both came around Red Rose and helped to lead the nationwide socialist youth organization Red Tide. Jean Allman, just arrived in the Chicago area to attend Northwestern, was someone I knew a little from St. Louis and eventually both a leading historian of West Africa and my partner for over twenty-five years. A few young Chicago workers soon assumed shifts at the store, with one also living there at times. Al Bodine and Ray Kohl had jobs in industry, and Ray soon held office in a Boilermakers and Blacksmiths local. Al worked a late shift and passed by my apartment, now further into the city, on his way home, so that my reading and writing for school often ended with him persuading me to hang out a little at what I considered bedtime.

We cohered as a store before we did as a political formation. A storefront opened on Greenleaf just a block off busy Clark Avenue, at 7000 North as locals would say, and next to the Ravenswood train track. Given that we had so little money, collectivizing mostly student poverty, the real estate choices were narrow. With one important caveat, we could not have made a better choice. Long and bright, it was a space broad enough to seat a hundred easily for a film or talk. The caveat involved the weather, not the two storied blizzards of the late seventies in Chicago but the fact that Red Rose had weather *inside* the store. With very high ceilings, little insulation, and huge windows, the store proved impossible to cool in summer and, much more miserably, to heat in winter. Drafts verged on creating wind chills.

Gathering some semblance of stock presented few problems. Used books appeared magically, as so many on the left had so many and moved frequently. Small left groups delivered little bundles of their newspapers on consignment and some pamphlets and magazines materialized on the same terms. A few presses also cut deals, making it possible for us to sell a few new radical books as well as old. My own first pamphlet, collecting articles on the working day by Weydemeyer, was published by the bookstore itself. We remained parochial enough to name the publisher after our address, Greenleaf Press. At the same time, we fancifully listed the little pamphlet's price on its cover in pounds and deutsche marks, as well as dollars.

Except during events, we seldom attracted a crowd to the store. Whole afternoons sometimes brought no one. The bulk of my academic reading therefore came while nominally on the (unpaid) job. I also read lots from the stock, more or less randomly. Italian Marxist Antonio Gramsci's work began to come into vogue within academia. History training included small doses of it, though more as a guide to why we don't have revolutions than on how to make one. At Red Rose I'd read much of the Gramsci available in English and enjoyed exchanges with Red Rose members and total strangers on its political import so many years after Gramsci's death.

The city came to us, by the ones and twos by day and by the scores for events. The customers who stayed—unwinding near either a space heater or a fan much of the year—included many autodidacts, with older ones strikingly broadly self-educated. Even the members of the most ingrown sectarian groups, bringing around their publications to sell on consignment, had much to say once they got beyond the party line. They often had fascinating stories of transformation by a strike or by the civil rights movement. One was an ex-nun, become direct action antiwar protester, become revolutionary, by then in a tiny group partly devoted to following Trotsky's admonitions even against gum-chewing. We also attracted Spartacist League members, bane of left meetings for their insistence on steering discussions, for example of a labor film, into the scoring of sectarian small points, driving ordinary neighborhood people away. One-on-one they were much better.

Some patrons occupied exalted places in the Chicago, and even the national, left. It was at Red Rose that Vicky Starr, the legendary organizer of industrial and then white-collar workers, who was featured as Stella Nowicki in Julia Reichart's 1977 documentary Union Maids, began a habit of bringing our family asparagus as a first vegetable of the spring, straight from land her family had outside the city. I think it must have been at Red Rose where I first met Studs Terkel, the charming Chicago radio host, actor, and historian who a little seriously credited his striking success at extracting life stories from ordinary people to his failures to use the technology of tape recording, with his misadventures breaking the ice and eliciting sympathy. We hit it off, and I spoke at Studs' huge "hundredth birthday" celebration at Newberry Library. (He'd died at 96).

Frequent Red Rose customer Eddie "Oil Can" Sadlowski led the rank-and-file union campaign Steelworkers Fight Back. He mounted a losing campaign for the international union's presidency and others for reform and militancy in the union locally and regionally. He typically arrived at the store with the wealthy veteran of the Trotskyist movement Frank Fried, who had himself been a steelworker during some of his Trotskyist youth, sent to factory work by the Socialist Workers Party after World War II. During a downturn in the steel industry, Fried picked up work promoting cultural events and soon became a leading promoter of folk music, in the late fifties and sixties a hot commodity and one associated with the left. He prospered in the entertainment industry with a career spanning "[Vladimir] Lenin to [John] Lennon," as he liked to say. Listeners hung on his every word—he'd reportedly bought a house Marilyn Monroe once owned, after all. Those of us in the Red Rose Collective vainly hoped he'd be charmed by the store and donate to it. Sadlowski's visits were all about the books, and he usually left with big stacks. Our most frequent and marvelous visitors, the surrealist artists Penelope and Franklin Rosemont, lived nearby and came sometimes with surrealist publications, and increasingly just to talk. They are central characters later in this chapter.

For most of our several years of operation Red Rose eked out the rent and replenished stock without great drama. We were fortunate in many ways to have as neighbors one of the major tendencies within the Iranian Students Association (ISA), the one most congenial to our politics. For complex reasons, it was better for them to have us buy and sell the classic socialist works that they read in Farsi in the runup to the Iranian Revolution of 1979. At times we may have sold more books in Farsi than in English, with translations of Rosa Luxemburg probably leading the pack. The exhilaration of an actual revolutionary process produced a kind of energy among our neighbors that I'd not see again until South Africa in the early nineties. However, the burdens of knowing how actively the Iranian regime's SAVAK agents and the Chicago police spied on their movement encumbered their activities. So did the exigencies of exile politics, which required over-reading meanings from very sparse information.

The factionalism in the wider ISA, at a time when so much was on the line, occasionally seemed fearsome. Our neighbors invited Red Rose to sell books at a big 1978 all-ISA meeting at Peoples Church in

Chicago's Uptown neighborhood. Those very Luxemburg titles became the center of fierce arguments about whether we'd be allowed to stay or not. For some, Luxemburg's thought was one key to thinking about revolution and for others reading her contributed to counter-revolution. It was not utterly surprising to us when the Iranian Revolution, in power, turned so bloodily on its own left wing.

Red Rose made me more of a public speaker, if mostly to introduce speakers and films, to referee intra-left squabbles in discussions afterwards, and to explain that the film projector had malfunctioned yet again and there would be a delay. At Northern Illinois, I'd organized events but rarely spoken at them. In Chicago what first changed this was our showing of the important and suppressed Gillo Pontecorvo film *Burn!* at the working-class campus of Northeastern Illinois University in the city. Hollywood had found Pontecorvo irresistible for a moment following his prize-winning gem *Battle of Algiers*, which had been budgeted on a shoestring. With quadruple that budget, and with Marlon Brando rejecting a role in *Butch Cassidy and the Sundance Kid* to star in it, *Burn!* became a lavish masterpiece reflecting on the limits of decolonization and emancipation in a world of white supremacy and uneven capitalist development. Vietnam never left the director's mind, nor the viewer's.

Set on a mythical Portuguese sugar island in the Caribbean, the plot of the film sees Brando's William Walker character cultivate a rebellious enslaved worker, José Delores. Walker encourages and enables him to make a revolution on behalf of emancipation and free trade, goals at the time congruent with those of the British imperial sugar interests for whom Walker worked. Years later, as continuing exploitation moves Delores to head a rebel insurgency, the sugar interests bring Walker back to overthrow the insufficiently bloodthirsty government and deploy tactics that look like anti-Indigenous genocide and modern counter-insurgency, destroying villages to save them and hanging Delores. The film premiered in 1969, stayed for a few days in a few theatres, and disappeared. Few had seen it—I hadn't—even a decade later.

Getting access to a print of *Burn!* thrilled us at Red Rose. We made it into a left event, cooperating with a Black nationalist group to show it. The discussion afterwards promised to be one where I'd offer a Marxist view of what made the film work and young Black nationalists would speak of ways it spoke to Black Power. I ended up feeling torn about that division of labor. Studying, as I was by then with Sterling Stuckey at Northwestern, I'd come to think of Black nationalism as itself often class conscious and sophisticated, opening on to Marxism. Moreover, Pontecorvo's Marxism informs the film but in a way usefully inflected by the ideas of Frantz Fanon. Brando's Walker character speaks in Marxist soundbites at times, expressing a hard-headed wisdom regarding how the world works. But the very persuasiveness of his materialist understanding of slavery, wage labor, and bourgeois revolution suffers for its bloodless callousness even as his actions drench the island in blood.

The film's climax undermined any schematic idea of following it with a race versus class discussion. Walker, having hunted down and executed Delores, wanders disoriented without an "other" to define his existence. As he carries his bags to the ship on which he is to depart, Walker mistakes a porter offering to relieve him of the burden for a resurrected Delores, who had carried his bags in order to filch them on Walker's arrival years before. The porter proves to be Walker's assassin, stabbing him, and causing the audience at the campus showing of the film to erupt into applause. I understood then how the movie couldn't have been shown in theatres in 1969 and how my task was nothing like as simple as merely learning a received body of Marxist wisdom. The term scarcely existed at the time but Burn! dramatized racial capitalism.

Hosting other groups' events, leafletting on shift changes as part of in-plant organizing, and discounting marked book prices, we made friends on the left. Red Rose could spark and participate in initiatives in the broader Chicago area. The biggest crowd I had ever addressed, before speaking in revolutionary South Africa in 1991, also occurred through involvement in Red Rose. The collective helped to initiate the Chicago Anti-Nazi League, as confronting Nazis became a particularly hot issue in Chicago in the mid-seventies. The Nazis were led by Frank Collin, himself said to be the son of a Jewish father who was a Holocaust survivor. They secured a hall, set up an incendiary White Power hotline, and built a base in the Marquette Park neighborhood where Collin once won 16 percent of the vote in an aldermanic election. Collin's group sought the ability to hold rallies in Marquette Park itself, where a mob of perhaps 700 white racists had bloodied Dr. Martin Luther King Jr.

in 1966. Home to a fair number of Chicago's white police, the neighborhood presented a perfect target for the Nazis, so much so that the city moved to require payments for permits to demonstrate in the park. Collin famously responded by enlisting American Civil Liberties Union legal talent and threatening to take his marches to more provocative venues, especially the suburb of Skokie, which had significant numbers of Holocaust survivors among its large Jewish population.

In organizing in opposition to the Nazis marching unmolested, whether in Skokie or in Chicago, Red Rose played a healthy role. We succeeded far less in influencing how those dramas are remembered, however. The Skokie events, or one corner of them, figure in US popular culture. One 1981 made-for-TV fictionalization carried the simple title of Skokie and saw the story as a battle between residents wanting to ignore the Nazis and deprive them of attention and others, sparked by the concentration camp survivor played by Danny Kaye, urging confrontation. A spate of documentaries has explored constitutional issues posed by the Skokie events and the irony of the ACLU having to defend reprehensible people for what they considered a larger good. Unremembered is the significant role of the left in building counter-demonstrations that included local residents of Skokie, even when most civic and religious leaders opposed mobilization. Red Rose and other left groups were there in the town center, ready to confront the Nazis. My talk from the city hall steps reached perhaps a thousand protesters. Collin's forces proved no-shows in Skokie when they got concessions regarding ease of demonstrating on the southwest side of Chicago, where they were a significant danger to nearby Black and Latinx neighborhoods.

We worked under difficult conditions to try to combat Nazi marches, even making brief efforts to cooperate with the right-wing but sometimes militantly anti-Nazi Jewish Defense League in such efforts. In one brutal stretch the great anarcho-pacifist street poet Joffre Stewart (self-described on a contemporary C-Span broadcast as a "war tax resister" through joblessness) suffered attacks twice. Once the Nazis did the beating, and in the other instance it was the JDL, as Joffre's anti-statism explicitly extended to the state of Israel.

We organized against the big Nazi Marquette Park celebration march of July 9, 1978. The counterdemonstrations gathered big, angry crowds, but overwhelming police presence prevented us from moving through streets to approach Marquette Park. Some of us in Red Rose found a rail line we could walk along and get into the park, but only to look, not protest. It was harrowing to see a crowd of perhaps 3,000, many young and not a few still with Rolling Stones' T-shirts from the concert the previous night. They partied and grilled as if being at a Nazi event were as normal a thing as being among the 70,000 hearing the Stones (and reggae freedom singer Peter Tosh!) at Soldier Field. A couple dozen Nazis marched. Some retrospective accounts hold that about a third of the crowd supported them, a third gawked, and a third protested. The last part is surely wrong, as it was so hard to move from areas where protest could occur to the park that open protest in the park would have been foolish. The dubious former Chicago mayor Rahm Emanuel boasts of having played a role in the mobilizations against the Nazis, but you couldn't prove that by me.

Shortly after the 1978 march, Collin spent three years imprisoned at Pontiac for child molestation, and the Marquette Park Nazis lost their grip. An opposing Nazi faction renewed attacks on Collin as Jewish, and some of his own associates found his child pornography at their headquarters and turned him in. The most enduring popular culture portrayal loosely based on him, Henry Gibson's Nazi character in the 1980 Chicago-based film *The Blues Brothers*, captured how ridiculous Collin and his crew ultimately were. But they were anything but harmless and their defeat was not foreordained.

The role of Red Rose in bringing Rock against Racism (RaR) to Chicago also deserves mention. We and others knew about the British RaR concerts responding after 1976 to the far-right presence in British life and (through both the National Front and Ulster Unionist Party) politics, to racist street violence, and to xenophobic statements by performers such as rock guitarist Eric Clapton. Perhaps 80,000 marched to Victoria Park in east London to hear the Clash, X-Ray Spex, Tom Robinson, Steel Pulse, and others. The local events—300 of them in 1978 and 1979 alone—were as impressive, consciously turning out interracial crowds and crossing lines of musical genres, especially punk, reggae, and ska. In helping to bring RaR to the US we followed that model. The historian Mark Lause, who had come around Red Rose, played an important role as did members of the Youth International Party, the Yippies. Punk, blues, and much more shared the stage and a large Lincoln Park crowd heard such bands as D.O.A., Lonnie Brooks Blues Band, Immune System, and La Confidencia.

Red Rose Collective began, and ended, with some confusion about what it could become. Its most veteran and voluble leadership, like the International Socialism tradition from which the collective emerged, believed party-building to be the hallmark of any serious left. A bookstore could build such efforts but the store as a gathering place for a broad revolutionary left hardly counted, by itself, as revolutionary practice in this view. I came to disagree, slowly developing the heretical view I'd spell out a decade later in the foreword to the joint memoirs of the radical journalists Harvey O'Connor and Jessie Lloyd O'Connor. There I argued that in many times and places the "fellow travelers" and independent non-party left constituted a healthy part of the radical movement, and we needed institutions capable of supporting them in staying left rather than only calls to join in building a party. In the collective itself we had frequent debates—again we typically numbered only a dozen energetic, overburdened individuals—over whether we should have a line on events of the day and of bygone days. Should we weigh in on whether the Soviet Union was a bureaucratic collectivist formation, a state capitalist regime, or a deformed workers' state? Should those disagreeing be disciplined if they did not appear to agree in public? Should Red Rose attempt to produce a newspaper when we felt lucky just to staff the store?

In general, even if we lost debates within Red Rose to those arguing for the need for more centralization and production, the "less is better" contingent prevailed in practice as there just were not enough minutes to implement whatever was proposed. Interestingly, the two workers in industry, my favorite members of the collective, tended to disagree with me on this, wanting a paper, or at least a statement of principles, that they could hand to co-workers. Red Rose included creative thinkers with a variety of experiences and taking ourselves too seriously was certainly exciting, leading to debates that riveted me as they proceeded, even against my better judgment.

Such debates did not kill Red Rose. The security culture produced by our awareness of spying by Chicago's Red Squad and of surveillance of our Iranian comrades hurt more, leading to a formal inquiry into whether one of our members was a cop. The results, a "probation" for a short term, drew no final lines and the accused stayed active in the collective. However, the process itself chilled things. More decisively still, and perhaps inevitably in a small group so thrown into each other's company, personal relationships, and in one case a romantic one, soured. By the time Jean Allman and I left to work in Connecticut in late 1979 it was clear that the collective could not revive itself. I'd learned something about the difficulties of building lasting left institutions, and still more on what the Chicago left had on offer. Working in the Kerr Publishing Company and with the Chicago Surrealist Group would have happier outcomes.

Surrealist Collaborations and Old-Time Socialism

As an undergraduate, my desire to become educated, but not look like I wanted that too much, had me haphazardly taking many art history classes. I started near the top, as mentioned earlier, with an upper-division class that met my criterion of assigning very expensive books, covered by my scholarship, that would generate enough cash for several good meals when sold back to the bookstore. My mother could draw anything she saw but I was hapless in doing the same. Art history and, as it got called, "art appreciation," seemed all that I could hope for. The class was great. I ended up not returning its lavishly illustrated textbook for cash, and I took several more such courses.

Even so, I learned only the smallest bits about surrealism in or out of class. I'd been listening to Jefferson Airplane's 1967 album *Surrealistic Pillow* for a decade by the late seventies and shared the album's and the broader culture's collective misunderstanding of "surrealist" as meaning strange, unexpected, and distorted. Indeed, the persistent misuse of the word "surrealist" by much of the left still impresses me as distressingly uncomradely. This is especially striking in that "surrealist" was not borrowed by the art movement's founders but coined by them to describe a specific set of spelled-out principles regarding imagination, revolt, and society. When I first encountered flesh-and-blood surrealists in Chicago, I was still likely to describe the Cubs scoring seven runs in the seventh inning as "surreal." I had no knowledge of the connection of surrealism to Marxism, nor even basic familiarity with radical scholarship on art.

I first met surrealists in the late seventies, when Franklin and Penny Rosemont began to frequent Red Rose Books. They registered with me only after the Chicago Surrealist Group's mounting of their spectacular 1976 "Marvelous Freedom" exhibition in the city. I missed it and missed the genius of the Rosemonts for a while thereafter. The two of them had visited Paris in 1965 and met with an aging André Breton, who had been a leader of the surrealist movement for artistic imagination, social and political liberation, taking dreams seriously, and opposing colonialism—especially in surrealism's heyday in the twenties and thirties. Upon their return to Chicago, the Rosemonts formed the Chicago Surrealist Group, attracting people in SDS, and especially their associates in the Industrial Workers of the World. The worldwide protests in 1968 often organized around a slogan flowing from the surrealist tradition: "All Power to the Imagination."

At Red Rose, I approached surrealism warily. We in the bookstore collective had staked out a particularly "workerist" politics, believing profound changes emanated from the point of production. Not knowing much, I mistook the surrealists for having a purely New Left project, at a time when I tried hard to see myself as a product of the Old Left. Although Penny sometimes took jobs as a chemist, the Rosemonts and most surrealists whom I soon met tried hard not to have a boss or an imposed workday. Franklin presented himself as a high school dropout. He had left school in Chicago's industrial suburb of Maywood, the same school and about the same time as the Black Panther hero Fred Hampton and the Chicago folk music legend John Prine attended. Most of our regular Red Rose customers would have spoken of their "revolutionary work." The Rosemonts, though fully serious revolutionaries, more treasured revolutionary play. A lot had set me up to dismiss the surrealists as probably disengaged from struggles and as bourgeois.

But not for long. For one thing Franklin, Penny, and other surrealists maintained such a persistent presence. They marched against Nazis, did strike support work (especially in the long strike of bituminous coal miners in 1977 and 1978), and proved the most indefatigable rebuilders of the Charles H. Kerr Company as a socialist publisher. Few of my rushes to judgment withstood scrutiny. The Rosemonts possessed not only an impeccable self-education but also had studied with the most important left intellectual in Chicago, St. Clair Drake, after Franklin managed to get into college without high school—at Roosevelt University in the Loop. The influence of Drake, the great African American sociologist, anthropologist, and historian, marked the Rosemonts' anti-racism and opposition to empire decisively. Franklin's dad, Henry Rosemont, worked as a union printer, wrote extraordinary working-class history, and had a radio show on WCFL—that is, W Chicago Federation of Labor. His mother played leading roles in union organization of women musicians.

As we met, Franklin was putting meticulous finishing touches on his fat collection of Breton's writings *What Is Surrealism?* The texts, plus Rosemont's book-length introduction, clarified how tightly woven surrealism's history was with that of the revolutionary Marxism of the Old Left, as much as it also spoke to the New Left. I read the book when it appeared in 1978. Over time I approached surrealism as an admirer of its political action and its personalities, especially Paul Garon, who collected and sold rare books and who wrote on the blues, insurgent imaginations, addiction, and poetry.

A moment marked out when I realized, or admitted, that my suspicions of the surrealists were unfounded. Franklin and I got into a discussion, maybe an argument on my part, about Marx and psychoanalysis. I had learned a lot from reading Herbert Marcuse and Wilhelm Reich on Marx and the Freudian tradition at Northern Illinois and agreed with the surrealist view that Marxism and psychoanalysis enriched each other. But in the moment I chose to quarrel over areas of difference. Since Franklin knew lots more of Freud than I it seemed best for me to reduce everything to a class angle. I argued ultimately that Freud's patients were bourgeois and from that poisoned fruit nothing that could come that would speak to the working class, which I held had completely other family structures, developmental experiences, and psychodynamics. The long exchange came after a late-running party at which bluesman Billy Branch played and Bugs Bunny cartoons were projected. I went to bed thinking I'd won an argument and woke up thinking I needed to listen and read more and talk less.

Coming to the Chicago Surrealist Group through such a route set me apart. Almost everyone in it had impressive artistic talents and deep creative passions, which made me an unlikely participant. They had a discipline around art that I remained far from possessing around my writing. I never did become comfortable sharing what little poetry I wrote, and still less any art. I drifted into surrealism and never left, more than I joined. But I did find my way to a collaboration with surrealists now nearly forty-five years in the running. I learned enough to write about the movement, especially in articles on surrealism and sports, the 1929 surrealist map of the world, and surrealism's place in US left culture. I helped cement the friendship, later a stunning collaboration, of Franklin with the young historian Robin D.G. Kelley. They ultimately produced the spectacular edited volume *Black, Brown & Beige: Surrealist Writings from Africa and the Diaspora* in Franklin's marvelous Surrealist Revolution series at University of Texas Press. It, along with Penny's edited collection *Surrealist Women: An International Anthology*, changed the way that surrealism is discussed, even in academia, even in the US.

Franklin and I drafted *Three Days That Shook the New World Order*, the collective surrealist statement of solidarity with the Los Angeles Rebellion of 1992. It became perhaps the most circulated and translated such surrealist tract of the last half-century. I finally did pick up art appreciation, not just art history, especially for the paintings of Penelope Rosemont, the drawings of Franklin, and the creative energy of such Chicago surrealists as Robert Green, Gail Ahrens, Joel Williams, Tamara Smith, and Beth Garon. Intellectually I became fascinated by the surrealist concept of miserabilism, the idea that widespread addiction to miserable social relations, to planet-killing development strategies, to overwork, and to debt underpins how rulers rule.

The national and even global range of the surrealist group's contacts was daunting. My kids came to know the African American beat and surrealist poet Ted Joans (who like me was partly from Cairo, Illinois) as well as such brilliant artists, musicians, and writers as Jayne Cortez, Laura Corsiglia, Philip Lamantia, Leonora Carrington, and Lawrence Ferlinghetti. At the time the kids much preferred the Rosemonts' house, stuffed with old comics, with toys and gadgets as well as art, to meetings at our house. A resident laughingthrush who sometimes talked on the phone, or at least raucously kept others from doing so, completed the scene and soundtrack at their place.

The arena in which I came to know the Rosemonts best turned out to be a central focus of my activity over the next twenty-five years: that of attempting to reach a broad US left through books from the Charles H. Kerr Publishing Company. I knew of the Kerr Company vaguely even before arriving in Chicago. In the Dekalb study group where I learned about historical materialism by reading classic short works by Marx, Lenin, and Engels, we occasionally splurged on classic editions published by Kerr, still inexpensive and much better-looking than the cheap China Books editions. The press's edition of the *Communist Manifesto* was a staple on the US left and we sometimes used Kerr's pamphlet editions of *Wage-Labor and Capital* and *Value, Price, and Profit*. Much more legendary than these was the Kerr edition of all three volumes of Marx's *Capital*, the authoritative English translation until at least the sixties, having originally appeared in handsome hardbound volumes published between 1906 and 1909. It was still the edition most cited by historians when I entered Northwestern. In Dekalb I knew I should read those volumes, and at Red Rose, with time on my hands, I did so—well, the first two anyhow.

Charles Hope Kerr, a progressive Unitarian from Georgia, had founded the company that bore his name in 1886. By the mid-1890s the populist movement for farmer-labor unity dragged Kerr and the company to the left and shortly thereafter the company entered its distinctly socialist stage with the inauguration of its sixty-pamphlet "Pocket Library of Socialism." The first title in the series, a socialist-feminist pamphlet by May Walden Kerr, appeared in 1899. Kerr's *International Socialist Review* debuted in 1900 and soon became a leading English-language organ of the left wing of socialist thought and language, famed far beyond the US. The company issued shares pitched to supporters, not to investors, and indeed promised to never pay a dividend, offering instead only discounts on literature and a feeling of having advanced the coming of the "cooperative commonwealth."

World War I, and the opposition of the best of the socialist movement to it, halted the company's rise. Both the US and Canadian authorities revoked the mailing privileges of ISR and the red scares following the war decimated the base of US radicalism even as much of the remaining left reoriented toward the Soviet Revolution. The political and the financial intertwined with the personal, most notably in the case of the 1922 suicide of the most talented intellectual associated with Kerr, Mary Marcy. In the twenties, Charles Hope Kerr sold shares in the enterprise bearing his name to members of the Proletarian Party (PP), a dissenting US faction of the Communist International growing out of the Michigan Socialist Party. John Keracher, a PPer, had already been doing day-to-day Kerr work before the transfer.

The new PP leadership proved apt custodians for a nearly undermined Kerr Publishing Company. Their activities as a party focused on education among a base of primarily skilled workers. They kept the Marxist classics in print, adding sparingly, for example with Keracher's own excellent 1935 short work on psychology, advertising, and capitalism, The Head-Fixing Industry. In 1971, as the party lost its aging members, the PP turned Kerr over to a group of veteran Chicago radicals, including Industrial Workers of the World historian and editor Fred Thompson, former labor defense activist and left opera critic (turned economics professor) Joe Giganti, Korean War resister Burt Rosen, and writer on Indigenous peoples Virgil Vogel. Publishing for, or in cooperation with, the Illinois Labor History Society gave the reorganized company some resources. Even so, the average age of that excellent, reconstituted group was very high. Thompson himself recalled to me that his goal in signing on did not exceed providing a "decent burial" to a venerable institution.

However, the new leadership quickly produced a new edition of the wonderful The Autobiography of Mother Jones, a Kerr book since the twenties. Completely new titles emerged, including Carolyn Ashbaugh's groundbreaking Lucy Parsons: American Revolutionary and Daniel Fusfeld's Rise & Repression of Radical Labor, a well-timed short guide to workers' movements and state violence. Kerr showed signs of being back in business, though the successes were uneven and created more work than the board could handle. The West Loop office was inconveniently located, and filling orders at the post office was grueling. My first visit to Kerr was perhaps in 1978, precisely to carry things and generally help out. My lasting memory of the working visit is of countless boxes of Bernard Brommel's just off-the-press biography of Eugene Victor Debs, a solid work but one even I knew could not sell in the vast quantities that had been printed and bound in hardcover. The board itself soon realized the need for assistance, adding the Rosemonts, and then me. By my late 20s, I had my dream job, however unpaid.

The rebooted board settled, not without frictions, into a working body, with Thompson, Vogel, and Giganti remaining especially active. Other old-timers also gave leadership, especially Theo Waldinger, a veteran of the Austrian Revolution of 1918, and the accomplished Latino printmaker and poet Carlos Cortez, born in Milwaukee to a Mexican anarchist father and German-American socialist mom, and the printer Martin Ptacek. When the offices moved to Clark and Greenleaf, a stone's throw from Red Rose, the Rosemonts staffed it, and we tried hard to make friends among workers in the post office in Rogers Park, where lots of our time was spent.

We had very little money but some resources. The Kerr inventory featured treasures, including old editions of *Capital* and sets of the Library of Science for the Workers, some of the books in the latter unspeakably beautiful and others marked by eugenic impulses. We sold what we could, with one of the science sets going to the socialist paleontologist and historian of science Stephen Jay Gould, who became a reliable supporter of the company. The collections of papers that remained in the office also had some value, and the University of Michigan's Labadie labor collection took on the Proletarian Party collection. Chicago's Newberry Library later secured the archives of the Kerr Company itself.

Gould and others participated in a Friends of the Kerr Company group, contributing funds and good words. Studs Terkel proved especially loyal, as did the historian David Montgomery, the poet Dennis Brutus, the organizer Vicky Starr, the labor leader H.L. Mitchell, the novelist Jack Conroy, and the brilliant surrealist artist Leonora Carrington, among many others. It was as a "friend" that Rawick blurbed one of our new titles as the "funniest book since Marx's *Capital*."

Paul Buhle reviewed Kerr books when and where he could, sometimes in the *Village Voice*. The *Nation*, *New Republic*, and the *New York Review of Books* stayed uninterested, preferring to review the most anodyne publications of the big New York publishers to anything declaredly revolutionary—and Midwestern to boot. The brave, long-living Chicago opponent of Richard Daley's political machine, Leon Despres, provided legal work. Friendships with leading writers on workers' self-determination who had their own small presses—Stan Weir's Singlejack Books and Marty Glaberman's punningly named Bewick Editions—led to Kerr being able to list their titles for sale, filling out our sometimes slim catalogs. Other supporters who taught in colleges committed to using our publications in classes in advance of our printing them. Publicity came in the form of mass mailing of catalogs in a tabloid newspaper format, enlivened by much art from Carlos, Penny, Franklin, and others.

The hundredth anniversary of Kerr's founding—we increasingly suspected that we'd reach that milestone—and of the Haymarket police riot and bombing loomed. Both came in 1986, and both energized the raising of money. The Illinois Labor History Society particularly supported work with local tie-ins, whether regarding the events at Haymarket or those radiating from the railway company town of Pullman on the southside. Franklin and I worked for years as editors of a massive, opulently illustrated, and determinedly internationalist *Haymarket Scrapbook*, the most ambitious title produced under the new Kerr collective. That book broke through to *New York Times* coverage, not in the book reviews but as a news story reporting on historian Paul Avrich's contribution, which identified a new candidate for who threw the bomb at Haymarket. I can brag full-throatedly about what an enduring book *Haymarket Scrapbook* is because Franklin did the lion's share of the of the writing and editing. With Penny, he also made it beautiful graphically.

Two even more oversized works came later. Franklin's *Joe Hill: The IWW and the Making of a Revolutionary Workingclass Counterculture* began as a projected slim fastback gathering the unknown drawings of Hill, the martyred IWW singer-songwriter. It grew to nearly 700 pages, offering everything Hill did and much that was adjacent to him. As Franklin planned the Hill book, we became close to J. Anthony Lukas, the Pulitzer Prize-winning journalist and historian who was finishing his fabulous, massive book on western US labor radicalism, *Big Trouble*. The sprawling example set by Lukas of following digressions and assuming they will come together is not foolproof, for me anyhow. But it worked in Franklin's *Joe Hill* biography. The other blockbuster Kerr book brought together contents of the many editions of the IWW's *Little Red Songbook* as *The Big Red Songbook*. The finest folklorist of his generation—and the originator of the term *laborlore*—Archie Green, did most of the intellectual work in this case but insisted that Franklin, Sal Salerno, and I be credited as co-editors. The current edition features a contribution by Rage Against the Machine stalwart Tom Morello.

We younger board members desperately wanted to change some things about the company but within boundaries set not only by finances but also by a reverence for Kerr's past. We regarded Paul Lafargue's 1883 *The Right to Be Lazy*, first a Kerr book in English translation in 1907, as being as on-time in speaking to our present as anything written the day before yesterday. Lafargue's publication represented the first book from Kerr by a Black author, with Hubert Harrison's "The Black Man's Burden" following closely in ISR. Still, we struggled to develop a tradition of publishing Black writers. We eventually changed that in many ways. With the help of Bobby Hill and Glaberman, Kerr added several important C.L.R. James titles to its list. One of them, *History of Pan-African Revolt*, sported an arresting introduction by Robin Kelley.

Through the efforts of the late historian John Bracey, perhaps the Kerr Company's best friend over the decades, we secured the important work of recollection and study *We Will Return in the Whirlwind: Black Radical Organizations, 1960–1975* by Muhammad Ahmad (Max Stanford, Jr.), a Revolutionary Action Movement leader in the sixties. Carl Cowl, a maritime worker, musician, and Yiddish scholar was a friend whom several of us knew as the only person who'd joined as many left groups as Rawick had. Cowl became Claude McKay's literary executor. Through him we brought into print the unpublished McKay novel *Harlem Glory: A Fragment of Aframerican Life*, another newsworthy event. Gail Ahrens' work on the mixed-race anarchist and communist Lucy Parsons and volumes of Carlos Cortez's poetry and art also reflected the changes at Kerr.

New Kerr titles often looked backward. That counts almost as an inside joke in the case of Franklin Rosemont's 1990 collection of Edward Bellamy's writings on "mystery and imagination" under the title *Apparitions of Things to Come*. Rosemont offered a Charles Kerr book about an author who decisively influenced Charles Kerr himself. Bellamy's influential 1888 work of utopian fiction, *Looking Backward, 2000–1887* had helped radicalize Kerr himself and sped the evolution of the company toward populism, and then socialism. When *The Communist Manifesto* turned 150 years old in 1998—by then it had been in print at Kerr just short of a century—a pretty new edition celebrated the milestone. Kelley contributed a striking new introduction.

Kerr's most commercially successful new title during this time was our reissue of Upton Sinclair's 1937 novel *The Flivver King: A Story of Ford-America*, first published as part of United Automobile Workers' organizing drives. An apt historical introduction by the leading expert on auto work, Steve Meyer, plus the lively and lean writing in the book made it a brisk seller in college classrooms, as we knew would happen based on pledges from professors to assign it. But we also appreciated that Sinclair had been a friend of the Kerr Company many decades before. His *Our Bourgeois Literature* had a place in the Pocket Library of Socialism. We soon learned that there was an unexpected further audience for *The Flivver King*. We'd produced it by photographing pages of the original novel, itself designed to fit in a worker's pockets. Soon auto retirees let us know that their young eyes in the thirties coped with the format, but the print was too tiny now. Subsequent editions got bigger.

In the case of the brilliant Kerr staffer Mary Marcy, an old-time Kerr author was being read again sixty years later. Her book, *You Have No Country! Workers Struggles against War* ranked as our hardest-hitting volume, page-for-page. Between the late seventies and 2009, when Franklin Rosemont died suddenly, Kerr published as many as 100 titles, if surrealist Black Swan books are included. These were produced without a single paid staff member.

Insofar as this book sets out to be about my life, the last words of this chapter's reminiscences should loop back the privilege of participating in Red Rose, the Chicago Surrealist Group, and especially the Kerr Company. Ten of those Kerr titles were ones I either edited or to which I contributed a foreword. These produced relatively immediate gratification, an especially appealing prospect when I was co-caring for two young sons. In some ways this involved having a separate Kerr "track" of work, in which an idea would arise and a year later a book would materialize. I anticipated no academic credit for this work, although it did dishearten me when a more senior scholar advised me early in my career to take those titles off my resume. These Kerr projects varied in intensity. For example, in writing on the charismatic Southern labor organizer Covington Hall, I became perhaps the only defender of the quality of his work as a poet, gathering selections of his verse for Kerr in the small volume *Dreams and Dynamite*. I then revisited Hall in a much more ambitious editorial project, providing context and annotation for his unpublished but much-cited masterpiece *Labor Struggles in the Deep South*. Given that my first job after finishing graduate school was as a junior editor of the Frederick Douglass Papers at Yale, I began to think of myself for a time as being more of an editor than a writer.

My best editing experience at Kerr involved a slim volume that took as much thought as many of the books I have myself written. Its story goes to the many ways Kerr experiences changed me in that its subject, Fred Thompson, set out to give me a political education, however un-obtrusively. Thompson, born with the century in 1900 in the Canadian Maritimes, participated vigorously on the Kerr Board almost until his death in 1987. He had been chosen to help in the "decent burial" of the company in light of an incredible life on the left: in the IWW by the twenties, in San Quentin prison that same decade, in editing the *Industrial Worker*, in teaching at Minnesota's Work People's College, in important labor organizing and strategizing in Cleveland and elsewhere, and in writing history. I wanted to tell that story but he professed not to see the need for his "ugly old mug" to appear on the cover of a book. It did, on *Fellow Worker: The Life of Fred Thompson*, but seven years after his death. The book stitched together oral history, brief autobiographical writing, and material gleaned from police spying on Fred in extended efforts to deport him.

Thompson fascinated me not only for what he taught but also for how. Kerr meetings tended to convene at his place in the Logan Square neighborhood because it was easier for us to get to him than vice versa. He hosted along with Jenny Velsek, his longtime IWW comrade. They offered Keebler cookies as refreshment, with Fred touting their being union-made each meeting and himself displaying something of the elfin magic associated with the product's ads, eyes dancing. If it were spring, he'd profess incredulity and sadness over that fact that Earth Day and the international worker's holiday of May Day were two different events a few days apart when they should have been one—a profound insight I was not quite ready to take on. He could recite considerable poetry from memory, reminding me of my mother in that regard, in his case especially William Blake and Robert Burns. He'd break into song a bit, especially an obscure snatch of music repeating "Karl Marx's whiskers they were eighteen inches long" as antidote to any threat that the gathering might lapse into abstraction or revolutionary posturing. He often repeated his waggish belief that a smart transitional demand for socialists was that any business with an incorrect time on its public clock immediately be considered the people's property. I never see a malfunctioning bank clock without remembering him.

One genius of Fred's interventions, in meetings and interpersonally, was to allow that he personally sympathized with a position while declaring it an impossibility. My most seemingly inspired book ideas almost invariably received dismissal from him with "That would be of interest to you, me, and a half a dozen other people in the whole world." I believed at the time that ultra-leftism, though theoretically possible, presented scant danger on the US left. Thompson therefore gently but repeatedly recalled old-timers of his youth cautioning him against his "getting so far out in front of the band" that all contact with the music got lost.

That he liked young people, and historians, and that he could relent made the interactions with Fred overwhelmingly positive. For example, amidst the defeats of unions during the Reagan ascendency of the eighties, the Rosemonts and I very much wanted Kerr to publish classic IWW pamphlets on sabotage as one useful tactic available to workers, who could engage in a "withdrawal of efficiency" or in more active attacks on production when provoked. Fred had a response to the proposal that we could not begin to answer: "I spent some of my life in San Quentin because of loose talk about sabotage." Those words left open the question of whether Fred opposed sabotage or loose talk. But he also softened on the book idea as we persisted and eventually *Direct Action & Sabotage: Three Classic IWW Pamphlets* did appear, under the editorship of Salvatore Salerno, though after Fred's death.

When Fred died, in 1987, I had already moved to Columbia, Missouri, but I joined the Chicago-based IWW in his memory and participated for two or three years. The Rosemonts likewise renewed their active membership during that period of experimental cooperation between the Wobblies and the radical environmental group Earth First! Fred's disquiet regarding the separation between May Day and Earth Day came to be addressed at least a little. We also edited a splashy TEAR DOWN THE CONFEDERATE FLAG special issue of the Industrial Worker in 1988, making a demand we all probably regarded as impossible before being happily proven wrong.

Connections to surrealism, radical environmentalism, and to the Kerr Company coincided with my growing perception that anarchism and Marxism needed elements of each other. Anarcho-Marxism—the "Chicago Idea" of the Haymarket martyrs and of Lucy Parsons—mattered in this connection. So did the world's growing examples of the horrors of state-sponsored violence and surveillance, whether in Chicago, Southeast Asia, Poland, or Iran. Impressive too was the fact that anarchists, and even anarcho-pacificists, sometimes seemed more ready to confront fascists and to engage in direct action generally than Marxists were. That the surrealists, their historic and present ties to Marxism notwithstanding, also sought insights from anarchism encouraged me.

In 1978, as I finished classwork at Northwestern, the slickest US radical academic journal ever, Marxist Perspectives, launched. Its elaborate, tiered hierarchy of editors predicted long life under the direction of its founding inspiration, historian of slavery Eugene Genovese. It barely lasted two years. I occupied the lowest possible rung looking up at that hierarchy and noticed the buzz about the journal within the profession. I could never much warm to the project or much mourn its speedy demise. Partly, I had an emerging critique of Genovese's work born of studying with Sterling Stuckey (see Chapter Five). But equally, for better and worse, the radical history with which I identified centered on the very different worlds of the Kerr Company, surrealism, and labor defense.

Interlude One

BRUSH WITH GENIUS: C.L.R. JAMES

For many years my favorite gathering of historians took place in Detroit. Sponsored by Wayne State University, the North American Labor History Society meetings defied the decline of industrial unionism in the city and the closing of almost every local hotel viable for a conference to convene electric gatherings of organizers and writers. I could depend on a meal accompanied by riveting recollections from William Santiago-Valles, the great Puerto Rican scholar-activist, Marty Glaberman, and others, once including White Panther Party former political prisoner John Sinclair reading poetry, and the sociologist Graham Cassano playing music. The legendary Black Marxist auto worker organizer General Baker often came, and the blacklisted historian turned movement lawyer Staughton Lynd spoke memorably. A full complement of more mainstream academic labor historians attended as well. One of them, Nelson Lichtenstein, greeted the leading young labor historian Robin D.G. Kelley and me in the nineties with the ultimate insider radical history joke. He approached us at a table, saying, "If it isn't Johnson and Forest." I puzzle over whether Lichtenstein meant to display arcane revolutionary knowledge or to convey a kind of dismissiveness, pegging us as the inheritors of a tradition gone for 40 years. We, maybe I should only speak for myself, were thrilled to be taken as allied with that particular lapsed revolutionary tendency. "I get to be Johnson," I said, though in truth I'd have happily settled for Forest.

The Trinidadian Marxist C.L.R. James had published and organized as J.R. Johnson in his movement work in the US from the late thirties to the fifties. His seminal historical and (what would later be called) cultural studies writings, including *The Black Jacobins*; *Mariners, Renegades, and Castaways*; and *Beyond a Boundary*, nevertheless appeared under the name of James. Similarly, Freddie Forest served as a pen name for Raya

Dunayevskaya, a Jewish immigrant from Lithuania, who joined James in defending the idea that the Soviet Union was a state capitalist society in fifteen years of collaboration with those inside and outside of the Socialist Workers Party. With the philosopher Grace Lee, whom I later came to know in Detroit as the important movement leader Grace Lee Boggs, Johnson and Forest reinterpreted dialectics searchingly.

For a waggish remark, Lichtenstein's carried a certain accuracy in terms of my political influences. I knew Forest, as Dunayevskaya, having met her in Chicago in the seventies at parties given by the small but intellectually productive News and Letters group, in which she was a senior leading figure. Her work taught me much about Marxist feminism. If contact with her did not change my life, it did change my research agenda for a time. When we met, I introduced myself as being from the St. Louis area. "Ahh, St. Louis," she beamed. "Home of our first soviet." I had no idea what she meant and later privately asked one of her younger associates to unravel the mystery. She directed me to a News and Letters pamphlet on the 1877 General Strike in St. Louis, one detailing the brief rule of the city by workers councils, or in Raya's term, soviets. I did not even know of the 1877 insurrection but made my business to learn about it, eventually publishing two substantial articles on the subject. It would have been the subject of my second book, but the article research sent me to a close analysis of those arrested in the strike and of its leaders, using city directories and census data to think about divisions of race and skill. The social portraits showed a much more divided working class than the heroic first days of interracialism within the soviet had suggested. I had only begun to move away from a search for a directly "useable" working-class past and even soviet makers did not make the cut in this case. I moved on to other research.

James, or Johnson, had a much more lasting impact on me. He had taught at Northwestern for a short time just before I came to school there, and I'd written a short appreciation of his work for *Minnesota Review*. My mentor George Rawick told endless and wonderful stories about being James' assistant in London in the sixties, emphasizing the mix of visitors to the flat where the James lived. The electricity of the place comes through at times even in V.S. Naipaul's dyspeptic novel *A Way in the World*, based on James and his circles. Rawick described James' own role in inspiring him to write the classic history of slavery, *From Sundown to Sunup*, by hosting his talk on the slave's view of slavery in that apartment. In the late eighties it became possible for me to visit James in his Brixton lodgings.

I remained close to librarians at the tremendous Melville J. Herskovits Library of African Studies at Northwestern, and they responded to my pleas that the library delegate me to write a description of the papers James held, with a view to acquiring them. Rawick, himself declining in health, and Marty Glaberman had said that James was ill, and from others I'd gathered an impression that he needed money. Through Anna Grimshaw, who provided some of his care, I scheduled a whole day at the flat, the morning with his papers and books, and the later afternoon with him. I'd visited his Brixton neighborhood before, but it seemed even more vibrant in light of getting to meet such a hero and knowing of the rebellions that had taken place in the district.

At first, I thought the lodgings were cold, but that's usually the case when I'm indoors in London. It soon became apparent that James' care, organized partly by the *Race Today* collective, featured solicitude and love. He sat watching cricket on television and I went to the room functioning as a library. The papers disappointed initially as they were sparse. Some of his personal papers had already ended up at the University of London and elsewhere. I did not know what kind of acquisitions case could be made. The working library of books redeemed matters. Many had fascinating marginalia. The work I had to do was completed before the morning was over. That cleared more time to be with James, I hoped, although I knew from his writings that he'd not abandon the cricket telecast lightly. He didn't, but it took a lull and my hopes rose, only to have him turn with equal interest to a soap opera. The everyday culture of working people remained very important to James.

I'd already rehearsed a hundred times just what I wanted the conversation to be about. As World War II had loomed, James had organized militant sharecroppers in southeast Missouri, the state's so-called Bootheel region, a short drive from Cairo, Illinois, where I partly grew up. I needed to know the local history, especially the racial dynamics of the movement and of the attacks on it. When the show ended and he had discussed it with a helper, I had my chance to ask questions. I blurted out the topic and probably five sub-topics we'd need to cover. With a circular pensive hand gesture he replied, "Ah, yes, Missouri," then a pause, "where I learned so much from Hegel." My script disappeared. It was the dialectic that he had decided I needed to learn about. The image of James reading Hegel's *Phenomenology* on the steps or porch of a sharecropper's cabin captivated me and a philosophy lesson suddenly seemed fine. James had only so much energy at that point in his life and he talked for less than an hour. Only well into the lesson did I realize that I was in fact learning about the sharecroppers. James realized that they were what some on the left and many in the broader society describe as "backward"—deeply religious, rural, not disciplined by wage labor and factory time, and possessed often of only what the later leader of freedom movements, Bob Moses, called a "sharecropper's education," designed by planters to be rudimentary. James nevertheless insisted that these organized sharecroppers and agricultural day laborers stood as the "most advanced workers" of their time. It was not just that James happened to be reading Hegel and witnessing sharecropper revolts at the same time. The opposites that the Bootheel region embodied demanded an encounter with dialectics. His books included marginalia on Lenin returning to Hegel in order to appreciate why it is necessary to "leap" philosophically—and Missouri's most marginalized workers were leaping.

5

THE CRAFT OF HISTORY
AND THE HISTORY BUSINESS

Almost all of the joys and problems I encountered in my late 20s and 30s in trying to work in universities remain our problems today but in much-altered—which is to say, much-worsened—material circumstances. Most historians of political economy tell us the shift to a neoliberal economy—austere where social spending was concerned but flush when spending to make wars and prepare for them, and wildly spendthrift in backing incarceration—occurred about 1970. It coincided with my entry into higher education almost exactly. The trends were there for the discerning to spot but mostly in their infancy: the reigning in of grand plans for expansion of universities, a far more difficult labor market for academic workers, shifting of costs to students, and increasing domination of higher ed by elite private universities and a handful of prosperous state universities. My early experiences thus speak to the ruin of universities, discussed mainly in the concluding chapter, but they approximated the miseries afflicting today's graduate students and young academics in neither degree nor kind.

The best example, the one I most need to remind myself of when thinking that I share the problems of today's graduate students but not the extent of those problems, lies in what gets called the "jobs crisis" in academic work, especially in the humanities. Such a crisis pressured students in the eighties. The largest annual meeting of historians featured a massive room, loud and chaotic, in which throngs of jobseekers signed up for and sometimes suffered through interviews for underpaid, insecure, far-flung work the following year. (The better positions tended to require conference interviews in the equally awful setting of the conference hotel rooms themselves). I had a great deal of trouble getting the security of a tenure-track job. Once, in the early eighties, a friend—he already had a good job—suggested that we disrupt the hiring hall part of the conference with a demonstration. I declined, and the action never happened, because I thought that the only form of protest appropriate to the heartless setting was a riot, and folks weren't ready for that. Plus the priority was to actually get a job.

When my own doctoral graduate students faced prospects of joblessness or precarious teaching, I used to rehearse this story as productive of insight and empathy on my part and hope on theirs. Now I don't. There's not a job crisis in the history business now, subject to being cyclical and ameliorated. There's a fully reorganized labor process condemning most who persist in the work to a career of precarious labor. The favored few avoiding that fate come with dismal regularity from elite universities. In the realm of academic labor, and all else in this chapter, I therefore offer not timeless truths—we get enough of those from my New Left generation—but personal experiences.

Northwestern: An Idyll and Its Opposite on the North Shore

Before I started graduate school, some intimate relationships and teaching tennis briefly had me around rich people and institutions not strapped for cash. But Northwestern marked a much more sustained excursion into what my friend Paul Gilroy has called the overdeveloped world. I found things to like: beautiful Lake Michigan views, studying a stone's throw from a beach; manicured grounds; and for that matter a tennis facility with well-maintained clay courts, a rarity in the North and indeed in the US. Faculty aside, it was the library that most made Northwestern magical for me. With an elegant older wing and a beautiful spacious new one, it housed lots of research carrels, some in the open and some in windowed and enclosed rooms, available to graduate students and professors, and bringing them into close contact with each other. The core library housed opulent couches and a collection of great books and more hard copies of current and recent journals than I had seen before or have since. My habit was to check on those in any field that even plausibly touched mine. My interests became interdisciplinary both out of a commitment to Black Studies and a desire to spend more time, with more journals, in that room.

Material facts made Northwestern pleasant for me. That its indoor temperature stayed a comfortable 15 degrees higher than the left book-store where I volunteered in winter and 15 degrees lower in summer made me study happily there. Moreover, I made disastrously bad apart-ment choices my first two years in Chicago, the first far too small, and in the second year a place transitioning to housing the elderly. These also made the library and the beach seem much better places to read. I was well-fed at Northwestern, especially after being appointed a fellow in a student residence, which gave me free food in return for eating with undergraduates.

Northwestern's Department of History, already rightly sensing a crisis in placing its PhDs in jobs, or at least in the kind of jobs thought to befit us, had opted before I arrived for small incoming classes. Mine had just four on the US history "side," all terrific and none from elite schools. We became close with classes admitted before us, including in my case the excellent African American historians Norrece T. Jones, Jr., my best graduate school friend, and David Dennard. Ample resources followed my small cohort around. These did not translate into more than subsistence pay but we did not teach until year four and then only a small first-year undergraduate seminar typically related to our dissertation research, though mine was instead on Herman Melville and social history. Northwestern's peer institution in the metropolitan area, the University of Chicago, seemed to take just the opposite tack, admitting many US history first-year graduate students with little aid initially but with a chance to compete, frighteningly to me, for support in subsequent years.

In a program as small as Northwestern's, faculty socialized with students to an uncommon extent. I played tennis regularly against an Americanist with whom I did not work and taught tennis to the son of one of my committee members. Particularly fascinating to me was the eagerness of the late George Fredrickson to hang out. George, who studied race in US and later in South Africa as well, was the best-known US historian at Northwestern, so much so that Stanford recruited him away in short order. He faithfully ate lunch in the student union and as faithfully asked if he could join my companion, Jean Allman, an undergraduate, and myself. Odder still was how uneasy he seemed even after we had become veteran lunch companions. George's voice quavered and his large body did likewise as he attempted small talk. It was extraordinarily sweet that he persisted in trying. Then at a certain point he'd rise and say something like, "Well, I have to get downtown" in order to be on some PBS telecast or radio show. I remember worrying at first that if he could scarcely make it through having a hamburger socially the shows would go terribly wrong. But tuning them in revealed a calm, laser-focused professorial presence on George's part. Later, when the Organization of American Historians chose George as its president, I needlessly worried about the stress of a presidential address and rejoiced in how triumphant his was.

My last long stay with George came near the end of his life. I taught then at the University of Illinois and wanted him to visit to give a talk. He agreed on the condition I would then drive him six hours south to Memphis for an OAH meeting. By then I treasured the awkward small talk as much as the easier exchanges over antiracist politics and writing history that invariably followed. George's politics remained liberal but taught me how much we would benefit from a fighting liberalism that could grow intellectually. When I later reflected on his unique moral compass—he became a supporter of the left anti-whiteness journal *Race Traitor* and a deeply engaged anti-apartheid activist—I came to argue that our problem in the US lies not only in the absence of a radical left but also in the paucity of fighting, principled liberals. To his great credit he learned a great deal about the Black freedom movements and Black intellectual life from his African American students, especially Sterling Stuckey.

When I returned to Northwestern as a visiting assistant professor in the early eighties, and Jean as a doctoral student in African history, we ate and drank with the brilliant Africanist Ivor Wilks most Friday nights, our toddler in tow. Sometimes we'd join important world intellectuals who taught at Northwestern in social settings, scholars such as the Palestinian political scientist Ibrahim Abu-Lughod (whom no less a figure than Edward Said called "Palestine's foremost academic and intellectual") or the South African revolutionary poet Dennis Brutus. The massive and sustained encampments against Northwestern's investment in South Africa in the mid-eighties brought us closer still to Brutus, who carried wounds from being shot twenty years before by South African authorities as he tried to flee incarceration for his leadership in the movement against apartheid in sports. Abu-Lughod, and Northwestern's outrageous decision to award an honorary doctorate to Israeli leader Menachem Begin in 1978, brought me into activism around what Said would call "the question of Palestine" for the first time.

On many days, and especially on days of protests, Northwestern seemed magical, but on other levels it was also dismal. Its leading founder and important donor, John Evans (thus Evanston as the town's name) had headed the university's board of trustees for forty years. He'd served as governor of Colorado during the horrendous Sand Creek Massacre of Arapaho and Cheyenne people in 1864. Hundreds died, two-thirds of them women and children. When the university prepared a report on Evans and Sand Creek on the 150th anniversary of the atrocity, it exonerated him from direct culpability—though he had urged the military to "pursue," "kill," and "destroy" Indigenous peoples resisting occupation. Evans' role in Colorado represented the new moment of wealth-making and a first turn to hard Republican Party racism. It is the subject of perhaps the best chapter by a US historian writing on race and political economy in the past fifty years, "Organizing the West" in my late friend Alexander Saxton's *Rise and Fall of the White Republic*.

The university's—so far in my experience all universities'—ability to countenance brutality while professing high-mindedness surely featured in my time at Northwestern: the honorary degree for Begin; aggressive CIA recruiting; heartless and procedurally irregular efforts to force out my colleague Barbara Foley after her direct action protest of a visit to campus by a leader of the Nicaraguan contras; florid self-praise for retaining, on freedom of expression grounds, a Holocaust denier in electrical engineering who taught for many years after the publication of his book on the "hoax" of Hitler's exterminationist policies; and a refusal to budge on divesting from South African investments. All of these were accompanied by broad suggestions that higher humanity shaped the university's actions and inactions.

The Historian's Craft: An Apprenticeship

Every couple years I teach a class at the University of Kansas called "The Historian's Craft." It's now my favorite course. My joining it started as a kind of a private joke. My appointment has me mostly in the inter-disciplinary field of American studies but a quarter time in history, the discipline in which my graduate training lay. The two fields exist in a state of bantering rivalry at best; stern warnings to students to avoid the other, unenlightened field recur. Historians suspect American studies is too soft in its standards of evidence—for a good while the teaching of novels was taken as a supposed sign of such lack of rigor within history departments. Historians also often regard American studies as too insistently political, too "woke" as it now gets said, and too inattentive to how things change over time. Like much in academia the battle is mostly a mock one. We in American studies are tempted to believe the hidebound among historians deserve the novelist Gore Vidal's indictment of them as "scholar squirrels," accumulating stores of facts without reaching hard enough for their meaning.

In fact, many of the American studies faculty trained as historians as had I, only discovering American studies when asked to chair it at the University of Minnesota in the nineties. I quickly warmed to it, so much so that I served on the executive council of the American Studies Association by 2001. There, a friend and I raised the question of Palestine, finding what a tiny minority we were in wanting to see it addressed, and puzzled over whether the dismissive opposition expressed bemusement or outrage. My partner, Betsy Esch, a former journalist in Palestine, particularly taught me about its tragic past and present. But some change was in the air, and by the time I served as ASA president in 2015 and 2016 an avalanche of legal attacks threat-ened to destroy the organization because it had taken a stand in favor of boycott, divestment, and sanctions directed at Israel.

Some US historians exercise little restraint regarding loose talk about lack of rigor or method, and over-indulgence of the dreaded bogeyman called theory within American studies. Students rarely resist detailing what they've heard to the potentially offended parties. Add the level of offense that adheres to the history department never having funded a single graduate student wanting to work with me in a decade, and I began to see myself a combatant in a meager culture war. When I saw "The Historian's Craft" listed among the possible courses the department needed to staff, I could not resist the irony of my offering it. My version carries the subtitle "Slavery from the Enslaved's Point of View." Weather permitting, I show up campily to class in a light History Channel jacket a friend gave me.

And yet graduate education for me hinged precisely on learning the historian's craft and realizing that I loved learning it. Explicit talk about history as a craft first reached me through the Welsh historian of West Africa, Ivor Wilks. I could have shrugged it off as boilerplate, even marketing, except that I liked the idea of learning a skill, an activity that had been so important to the survival of prior generations of my family. Wilks had been a militant in the Welsh nationalist movement as a youth and on his own account left Britain for Ghana a step ahead of the law and without a doctorate. His work in Ghana as an adult educator during the attempts at decolonization under Kwame Nkrumah's leadership led him to the Ashanti region often, and he became the leading historian of the land, the rulers, and the ruled there.

His writing was meticulously documented in a way characteristic of radical historians at the time, who acted on a belief that evidence had to be unassailable. In Wilks' case, his lack of credentials surely added to the methodological zeal. The organic quality of his emphasis on craft—it clearly flowed out of the archives and local knowledge, not bureaucratic rubrics of departments—appealed to me. His seminars, and discussions outside of them as Wilks served as undergraduate advisor for my partner, made me realize how deeply periodization spoke to our understanding of what most mattered in the history of a place. He soon announced that he was to be in future also a historian of Wales, undertaking a book on a "rising" of the people in South Wales in 1839. It soon became a prize winner, with Ivor noting that once one knew the craft of history it could be applied in different times and places.

What I fell in love with at Northwestern was the craft of research. I still love it. Stuckey, important to me in so many ways at Northwestern and after, showed the way. My first seminar with Sterling met in a small group in his apartment, about ten minutes from school and across from Evanston's main post office, meaning I could do Red Rose Bookstore tasks on the way. Sterling was still at work interpreting the primary sources that he included in his documentary history, *The Ideological Origins of Black Nationalism*, which had appeared four years earlier. In it he collected writings from nineteenth-century nationalists who did not champion repatriation to Africa or other emigrationist projects but stay-at-home fights that sought meaningful alliances across the color line. Such a redefined lineage, as his later classic *Slave Culture: Nationalist Theory and the Foundations of Black America* showed, centered Black nationalist history not on a separatist trajectory stretching from Martin Delany to Marcus and Amy-Jacques Garvey to Elijah Muhammed but rather on one linking the enslaved themselves to free Black militants including David Walker, Henry Highland Garnet, W.E.B. Du Bois, and Paul Robeson.

Ideological Origins featured several essays by an African American thinker who signed himself simply "Sidney." In many ways, Sidney's pieces best exemplified the flexible left nationalism that Stuckey found coursing through antebellum Black writing and folk sources. Our seminar spent exciting weeks trying to figure out Sidney's identity, comparing his writings with the signed works of other African American theorists from the antebellum period. The detective story operated on several levels. Where and how did authors punctuate? In cases of variant spelling, which did they use? Whom did they quote or paraphrase in the many allusions to canonical works? What small political points did they particularly insist upon? What did they call Black people in the US collectively? And, for that matter, who (among several historical possibilities) was the Sidney from whom the pseudonymous author borrowed a name? This came very early in graduate school, and it was the closest close reading of a source I'd done or would ever do. Moreover, brainstorming took a fully collective form, one strengthened by the knowledge that none of us, including Sterling, came to class with the answer to the riddle.

Misunderstandings of Sterling have represented him as a Black separatist and even as anti-white. I want therefore to emphasize how little this squares with either my experiences with him or his writing. The main source of such an erring view is the treatment of him in August Meier and Elliott Rudwick's *Black History and the Historical Profession*. Although at times careful to point out that Sterling later returned to more "universalistic" positions, they see him as a separatist at key moments. Such a view rests on misapprehending the trajectory of Black nationalism that Stuckey elaborated—one intensely interested in interracial alliances—by collapsing it into the narrower and sometimes separatist nationalist traditions whose centrality to Black nationalism Stuckey himself contested. That Sterling risked much very early in his career to rightly query why historians of Africa remained so overwhelmingly white and that he commented critically on a presentation by the fine young white historian of slavery Robert Starobin around the time of Starobin's suicide stitch together the case against Stuckey. Meier and Rudwick also derided Stuckey as taking an "instrumental" approach to history, putting study of the past into the service of social protest.

My experience with Stuckey, as well as my reading of his work, was just the opposite. He not only welcomed white researchers but also deeply wanted to hear everyone doing the work defend their views. He was a warm and fiercely loyal friend. Throughout the years in our conversations, too often by phone and too seldom in person, Sterling would interject the word "man" as in "Oh, man, I hear you" or just "Oh man." Near his life's end when I interviewed him in Riverside he looked for a way to describe the loneliness he'd sometimes felt in graduate school at Northwestern and ended saying that it was so hard to find anyone to whom he could comfortably say "Man."

Sterling's seminar then turned to perhaps his most challenging set of interests, namely whether and how it was possible, given sources surviving and the layers of subtlety necessary for the self-preservation of the enslaved, to imagine writing a history of slavery "from the slave's point of view." His famous article, "Through the Prism of Folklore," written while he was a Northwestern graduate student, had provided the most resolutely positive answer ever to the possibility of writing such accounts, particularly mining folklore and song to reconstruct an "ethos" that the enslaved created and sustained. But even the sources used in that ground-shifting paper—first presented at a 1966 conference of Southern civil rights activists—frequently passed through the hands of whites and the humor, dreams, and even audience of the folklore required careful interpretation.

When I met Elma Stuckey, Sterling's mother, I came to understand more what I was learning from him. A brilliant poet, she based much of her work on stories heard as a child in Memphis from ex-slaves. She saw folklore as evidence, art, and the basis for more art. I later interviewed her for Black American Literature Forum and wrote on her poetry. She spoke with pride of both Sterling's career as an historian and his "career in the civil rights movement." To see these as two distinct things helped me to regard history as something more creative and profound than writing one's politics back in time or even than producing accessible accounts of prior struggles as a usable past. It could ultimately become a place to test political ideas rather than to garner endorsements for them.

This is not to say that Sterling traded one career for another. He remained a committed activist. He confronted former Black Panther Eldridge Cleaver when the latter visited campus as a born-again Christian conservative and advocate of Black capitalism. "What," Sterling asked Cleaver, "would you have to say to Fred Hampton's mother?" It was rare for senior professors to move classes to the massive shantytown encampment protesting university investments in South Africa in the eighties but Sterling did, delivering a memorable lecture to the whole gathering on one of his visits. But in classes the politically charged content remained distinctly within an intellectual, even literary, set of concerns. When he asked, after we read sources on the atrocities for which the master class was responsible, "What is the appropriate tone in which to write about such a record of brutality?" I thought and more or less said, "The angrier the better." He countered that to shout was less of an accomplishment than making readers want to shout. When we read in seminar documents from the "Negro Convention Movement" in Northern states before the Civil War, I wanted them to reflect that free Blacks were the best abolitionists. They were—next to the enslaved themselves—in other contexts, but Sterling rightly insisted that the convention proceedings often paid more attention to a range of other issues bearing on the interests of those in the North.

My first-year graduate school project came to focus on death, heaven, and funerals in slave communities precisely as an attempt to think about how we could know the mind of the enslaved on matters vital to them. I mined the same music and folklore collections that Stuckey did. My carrel in the library lay near the two major Dewey Decimal locations in which slave autobiographies sat on shelves and I moved through them by the score, training an eye to see the keywords I sought and scanning pages fast. I'd then spend an hour pondering a single passage like "I got shoes. You got shoes. / When I get to heaven gonna put on my shoes / Gonna shout all over God's heaven." The material culture of grave decorations, and its incorporation and transformation of African antecedents, likewise fascinated me. Finally, I researched the thousands of pages of testimony from surviving ex-slaves collected in the thirties by the Federal Writers Project and published in the sixties and seventies by my friend and mentor George Rawick. That whole body of sources is digitized now. Entering search terms like "grave," "burial," "funeral," and "heaven" can reduce what was months of research for me to a week's work. But I'd have missed a lot, including hosts of variant spellings of keywords. My paper appeared as an article in *Massachusetts Review*, as Sterling's "Prism of Folklore" had and on his recommendation to the editors. As I came to keep an eye out for all references to Africa in the sources, my next very early article took up the meaning of Africa for US slaves.

Clarence Ver Steeg, an eminent historian of colonial America, was retiring from Northwestern when I arrived but I did get to take his very last graduate class. As it ended, he offered sound advice for those of us who would be writing dissertations and books. "First of all," he said, "figure out the places where you are going to sit." This meant what archives would have the appropriate materials but also where in the library or home one could be close to the notes, xeroxes, books, coffee, tablets, pens, and typewriters that made writing possible. Ver Steeg also meant to signal that patient sitting was a key to history-writing. I'd long thought that in tennis an unwillingness to be "out-worked" had papered-over weaknesses deriving from a late start and middling talent. Now there was a new goal: not to be out-sat. Varying in the course of a day working outdoors or at the kitchen table, a library carrel, coffee shop, or bar, with or without the Cubs game or *Rockford Files* on television, became how I changed things up. My mother's annoying old-wives' motivational advice had always been, "A change of occupations [meaning tasks] is like a rest." I came around to the view that even a change of background music could function that way. Often it switched from Leonard Cohen to Tina Turner to the Ink Spots.

African American history cherished appeals to evidence and to careful reconstruction of meaningful dramas against what Du Bois called the "propaganda of history." So, in the sixties and seventies, did the new trends in working-class history. To those writing in that vein, as my deceased friend Jesse Lemisch wrote, the charmingly over-long footnote reflected a need to be taken seriously in making novel claims as well as the joy of discovery. The Northwestern department also stressed "historiography," the changes in history writing over time and through debate during changing circumstances, as central to the craft of history. At the time, and perhaps still, debates over slavery provided the best example of controversies within historiography. I had a front-row seat to Sterling's and others' painstaking accumulation of evidence to dislodge the position, developed by Stanley Elkins with scant need for evidence, that enslavement had reduced its victims to pliant "Sambos" without possibility for collective mental health and political mobilization. We still need such rigor in order to combat attacks on radical interpretations of US history.

The idea of history as a learned craft served me in one final way. It meant that I could learn methods from people whose political views on the meaning of the history I'd have questioned. One of my professors, almost certainly a Republican, once eagerly confided to me that he'd realized that had he lived in the seventeenth century he was certain he'd have been a Marxist. I pointed out that he would have had to invent Marxism, or time travel. But his views made little difference to me in terms of whether there were things to learn from him. I worry now that some graduate students arrive with so fully formed a critique of a program and/or professors within it that the opportunities to learn are attenuated. To take on so much debt as getting a doctorate now requires without knowing that one has a lot to learn puzzles me.

Academic Labor and the Rhythm of Work

Among the most important pieces of writing by a historian for me was "Time, Work-Discipline, and Industrial Capitalism" by the British Marxist E.P. Thompson. I read it in an undergraduate class and then again in graduate school. It sticks with almost anyone reading it as a perfect example of how fundamentally changes in class relations and the processes by which things are made impact everyday life, especially in the way humans regard time. Thompson showed how "pre-industrial" workers, on farms but also in small workshops, labored without constant awareness of clock time. Instead, changes of season and the movement of the sun shaped workdays. Factories and railroads made not only for more exactitude but also lessened flexibility through which farmers and artisans took off for stretches of time during slack seasons, working feverishly before and after those times, making hay while the sun shone and shoes before the canals were impassable due to cold weather.

Thompson's article also stuck with me because it briefly considered academic labor and student schedules as examples of pre-industrial work patterns. This engaged not only my academic interest but also pressing personal concerns about my own class position as a graduate student and then a faculty member (not) proceeding toward tenure. Whenever I went home, questions emerged around how hard a time I had explaining my existence in Chicago to friends from high school. The idea of reading constantly, making very little money, to qualify for a possible future job, itself not particularly well-paying, seemed mad to them and, I only later realized, to my mother. Among my not exactly hell-bent on upward mobility friends the freedom from a boss and schedule struck a chord though.

Even after 1980, when I had an insecure but full-time teaching job, my schedule amounted to just six hours a week teaching and another three for office hours. We worked three ten-week quarters annually, though I taught in summers too. No one ever observed my teaching. Nevertheless, I worked constantly, perhaps sixty hours a week, fifty weeks a year, preparing lectures and writing things that might lead to a better job. I almost completely set the hours. I was like Thompson's pre-industrial worker, writing in bouts fueled by coffee and for a few years by pipe-smoking, sometimes all night and then sleeping all day. But all this came during the reign of capitalist work-discipline that seeped into jobs of those far outside of factories and led to my obsessing regarding clock-time and productivity even when I did not have to.

The contradictory, but ultimately working-class, position of academic workers had and has important personal and organizing implications. I'd had a taste of the problem growing up. My mother, said to have "summers off" as a grade-school teacher and therefore deserving to be paid less, in fact worked lots in summers to revamp courses and take college classes to learn new things, especially about learning disabilities, and to get small raises. Her family members, me included, nevertheless saw her as fully leisured and available from Memorial Day to Labor Day. The tiny numbers of set hours in my college teaching job and my partner's yielded problems with family visitors who were uncertain why we were only sometimes ready to stay up and sleep in or entertain them all day. That the kids were in childcare when we had so much apparently free time seemed to my relatives spendthrift at best and at worst—my mom's view—taking a stand in favor of childhood ear infections. At various moments I experienced overwork as freeing. In the mid-nineties, after a group of lesbian doctoral students at the University of Minnesota found themselves without an adviser, I was able to teach group independent readings for them in order to learn queer studies. I recently did the same with an Alaskan dissertator teaching me about Indigenous Alaska, so that I could advise her dissertation. These moments of both self-exploitation and self-improvement are experienced as glorious, but they are harder to justify as more students and fewer faculty make the university a place of enervation.

Getting Through

In the history department's doctoral program at Northwestern many years ago, students read and did course work for only about two years. We then secured formal entrance to the PhD program by passing a qualifying examination. The descriptions of the program left open the possibility of completing a doctorate in four years and, not knowing how hard it is to write a dissertation, my anxieties focused on the qualifying exam as the only roadblock to speedy completion. The stress made me appreciate the great story my late friend John Bracey told about the origins of qualifying exams. Bracey, himself a Northwestern student just before me, described himself in the tale as being so old that he sat in on the meeting inventing the exams. "I was there when it was all decided," he'd tell young scholars. "Some of us wanted a comprehensive test like the one you complain about," he continued, "and others wanted to make you carry a brick everywhere you went for two or three years before moving to the dissertation stage." Bracey's story concluded with the fraternity-style brick-toting hazing narrowly losing out to the more bureaucratic style of hazing that continues, sometimes usefully, to credential dissertation writers.

My worries centered on the format of the exam at Northwestern and on the likelihood that I'd become nauseous during it. The entire process was oral, with four or five faculty quizzing the candidate serially about a range of specializations within history. Mine were slavery, labor, immigration, colonial North America and, as a very serious minor field, African history. If the oral went badly, and the student failed, the same committee reconvened later. In the event of a second failure, the program terminated the student. I knew if I failed in the first instance, the second would be more pressured. I relied on those who'd made their way through the exam before and on good, calming advice from Stuckey who'd also himself gone through the same program not too many years earlier. The more recent examinees revealed that some questions recurred from the same committee member time after time.

The toughest nut among the examiners habitually asked factual questions about agricultural history, as in "What were the tasks on a tobacco plantation in the fall?" I'd have had little clue had I not been prompted by prior victims. The same examiner likewise repeated the stunt of putting on the table a brand-new work of history. Seeing this book for the first time, the student had three minutes to look at it and produce a quick take that was intelligent and professional. There was a right method apparently, utilizing blurbs, acknowledgments, and sources cited. My qualifying exam had another question with a putatively right answer that almost tripped me up, on the impact of the American Revolution. I ran through a little litany of "history from below" answers—some of the enslaved found freedom, the franchise vastly expanded, a Bill of Rights—and some gloomier ones, including sixty years of Southern domination of federal power. The committee fidgeted. Finally, it hit me that I was meant to say, "A commitment to liberty for all, however deferred." I choked out that supposedly right answer although I wanted the words back as soon as they left my mouth.

The final bit of advice from those who had previously passed their exams remains a good one in such situations. Friends urged me to get faculty members talking with one another and this I did well, probably not speaking myself for more than thirty minutes of the two hours. Most of the big, flagship state universities at which I have since taught require very lengthy written exams. Some have students writing frantically for up to a week on three different areas of specialization. Then they have a two-hour oral defense of the hundred pages or so of writing produced. I'm sympathetic to the fact that this seems to students like having to carry two bricks around. But I'd have much preferred it to letting everything ride, after two years of intense work, on two hours of unpredictable talk.

A Plan and a Mistaken Change of Plans

Fifty years into this line of work I have only one big and lasting academic regret. Coming in my third year of graduate school, in 1978, the misstep did not turn out as badly as it could have but it was a failure of both vision and judgment. I had come to Northwestern wanting to work with Stuckey and Fredrickson. As the latter's staggering research agenda on race and slavery in the US and Southern Africa became clear, I noticed that its comparative dimensions complemented the transnational work Stuckey pursued on the slave trade, the peopling of plantations by Black workers of varied ethnicities, and the creation of an African American culture from that variety.

At almost any other US university at the time, comparative study of race and slavery would have brought the US into dialogue with the history of Brazil or perhaps Cuba. Northwestern's very strong African Studies resources sent me instead to thinking about so-called "African slavery" as it shaped the experiences of the enslaved in the American South. My partner Jean had become an undergraduate concentrator in African history, studying with Wilks. She won an incredible grant not to be an exchange student but, barely 20, to go to Ghana and find a way to conduct her own independent research. I tagged along for part of the time, an incredible experience for young people who had never before been outside the US.

My paternal grandfather
holding my mother, not
long before his death.
Author photo.

PRIVATE POOL
MEMBERS ONLY

1962 Cairo, Illinois swimming pool protests as captured by the celebrated
photographer Danny Lyon. Copyright Danny Lyon, Magnum Photos.

Top: Masthead of high school underground newspaper. Author photo.

Middle: Starting college. Author photo.

Bottom: P. Sterling Stuckey, historian, role model, and friend. Courtesy of University of California Riverside History Department.

Speaking before occupation of president's office in Northwestern University protests against investments in South Africa, 1985. Courtesy of Jean Allman.

At the Northwestern shantytown protest against South African apartheid were the poet Ted Joans (upper right) and below him Penelope Rosemont, and Jean Allman. In the baseball cap is the South African poet Dennis Brutus and to his right the surrealist artist and thinker Franklin Rosemont. Courtesy of Jean Allman.

With son Brendan and the Africanist scholar Phyllis Boanes and the graves of the Haymarket martyrs. Courtesy of Jean Allman.

Fred Thompson with Charles H. Kerr Company books, old and new. Courtesy of Charles H. Kerr Publishing Company.

Speaking with blues legend Honeyboy Edwards at a table of Kerr books, including a volume featuring Edwards edited by the great surrealist writer Paul Garon. Franklin Rosemont is to my right. Courtesy of Tamara L. Smith

With son Donovan and a teammate from Ashanti Tennis Club in Ghana. Courtesy of Jean Allman.

With Donovan in Ireland. Courtesy of Jean Allman.

Some contributors to a remarkable left initiative at the University of Missouri History Department. Counterclockwise from myself on far right are Jean Allman, Sundiata Cha-Jua, Susan Porter Benson, Donald Lowe (a frequent visitor), and Tani Barlow. Courtesy of Jean Allman.

Top: Joffre Stewart, anarchist, pacifist, and poet. Photo by Viewminder on Flickr.

Middle: With Penelope Rosemont, painter, author, and central figure in both the Charles Kerr Publishing Company and the Chicago Surrealist Group. Courtesy of Tamara L. Smith.

Bottom: Activist Megan Jones' art from the movement against guns on the University of Kansas campus. Courtesy of Megan Jones.

At 2024 celebration of Robin Kelley and others by the Center for Political Graphics. Left to right: Natalia Molina, Sara Johnson, Danny Widener, George Sanchez, the author, Elizabeth Esch, Fanon Che Wilkins, and Kelley. Courtesy of Fanon Wilkins.

Alongside Andrew Ross at 2023 Palestine march in Montreal. Photo by Robert M. Zecker.

In multiple classes I had read the work of the great Guyanese historian and pan-African revolutionary Walter Rodney, especially his short 1966 article "African Slavery and Other Forms of Social Oppression on the Upper Guinea Coast in the Context of the Atlantic Slave-Trade" in the *Journal of African History*. He argued there against the glib use of "slavery" to describe both African societies from which the cargo of slave ships originated and the plantation societies where they disembarked. The Upper Guinea Coast, he observed, had no mode of production corresponding to plantation slavery and West Africa generally lacked the practice of hereditary bondage in its constellation of what Rodney called "other forms of social oppression." Rodney was assassinated just after I finished my dissertation; one of the highest spots of my lecturing experiences was to speak at a series named in his honor thirty-plus years later. The two very different Georges, Rawick and Fredrickson, each played roles in honoring Rodney's work posthumously and pressing for investigation of his death.

A project comparing unfree labor in specific areas of West Africa to plantation slavery in a specific part of the American South held great promise for me. It fit with Stuckey's emphasis on the lived experience of the slave trade as an "incubator of Pan-Africanism," or as the wonderful Baltimore mystery writer Laura Lippman, a former Northwestern undergraduate, put it in a novel that lovingly remembered Stuckey's lecturing, the process in which "old ethnic divisions melted in the face of slavery." The project afforded me an opportunity to explore my growing conviction that slavery in the cotton-producing South was a capitalist economic formation. It also countered what have turned out to be persistent right-wing falsifications of history turning on the idea that slavery inheres in "human nature" and/or that African rulers and patterns of war were to blame for the horrors of the slave trade and its aftermath.

I gave up on that great dissertation idea for two understandable reasons and one bad one. First, I knew from Africanist fellow students that work in African archives and "in the field" inevitably increased time until completion of a dissertation or book, and I prioritized finishing. That it was an open secret that Fredrickson would be leaving Northwestern soon pressured this timing issue as did my lack of any African language. Secondly, I could not quite imagine the research design that would let me address a specific African group transported to a specific US place. Research on "survivals" of African practices in the US, or what were increasingly called "syncretisms" creatively refashioning such practices, operated on a big canvas. I saw the desirability of more specificity as to times and place but did not know how to operationalize the research. Later, after the work of Michael Gomez and others, models for doing so existed.

The third and worst reason for abandoning the projected study of the "Rodney thesis" flowed from my allowing other faculty and a fellow student or two to create doubt about whether it would be possible for a white scholar to succeed in the job market studying Black history. It could have been a serious and difficult discussion involving the ways in which academic units so seldom diversified by aggressively recruiting faculty of color for positions not "about race," and taking note of the remarkable extent to which Black Studies, for example, has in fact welcomed white scholars. Instead, the discussion of the alleged impossibility of making such a career proceeded by way of assumption and insinuation. But I did hear it, and did not directly talk to Sterling about it. It did not move me to actively seek a new topic, but I became open to other possibilities during my third year of graduate school.

Enter Philip Foner. The most prolific Communist-inclined historian of his generation, Foner visited Chicago in 1978. We at Red Rose Books had just published his small book *Karl Liebknecht and the United States*. I expected to like him only so much. Our political differences seemed daunting. My one prior experience with a leading Communist historian had been mixed. I'd enjoyed meeting Herbert Aptheker, the Communist historian of slave revolts, when he spoke at Northern Illinois and I sent him a copy of a long paper on his work I'd done with Sterling. The paper appreciated his courage—he was an anti-peonage activist as well as a historian—and his scholarship. It resisted the ridiculous commonplace criticism that his work inflated the importance of slave resistance, but it stopped short of accepting that his book about Hungarian Revolution denial was to be taken seriously. When I next met him, in New York City, I reintroduced myself and he frostily said "I know you" before falling again into silence.

Foner proved very different—talkative and funny. We bonded over a strange coincidence. He stayed at our house, and in the afternoon mail I received a copy of a very early publication of mine, reviewing a book in a journal on Black education. I was excited but somewhere between submitting the review and seeing it in print it had registered that the spelling of the name of the greatest US historian of the twentieth century was Du Bois, not Dubois. Seeing the error in print left me so disconsolate that I told Foner. He sympathized, adding that one of his earliest publications managed to misspell Frederick Douglass as Douglas. This held out quite a possibility of redemption in that Foner had gone on to write a major biography of Douglass and to collect the latter's works in an impressive five-volume set.

Foner told stories of being prematurely blacklisted, before the Joseph McCarthy red scare, and indeed while the US and the Soviet Union were allies during World War II. He'd lost a job at City College in New York and would not teach for twenty-five years, until the historically Black Lincoln University in Pennsylvania hired him in 1967. Also blacklisted from New York jobs in education were his historian brother Jack Foner, father of the distinguished historian Eric Foner. The older Foners—brothers Henry and Moe also fell victim to political repression—tried briefly to support themselves as a jazz band. Phil also surprised me with stories of how quickly he left the Communist Party, which I had assumed still counted him as a member. The bone of contention, he added, was his wanting to publish more of Du Bois' work as quickly as possible, therefore turning to a Trotskyist publisher. All of this made me like Foner more.

On the day before he left Chicago, Foner asked if we could meet so that he could run a proposal by me. He had photocopies of lots of labor newspapers and other material mostly from the nineteenth century, much of it bearing on struggles to decrease the hours of labor in a normal working day. He proposed sharing those with me. They could become the basis for a dissertation on shorter hours movements by workers in US history through the Civil War with all the writing and the further research mine. After my dissertation, the project could then continue its story up until the present, with Foner writing only the chapter on the Great Depression and the working day. We would be listed as co-authors on the completed book.

The idea grew on me, pulling first on my desire to be finished and to have an adequate income with job security. As I thought more, the intellectual attractions of the project became clearer. Most of the great moments and movements of labor sought greater control by workers over their own time. Marx's *Capital* made the working day the key to understanding exploitation. The shorter hours demand united labor across lines of skill, race, and gender. The connection between the emancipation of the enslaved and the organizing momentum that sent US labor to world leadership in the struggle for an eight-hour day—with eight hours for "what we will"—remained to be untangled. After some time, I took Foner up on the proposal with just an oral agreement.

The arrangement worked; my dissertation was done within sixteen months. The talented historian of immigration Josef Barton took over the dissertation supervisor role and Stuckey graciously continued to help me in all possible ways. That he admired Foner as a Douglass scholar probably helped. The larger costs of the decision in delaying my career only emerged over the next decade. But even as I finished graduate school, some career problems presented themselves. One was that I had moved into the field of labor history but without any association with a labor historian at a PhD-granting institution to champion my work in job applications. The "new labor historians" who dominated the field had emerged in the sixties professing to turn from the history of unions and labor economics to the everyday lives and social history of workers. Philip Foner seemed stodgy by comparison in this framing of things. Lots of new labor history works began with a ritualistic declaration that the author departed from both Foner and his more conservative predecessors.

Foner's reputation also suffered because he had been credibly accused of plagiarism before we met, unbeknownst to me until after we'd begun the book. Other similar charges would recur later, one in which a friend argued that his graduate work was lifted. Foner's most consistent explanation to me was that he had an incredible memory for words but not so much for sources. In his haste to produce works he regarded as politically urgent and to vindicate his academic prowess in the face of the blacklist, he hurried too much. His scores of books have a certain have-to-get-done quality. He brought, a relative of his later told me, his yearly harvest of titles to family reunions. The research materials he shared with me reflected how he'd trained his helpers to examine and photocopy—with considerable resulting disarray, which lengthened the process of my writing. At the dissertation stage all the words were mine, so plagiarism was not an issue. His later book chapter on the thirties required some checking but I found no irregularities. Our one disagreement as I wrote centered on my realization that the long book, all but entirely written by me would, alphabetical order prevailing, appear with Foner as the first author. I raised the matter but got nowhere. In the resulting exchange he mentioned organized-left practices regarding authorship in a way that I still find fascinating. He noted that he had as a young Communist written some of the history credited to party leader William Z. Foster, implying I guess that these things even up over the years.

Karma had me paying for my mistake in switching dissertation topics and supervisors and there would be more karma to come. Ironically, after all the misadventure, it was still my work with Stuckey, and Sterling's direct intervention, that saved my career in the short run. As I rushed the dissertation to completion, and as labor history began to decline as a field, I found few jobs I was fit for—my best ideas and strongest recommendations coming still from the field I had left. There was, though, a job at Yale, helping the esteemed African American historian John W. Blassingame edit for publication the papers of Frederick Douglass. The person hired would do that long-term work full-time, and teach for Yale's history department every other year. For this job, Stuckey's recommendation, and Fredrickson's, would count lots and the association with a Douglass scholar like Foner would not hurt. I prevailed in the search and left for New Haven nine years after I'd decided not to attend Yale as an undergraduate.

Yale After All, Briefly

I first lived in Ghana in 1978 and first saw Yale in 1979. The latter seemed the much more foreign place. The good parts of a year in New Haven—it wasn't even quite a year—are easily enumerated. The Frederick Douglass Papers Project provided excellent company. The superb historians Julie Saville and John McKivigan did work like mine, under the direction of Richard Carlson. Everybody wanted the time of John Blassingame, even more so from the larger academic world than the project. He was hopelessly overextended on worthwhile projects and took to hiding out in a legendary Italian eatery near both the history department and the Douglass Project offices. I'd sometimes get word he wanted to meet, and I'd go there. The work itself included varied research. We were producing what became the second fat volume of Douglass' speeches. The labor involved comparing texts, since Douglass toured and spoke incessantly using variants of existing texts as he incorporated new materials and was excerpted in different ways in the press. When Douglass' hosts, comrades, or adversaries entered the documentary record, or when Douglass himself mentioned or quoted others, brief biographies and identification of the sources of quotations needed to materialize as parts of the lavish annotation.

Funded generously by Yale and the federal government, the project functioned much like the projects on the papers of major US presidents, sending implicitly a healthy message about Douglass' stature. It generated tremendous new knowledge, especially regarding the secondary leadership of abolitionism, spinning off the Black Abolitionist Papers Project. I began to understand anew why elite institutions, and especially their funding and their libraries, held attractions. Even beyond the treasures of rare antislavery material in its Beinecke Library, Yale's open-stacks Sterling Library held priceless abolitionist pamphlets sometimes shelved in boxes of several publications with ABOLITIONIST PAMPHLETS lettered on the side. I worked long hours in part because, with Blassingame's blessing, I could detour to look at items on labor and the working day. Beyond school we had much fresh seafood and a pleasant rental house near Edgewood Park. I was in a good tennis league.

Almost everything else produced dread. Compared to Chicago, New Haven had a very slight intellectual life. I could imagine its appeals for undergraduates, who scared me in their propensity to occupy the entire sidewalks, running off those moving in the other direction. And senior professors of course were well-paid and well-supported with research assistance. If they had a good idea, they could test it in New York, Paris, or London and tended not to do much on campus. (The great labor historian David Montgomery, who moved to Yale from Pitt the year that I arrived, was an exception. His activism in support of the fall 1979 strike at Winchester Arms, one of the last gun manufacturers in the area, taught me lots. But we only came to know each other well later in life.) The mood among junior professors seemed especially grim. Like much of the Ivy League then, Yale still regarded wholesale tenure denials as a gauge of excellence so that either isolating to write or worrying about not doing so burdened the untenured.

Jean and I moved to New Haven together just after she graduated with the highest honors from Northwestern. She spoke French, Russian, and Twi and qualified for library jobs. But the pay was woeful. So too, Yale setting by example local standards, were white-collar wages in the city. She ended up driving a forklift at the Yankee Metal factory but had to quit some months later because of pregnancy. Her co-workers hated Yale, to the point that she did not much talk about being connected to it through me. Yale faculty professed little interest in her job. We grew increasingly lonely and, as the baby's delivery date approached, attracted by the prospect of free child care from Midwestern grandparents. One spring day, with no other job prospects except Jean's getting a fellowship to do doctoral work with Wilks at Northwestern, I met with Blassingame and simply said I did not like it at Yale and had to leave. He smiled and said he often didn't like it either but did not get to leave.

Soon we were back in Chicago, insecure but happier. I scrounged up a few courses to teach at Northwestern, including evening ones with the excellent, more working-class student body at its downtown Chicago campus. I also became the first books editor at the new socialist newsweekly In These Times, where I made more money selling review copies of unreviewed books to bookstores than from my salary and learned for the first time how to use "which" and "that" properly. The following four years Northwestern employed me as a Mellon Assistant Visiting Professor of History.

A Book that Almost Wasn't and Its Costs

By the time I submitted my dissertation, at 27, I had published five articles, not something I would advise for students but a measure of how I took to research and how badly I craved validation. Two were on the history of labor and race in St. Louis from the Civil War until the general strike of 1877, and the balance on slavery and Black culture. I'd found a regular gig reviewing books for a leading broadly left publication, *The Progressive*, where editor Mary Sheridan took Stuckey's word that I'd catch on to the style required for their excellent reviews. When I sent to Aptheker a draft copy of my *Progressive* review of his collection of W.E. B. Du Bois' writings, he wrote to say that it would never see publication. He maintained that the magazine had never published positive things connected to Communists. Sheridan proved him wrong. I thought I understood at least a little corner of the world of publishing and of the ebbing of academic anti-radicalism and didn't worry much, in 1980, about finding a secure job after abruptly leaving the Douglass Papers.

It turned out that I was mistaken about both the publishing world and anti-radicalism. The two came together as I turned toward publishing the book based on my dissertation. In choosing late in graduate school to work with Foner on a study of the working day in US history, I had calculated that the research materials he'd provided would speed completion of a dissertation reaching through the Civil War. That worked. I then turned to research and writing on the second half of the story, with Foner contributing his Great Depression chapter quickly. It took me longer, but in three years the manuscript was ready to be sent to press.

By that time, the young staff at Yale University Press had impressed me with their list of titles and their interest in the manuscript. I think Foner had his doubts, along the lines of Aptheker's, on the fate of the *Progressive* review. Foner had published his wonderful first book, *Business and Slavery*, with the University of North Carolina Press, but that had come forty years before, as his blacklisting unfolded. Since that time lots of his many books came from International Publishers, associated with the Communist Party, or with Pathfinder, the press of the Socialist Workers Party. Others were published by Citadel, a publisher at which he was chief editor, the main source of Foner's livelihood during the years the Red Scare victimized him. He'd more rarely published with university presses when we submitted the manuscript, *Our Own Time: A History of American Labor and the Working Day*, to Yale.

Nevertheless the process began swimmingly and seemed destined for speedy success. Then as now, the procedure began with the manuscript being sent out by the press to two or three readers who report back on the book's merits anonymously. In our case, the readers enthusiastically supported publication. The excellent young editor assigned to the book happily relayed the good news. This meant a major boost for a book that we thought carried a critical message about what animated and unified the labor movement in its healthiest moments. It also carried important career momentum for me, since in much of the liberal arts the word of anonymous readers shaped decisions on tenure and promotion. But it was not to be. There was a second, nominal, step in the process of offering authors a contract. A press board of scholars and others received the reports of the readers and were to approve a final offering of the contract. For a manuscript very positively recommended by its anonymous readers, this was understood as pro forma. Nevertheless, the board mysteriously demanded that the book be sent out to a new set of readers, who proved to be more skeptical. The editor was mortified and offered to give us the highly positive initial reviews to pass on to another press.

We settled on Cornell University Press, working again with a discerning and energetic young editor near the start of a distinguished career. When he and I met at the next major history conference, the young, then leftish, labor historian Sean Wilentz wandered up and we told him the story. He enthused over the possibility of rescuing the book saying, "It's like one big floating crap game," in which we, or maybe he, seized chances. I somehow knew in that moment that all would go poorly. One of the Cornell reviewers oozed vitriol. If the book were to ever be published, they allowed, the appropriate venue should be a Xerox, the photocopying giant whose brand name then stood in for mere duplication. That sunk any chances for publication.

There was plenty wrong with Our Own Time. Our divorcing of the history of white labor from that of slavery was as bad or worse than the norm for labor history at the time. Moreover, our prediction of a revived movement for more free time proved quite naive. Nevertheless, it was shadily ganged up on in the secret stage of the publishing process. It remains my view—and I had plenty of time to think about it—that the extra scrutiny the submission received at Yale University Press was a product of anti-communism, albeit of a liberal stripe. Therefore, it was directed more at Foner than myself, although the seventies had seen a bitter conflict at Yale in which I'd taken part.

The history department had refused to allow Aptheker to teach a student-initiated seminar at Yale and a significant protest movement developed. Though a graduate student I joined it on academic freedom grounds and because I so admired the late Staughton Lynd, whose academic career Yale had earlier helped to ruin, who provided leadership. At the least I think the self-righteousness of some at Yale around the "Aptheker affair" and around Lynd's case made Foner's victimization and mine more likely. It was not, to my knowledge, a time when plagiarism charges against Foner were being actively discussed, and no part of the process suggested that they played a role.

History being a "book discipline," my having edited but not written published books cast doubt on the weight of the many articles I was producing. Nor did I get work done on the second book—there not being a first. Because I had a Mellon visiting assistant professorship and strong reasons to be in the Chicago area, I applied for jobs selectively, and I suffered more from bad book news than from disappointments in the job market. But lack of a tenure-track job made me doubt the leaps I'd taken into a kind of job so far from my family's traditions, particularly in the fourth year of the Mellon contract as the job at Northwestern was about to end.

Not long ago, my older son, who was only four when we finally left Northwestern in 1985, recalled the only time he could remember seeing me really mad during his early childhood, at and after a party at Ivor Wilks' house where everyone drank too much. Ivor attempted to mentor me publicly that night regarding political outspokenness and getting ahead in academics. I heard it as an attack. I perhaps knew Ivor was not wrong but also that I could not withdraw from the protests swirling on campus and in Chicago over apartheid. I'm not much impressed when junior faculty proclaim that they'll be hell on wheels politically once they get tenure, though I do advise at times against being what Fred Hampton called "Custeristic." The loudest such proclaimer of his future leftward lurch, a colleague at Missouri, made a dramatic post-tenure leap—but to the right.

At Northwestern the anti-apartheid movement had radicalized several undergraduate students whom I'd helped to introduce to left history. I felt responsibile for them, especially as they came for advice about which small revolutionary groups to join. The wildly different Progressive Labor Party and International Socialist Organization exhausted the choices on campus, and I urged neither. Four or five students joined ISO after asking my view, some becoming leaders. I'd said that group probably did less harm than others on the sectarian left. Maybe that seemed like an endorsement. Two tremendous undergrads lost part of their lives to Progressive Labor. The day that I most tried to urge them to not join was the very one when Northwestern's history department discussed whether to make my position more permanent. One of the uninformed opponents of the hire raged against me—some things done in secret don't stay that way—as a "Stalinist."

As possibilities at Northwestern dwindled, few other Chicago-area jobs appeared, labor history continued its decline, and Jean neared finishing her doctorate, I applied for jobs far more widely, even desperately. I got a little better at it and went far in searches. I think as it became clearer that my success in getting a job was not a foregone conclusion, my recommendation letters were made to glow a little brighter. Stuckey remained my biggest booster, but his networks tended to be in the very fields I'd largely abandoned. He regarded me as still an African Americanist and charmingly if hopelessly nominated me for Ivy League jobs in that field.

It was a job in Southern history at the main University of Missouri campus that finally worked out for me, a mismatch given my then-current research but reflective of my best work still being with Sterling, on slavery. The great Southern historian already at Missouri, Tom Alexander, supported my hire. He was nearing retirement and another exemplary fighting liberal. I think Alexander first liked me because I was the only candidate up for drinking a small glass of bourbon with him after a long day of interviewing. By the time Our Own Time finally appeared in 1989, I had been at the University of Missouri for almost four years and had tenure there, getting it with no book except the co-edited *Haymarket Scrapbook*.

Good News for a Change

Those of you not inclined to happy endings, preferring the sad stories coursing through much of previous passages, can skip now to the next chapter's end. Given all the setbacks, taking almost seven years from when we'd first submitted it, Foner, aging and wanting to see *Our Own Time* out, finally submitted it to Greenwood Press. He'd published there before. It was distinctly a second-tier press but with a strong working-class history list, including Rawick's massive *The American Slave* collection, the introductory volume of which was his brilliant history of the enslaved, *From Sundown to Sunup*.

Once in print, *Our Own Time* got overwhelmingly positive reviews, including from the *New York Times*, sold well, and garnered lots of citations. More amazing, and completely unsolicited, was the offer by Verso Books, a few months after the book appeared in hardcover, to buy the rights from Greenwood and publish a paperback as part of their Haymarket series. Under the editorship of the left historian and polymath Mike Davis and the Marxist literary scholar Mike Sprinker, the Haymarket imprint was bringing out a raft of superb US-related books from the leading left press in the UK and around the world.

Davis and I had not met when he started calling in the late eighties. He still worked as a long-haul truck driver and would propose things like: "On the way back from my haul to Toronto I could stop over in Missouri [where I then taught] and we could hang out a couple hours, but I have to be back for my seminar on Tuesday." Such plans never materialized, but I liked hearing from him and we soon met. His unfortunately titled but otherwise marvelous essay "The Barren Marriage of American Labour and the Democratic Party" in *New Left Review* in 1980 had shaped my thinking and taught me that it was possible, if barely, to be a major US intellectual with a devastating critique of the Democrats. His earlier *Radical America* piece on scientific management, sabotage, and the Industrial Workers of the World ("The Stopwatch and the Wooden Shoe") helped guide my approach to the working day and the intensity of labor.

I'm not sure how Mike Davis, or maybe it was Mike Sprinker, found the Greenwood hardcover edition of *Our Own Time*, not an easy title to run across in 1989. I'm glad they read it because their publishing of the Verso edition saved the book from obscurity. Moreover, the two Mikes, and the great chief editor at Verso Colin Robinson, quickly asked "What's your next book?" at a time when I thought of myself as a writer only of articles and of a book that took a dozen years to appear.

Interlude Two
BRUSH WITH GENIUS:
RADICALS AND THE COUNTRYSIDE

After moving from Chicago to Columbia, Missouri in 1985, we missed our webs of contact with much older radicals but I soon made friends with a raft of wonderful new old-timers. Their artistry and activism fit well with the rural setting where we lived, now with two children, for several years in a log cabin. One new friend, the celebrated—but not nearly enough—novelist Jack Conroy, was back in his hometown of Moberly, Missouri. I first met him through the important preserver and creator of Missouri and Kansas radical history and worker's culture, Fred Whitehead. Fred brought Jack to Columbia in the late eighties, as Jack approached his ninetieth birthday. Although most famous for his novel on mining, The Disinherited, Conroy had also co-authored, with his friend Arna Bontemps, a noteworthy children's book, The Fast Sooner Hound. I'd bought a copy for our older son Brendan. Jack excelled as a storyteller, eyes twinkling and doubling their gleam when in the presence of a nine-year-old fan seeking his signature on their book. The relationship ended in correspondence, and, when some of us at the Kerr Company helped to place Jack's papers at the Newberry Library in Chicago, the back-and-forth between him and Brendan became part of the collection. Jack was a big supporter of the Kerr Company, having learned some of his radicalism from their books many decades earlier.

In 1988 the University of Missouri at Columbia welcomed the Peter Tamony collection to its archives, changing my research agenda and enabling me to meet Archie Green, the son of Ukrainian working-class immigrants who became a folklorist and the leading scholar of US working-class culture at the time. Tamony, partially disabled by respiratory illness by age 20, became the leading expert, academic and otherwise, on US slang. From the early 20s until his 1985 death he researched countless words. Typically, he clipped the end from an envelope he'd received in the mail at his home in San Francisco, wrote the word on the outside, and stuffed it with references drawn from dictionaries, literature, and the press. His passion emerged from enthusiasm for the vocabulary of sportswriters and came to include words from popular music (especially jazz), sex, work (particularly on the waterfront), queer life, and Black vernacular speech among much else.

A graduate of the University of California at Berkeley who then chose waterfront work mostly as a shipwright, Archie returned to college—a master's at Illinois and a doctorate at Penn—at 40. He apprenticed himself to Tamony and became a leading expert in working-class slang, the music of rural miners, and the field of "laborlore," which he originated. Green's 1988 visit to Missouri was in connection with the move of Tamony's eccentric collection to the university after his death. (It gave me material and confidence to write on such words as *greaser* and *guinea* when discussing the racialization of the immigrant working class in the early twentieth-century US.) Archie gave a welcoming lecture, having been instrumental in the papers finding a home.

The program included a requisite number of administrators introducing other administrators, and then the librarian and faculty member who'd actually made things happen. The introduction of Archie appropriately chronicled an incredible life of achievements, and then he spoke at length, reminiscing about Tamony and thinking about the importance of slang. The venue, shiny and new, included huge windows letting in light from a spectacular spring day of new greenery, birds, and sunshine. The program was to end at 5 p.m. with my panel's little contribution. It was already past five o'clock when Archie ended, and the moderator enjoined the crowd not to leave as there was more to come. Archie simply said that was all well and good, but he would be leaving to join the beautiful day outdoors, not knowing how many more of those he'd get to enjoy. Perhaps some compromise was reached around presenting a very abbreviated program, but Archie went outside quickly. I had long loved Archie's writings but now was a convert regarding his spirit as well. I soon learned that part of his irreverence stemmed from the fact that his years as a shipwright left him with an occupational disease that he thought would kill him soon.

He ended up living another thirty years, till 91, and vigorously. He was working when we met on a book on words connected with labor. Some of it concerned "Wobbly," as it applied to the members of the radical union the Industrial Workers of the World (IWW). He asked to interview me about the word. Folk stories about its origins are legion and varied—Archie insisted it was not a matter of a single correct origin with the really important and mysterious words. I knew some of the stories but nothing special, and thus took a longer view in the conversation with Archie. Since IWWs embraced the term Wobbly, the question became why. The contrast with other groups on the left, who claimed to speak with the confidence of socialism that was scientific and swore that they knew where the future headed, struck me. The IWW did wobble through history and, more importantly, loved its own wobbles. The whole interview ended up appearing in Archie's *Wobblies, Pile Butts, and Other Heroes* in 1993.

I saw Archie lots, as he came to Missouri and I sought him out on Bay Area visits. His labor history walking tours of San Francisco walked me right into the ground. They embodied his conviction that since all buildings were built by workers they each had a labor history claim. He mounted a campaign for requiring that all large new buildings should display a photo of those who did the work of creating them. The more traditional high spots of the tour included the place where the city's anti-Chinese riots began, the beautiful former Workingmen's Library, reborn as a chess center, and the bar at the hiring hall of the Sailors Union of the Pacific. I later saw him for an extended visit at the Iron Workers Hall in Benicia, California in 2006 when in his late 80s he convened a big and electric "laborlore conversation." The following year I spoke on the closing plenary at the event at which the Library of Congress honored his life's work. We talked about finishing touches on *The Big Red Songbook*, a Kerr project collecting material from all the many IWW editions of *The Little Red Songbook*. Archie had inherited the most complete collection of the little editions from the Wobbly machinist John Neuhaus in 1958, and we brought the big edition to press a half-century later.

An even more frequent visitor to the University of Missouri was H.L. Mitchell, the Arkansas-born founder and longtime leader of the Southern Tenant Farmers' Union (STFU) and its offshoots. I had first met "Mitch," as friends called him, in Chicago in the mid-eighties. He published a long autobiography, Mean Things Happening in this Land, and came to us at the Kerr Company with a proposal for a shorter account, more packed with photographs and more focused on the union than on himself. It became Roll the Union On, with both of his book titles sampling the songs written in STFU struggles.

Lacking skills to lay out the images in Roll the Union On, I worked hard on the text, so much so that when Mitch signed my copy, he thanked me for editing the book. When the book came out, we sat together with Studs Terkel at an event sponsored by the Illinois Labor History Society and Mitch made a strong pitch that all should buy his book then and there. "You know how to write books," he said to me afterwards, "but I know how to sell them." Mitch had sharecropped (on his in-laws' farm) but also had run a fragile dry-cleaning business and a gas station. He was, he said proudly, an effective salesman and fundraiser, keeping STFU's example as an interracial union alive. Both he and Green ratified by their examples my conviction that radicalism emerged sometimes from ordinary, fathomable white life, and not only in rebellion against it.

Part of Mitchell's fund-raising, I learned after moving from Chicago, involved driving around a circuit of campuses that would invite him to talk again and again. He had lots of support at the University of Missouri, including my fellow historian Arvarh Strickland and the linguist Donald Lance. Mitch unfailingly stayed at the Red Roof Inn, a mile from our house. He liked how cheap it was but also accented the Red in the name as if it were a people's motel. He often came with materials packed in his car to perform a task and would sit in the room, entertaining me and whoever else came while getting some help stuffing the mass mailing envelopes he was preparing. He honed and repeated stories. I'd grown up, while in Cairo, a mere half hour from where the STFU's most important mass action had occurred in the Missouri Bootheel in 1939. I listened with rapt attention to stories that were so great in part because they were perfected by repetition. I became close enough to an expert on the STFU that I was an adviser to the film on the union, Oh Freedom, an Emmy winner in 2001. Mitch's attitude to his own longevity differed fully from Archie Green's. He often referred to the possibility of his living to 100 as if it were a certainty. When he died at 83 in 1989 it seemed a tragically early demise.

Only weeks after Mitchell's death a spectacular and improbable performance for which he was largely responsible took place on the University of Missouri campus. The bard whose lyrics gave the titles to both of Mitchell's books, John Handcox, had disappeared for decades as a movement artist and leader, first removing himself from his native Arkansas ahead of a lynch mob. Later, as STFU defeats accumulated, he left for California, where he worked as a carpenter and sold produce. The author of STFU classics like "Raggedy, Raggedy Are We," and "Mean Things Happening in This Land" and the broader labor anthem "Roll the Union On" seemed to have vanished. His brothers and sisters in the STFU presumed Handcox was dead, but he reappeared in the eighties for the fiftieth anniversary of his union. Scholars and performers, including Pete Seeger, rediscovered Handcox. He began to perform in public again and even to write new songs. One skewered Ronald Reagan.

We at the University of Missouri invited him to campus as soon as we knew of his availability. He flew in during the fall semester of 1989 wearing a big tag on a cord around his neck with his contact information in its clear plastic pocket. Handcox performed in a beautiful light-yellow sportscoat to an overflowing crowd of more than 200. Even those thinking "extra credit" on arriving soon settled into realizing they were witnessing something special. Archie Green delivered a short talk and gave big hugs to Handcox. I hosted, not so much nervous as overwhelmed with emotion. John bantered, read poetry, and sang his classic songs before pulling out his own copy of the Little Red Songbook and searching until he found "Solidarity Forever." He then immediately lost the place again and sang from memory, speaking between verses with a personal closeness to the song that made the words seem as much his as songwriter Ralph Chaplin's.

The striking "Solidarity Forever" lines "In our hands is placed a power greater than their hoarded gold / Greater than the might of armies magnified a thousand-fold" became in Handcox's performance "In our hands is placed a power greater than their horrid gold / Greater than the mighty armies magnified a thousand-fold." The whole set showed how music changes. In Handcox's original "Roll the Union On" it was a notorious anti-STFU sheriff (or the boss) who was in the way and needed to be rolled over. The 1989 lyric became: "If Bush gets in the way, we're gonna roll it over him." Long after Handcox's death, Michael Honey, accomplished as both historian and folk singer, teased from fugitive sources a moving biography, *Sharecropper's Troubadour*. Seeger's preface to that book ended by addressing Handcox and concluded, "Children not yet born will carry on your work."

6

PRESENT AT THE UNMAKING
Critical Studies of Whiteness and Critical Race Theory

I became low-key famous—academia famous, that is—in the early nineties following the publication of *The Wages of Whiteness*. The same book, plus three or four sequels and spin-offs, also made me low-key infamous by attracting extreme right-wing and not-so-right-wing political attacks. Before that, I was a labor historian, reliably providing quotes on efforts to gain a shorter working day in the US or explaining why those efforts had so dwindled. I taught, with tenure and a full professorship, at the University of Missouri and aspired to little more career wise.

Wages of Whiteness pretty much wrote itself, out of conversations, political arguments, and wisdom acquired from readings a decade before, as I tried to process the defeats of the left and labor. It is far from my best book, but it is the one most a part of its historical moment and most approximating in some parts of its drafting what we surrealists call "automatic writing" with brain and typing—or in my case, handwriting, as I seldom typed first drafts—in sync. The result was a slight volume, not 200 pages of text, and thus perfect for the diminishing expectations of what undergraduates might read in a couple weeks of a course. It compactly located the formation of a US working class alongside a much larger enslaved, racialized African American labor force. It placed that history in the wake of the American Revolution, which made the identity of the "white worker" especially resonant and ensured that the accent in that term fell upon the adjective.

When the great sociologist of race, policy, and science (and grandson of Ida B. Wells) Troy Duster quickly adopted the book as a text in his large, legendary introductory classes on race at the University of California, *Wages of Whiteness* was on its way. It has sold nearly 100,000 copies and now approaches 10,000 citations, unheard of for a work of nineteenth-century US history. One of the several editions features an introduction by the radical law professor and former Black Panther Kathleen Cleaver. Another is elegantly led off by a historian of South Asia, Priyamvada Gopal. It won a major prize from the Organization of American Historians and put me in close association with Toni Morrison. Translated into Japanese, French, and Chinese, it landed me in debates in much of world.

Conservative attacks on the book came fast and liberal ones later, the former doing it no harm and the latter lots of good. As importantly, and unbeknownst to me or any of us, it turned out that the idea of studying whiteness was in the air. A dozen serious books on the subject appeared in the nineties, from Alexander Saxton to Ruth Frankenberg, from Toni Morrison to Matthew Frye Jacobson. By the end of the decade what had been a group of individuals thinking through common problems had crystalized into what was termed a school of thought: Critical Whiteness Studies for those taking it seriously and mostly White Studies or Whiteness Studies for those predisposed to snark.

Those writing about the critical study of whiteness varied greatly in approaches and conclusions but generally took care to think about whiteness as a problem, as something created, embraced, and rejected in specific times and places and for identifiable purposes. Considering how many of us were on the left, we avoided magnifying disagreements into eviscerations. Especially within the fields of labor history and immigration history, the new scholarship fundamentally challenged established narratives. Such studies overlapped with what had come by 1989 to be termed Critical Race Theory, eventually a *bête noire* of the right.

Problems, Possibilities, Defeats

It is difficult in several ways to write about this period of my career with balance and without some sadness. First, as I began to write this chapter giving my account of the origins of Critical Race Theory and critical studies of whiteness, the governor of Florida promoted attacks on both as his hoped-for ticket to the White House. To comply with his broad bans on the teaching of CRT in state schools, biographies of such baseball superstars as Hank Aaron and Roberto Clemente have disappeared from libraries amidst worries that the descriptions of racism in them could disrupt ancestor worship among whites and make schoolkids encouraged to identify as white feel bad about their patrimony. Florida's now much-emulated goal is to prevent that at all costs.

I abbreviate CRT not only for convenience but because a broad swath of the US public now somehow recognizes those initials. Many on the right believe that the letters are another mark of Satan. Democrats are trained by their leaders to announce that CRT identifies an esoteric legal theory, scarcely practiced in the wider world and so universally un-taught in schools as to require no defense. White nationalism is something that US conservatism plays at strategically and embraces far too often. Where it wields power, the right is tempted to enforce that erasure of history. They don't resist temptation.

Parts of the left and liberalism proved almost as lacking in seriousness concerning the study of race as the right, taking potshots at the critical study of whiteness and sometimes at me. In his 2023 jeremiad *I'll Burn that Bridge When I Get to It*, Norman Finkelstein writes a sad new chapter in what's been an estimable and admirable career studying Zionism by joining the ranks of those denouncing "cancel culture" and "identity politics." He writes that "Whiteness studies" is "as much an academic discipline as hula-hoop studies." He reaches such a conclusion from a not very close reading of the excesses of one popular self-help book on white identity, Robin DiAngelo's *White Fragility*. As much as I lack interest in making the critical study of whiteness into any kind of an "academic discipline," it is a body of thought that includes Ida B. Wells, Gloria Anzaldúa, Toni Morrison, Alexander Saxton, W.E.B. Du Bois, bell hooks, Theodore Allen, Cheryl Harris, James Baldwin, and other leading left thinkers. In a book as breathlessly devoted to questioning "cancel culture" as *I'll Burn that Bridge* is, it rings false when a case is made for abolishing such an area of inquiry.

Finkelstein comes for me specifically on the basis of a supposedly glowing review of *White Fragility* that I allegedly wrote for the *Los Angeles Times*. I'm billed as the "reigning guru of 'whiteness studies.'" No such review exists. I actually wrote critically on the book and the diversity consultant industry in the *Los Angeles Review of Books*. On the basis of such misreading, I become in *I'll Burn that Bridge* someone urgently needing to be "retired," along with the whole in-scare-quotes field of "whiteness studies."

Even a more weighty and lucid account, the radical political scientist Cedric Johnson's "The Wages of Roediger: Why Three Decades of Whiteness Studies Has Not Produced the Left We Need," can abandon good scholarly habits characteristic of some of the author's work when "whiteness studies" enters the picture. The boom in studies of whiteness was not thirty years old but instead nearer forty when Johnson wrote that article in 2019. Adopting the shorter time frame cuts out the most noteworthy, and often Marxist, modern works on the problem of whiteness—those of Allen, Saxton, George Lipsitz, Matthew Jacobson, Noel Ignatiev, Karen Brodkin, Cheryl Harris, and even the reason for the very title and the ire of Johnson's indictment, my own *The Wages of Whiteness*. Removing those works by periodizing so oddly makes it much easier to cast the whole enterprise as one centered on corporate antiracist training and individual microaggressions, not systems. Critical whiteness studies becomes the project of a very loosely defined "professional-managerial class," bent on undermining unity among workers and minimizing class conflicts, not, as we aimed to do, on deepening struggles and making meaningful class solidarities possible.

Finally, it verges on the impossible to get the *tone* right in writing retrospectively on critical studies of whiteness. It won't do, in the face of hostility, to inflate the importance of critical studies of whiteness or CRT. Blowing out of all proportion the influence of antiracist scholarship is in fact the preferred tactic of those hostile to such work. Alarmists on the right imagine juggernauts bulldozing white self-esteem and taking society to the doorstep of making reparations for past injustices; left critics meanwhile conjure up a whiteness studies "industry" as what separates us from the left that we need. The hard truth supports neither accusation, especially where critical study of whiteness is concerned. It remains a subspecialty, rethinking and deploying insights long available within ethnic studies traditions. Part of my refusal to convert critical studies of whiteness to the initials "CWS" stems from not wanting to participate in the hype or to raise the false expectations.

An example undercuts the claims of critical studies of whiteness to produce prescriptions for social movements. Almost a decade ago I participated, mostly just by bringing snacks to my son and other activists, in a planning meeting for a St. Louis demonstration after Mike Brown died at the hands of a cop. One of the proposed chants alternated the lines "Hands Up" and "Don't Shoot" with marchers raising hands on the first line. A discussion ensued, with some in the group saying that white protesters should not raise the chant, as their risks from the police did not in reality approach those of Black participants. Others—and race by no means predicted who argued on which side—insisted that taking up the chants and motions performed allyship, choosing to join in the risk and maintain common purpose in marching.

I went on a speaking tour about something else shortly thereafter and in talking about my interest in the exchange around the "Hands Up" chant found that people in two other cities reported almost the same debate in their local movements. Others had similar discussions over white participations in "die-ins," a part of the street theatre of some demonstrations against police murders. In hearing more, I realized that critical whiteness studies, or my version of it anyhow, was not really situated to provide an answer to what whites should do, or be asked to do, in that situation. What it can do is explain why the tensions between the two positions are enduring ones, worth airing.

Disappointment, even disillusion, arose from the ease with which our ideas quickly achieved some national attention and then receded. We gained some ground and more recently lost it. We exercised too little care in what we wished for in terms of notice in the press. We failed, so far, not only in the unequal battle with conservative media to give CRT serious meaning but also in the fight with racial liberalism by failing to make "white privilege" a weapon in contesting the class and racial structures of racial capitalism. Originating on the left, critical study of whiteness has too often ended up as the property of diversity consultants who may do some good, but not the good that we envisioned, and also do harm. Thus, bad-faith efforts by white nationalists and others on the right only account for part of the problem. The very term "white privilege" came to have a meaning very different from what we hoped to convey, now referring to matters that are more interpersonal than structural.

Different emphases existed from the beginning of critical whiteness studies. One was therapeutic, offering exercises designed to make healthier and more aware white individuals and communities while lessening implicit racist biases. But the extent to which antiracist "trainings" have come to take place under corporate, military, and university diversity and equity bureaucracies almost ensured that they would fail to also emphasize larger points concerning race and capitalism, which were foundational to the critical study of whiteness. To the extent that we have sparked a dialogue capable of losing track of structures of class, empire, and even of systemic racism, we have failed.

But losing does not mean we're completely wrong, let alone faithless. The specific charges against those studying whiteness critically are largely bullshit. We were not interested in homogenizing the experiences of so-called white people across lines of class or in blaming individuals. Most of us began by thinking expressly about the class differences among whites papered over by a belief in a common racial identity and interest. No writer I came to know in studying whiteness desired to make anybody feel bad for their race, which we regarded as an ideology and even, as per James Baldwin, as a lie. We were, and are, trying to make a society in which poor and working people feel and actually *do* better. In the case of both CRT and the critical study of whiteness there are such straightforward commonsense reasons explaining their origins that conspiracy theories regarding a plotting professional-managerial class are not only mistaken but superfluous.

CRT Happens

Remembering the development of CRT and the tasks it responded to situates us to understand my experiences as a sometimes participant in it. After *The Wages of Whiteness* appeared, invitations into debates over CRT proliferated. When I began writing *Wages* in 1989, I had neither heard nor read the words Critical Race Theory, at least not in that order and capitalized. Until the late eighties there were only bubbling bodies of thought, awaiting an assigned name and initials. These had very deep roots and drew less on ideology than on deeply practical (and in legal matters often technical) concerns.

CRT barely predated the critical study of whiteness as an identifier of a school of thought, although both have long and distinguished lineages, making it hard to identify a single date of origin. Critical Race Theory started to attract attention under that title in 1989 when the legal scholars Kimberlé Crenshaw, Neil Gotanda, and Stephanie Phillips convened an event using that title at the University of Wisconsin. I would not have heard about it. The conference's very title, "New Developments in Critical Race Theory," caught the way that the sub-field already had a vibrant, evolving intellectual life even as the workshop organizers could claim to have originated the actual name Critical Race Theory.

That vibrancy owed much to the prior work of the towering scholar-activist Derrick Bell, who had litigated important cases leading to the ending of segregation, especially in education. With civil rights victories in court, and by the mid-sixties in Congress, Bell moved to reflect on the extent to which broad racial inequalities were bound to persist, now in some ways harder to mitigate, or even question through Black self-organization and legal actions. The challenge for Bell, and for other civil rights movement lawyers, became how to introduce the impact of inherited inequalities and internalized biases into court cases in which the statutes, but not the broader practices of law and society, were seemingly "color-blind."

Bell did so in part through telling stories—asking, for example in "The Space Traders" how the US would split if extraterrestrials offered to solve economic and environmental problems if the nation gave up its Black population. The broader goal remained to introduce histories and habits into the record as part of a strategy showing how inequalities were produced and reproduced within social structures. The plain imperative to include such expansive context—and equally the goal of opponents to exclude it—lies at the heart of what is now a half century of attempts at dismissal and then censorship of CRT. Bell and his associates did not make this up as a problem in legal practice. They lived with it. In 1989, as CRT was named, the Supreme Court decided *City of Richmond v. Croson*—this I did know at the time—and included in their ruling the stricture that racial justice "remedies that are ageless in their reach into the past" could not prevail. It is now clearer than ever that the right understands the battle as precisely over the production and dissemination of knowledge about the racially unequal past and its impact on an unequal present.

One recent distillation of this conflict into which I was drawn involved screenings in schools of the animated short film *The Unequal Opportunity Race*. The film animates US history as a multiracial track competition, promising fairness to all runners at the outset, but with obstacles—from slavery to manifest destiny to Jim Crow to mass incarceration—cropping up to impede the runners who are not white while advantaged white runners, unimpeded, sail into a widening lead and accumulate rewards. Those who lobbied to stop the film from being shown in schools, especially in the election year of 2016, labeled it a "white guilt" cartoon. The controversy looks in retrospect like a rehearsal for current efforts to ban CRT. It underscores how the legal strategy problems faced by Bell and others bled into the realms of education, popular culture, and electoral politics. CRT became one worthwhile part of the pedagogy of social justice, originally forged in sternly practical legal strategies but drawing on and enriching wider knowledge.

Central to CRT, and as miscast by the right and parts of the left and liberalism, was the idea of "*intersectionality*." Crenshaw originated that term, at least in a form that persisted in use, also in 1989. Intersectionality quickly became one centerpiece of CRT. The term described the ways in which systems sometimes require, and ideologies often encourage, the reduction of identity to a single "essential" one, but life insists otherwise. "Nobody," I heard the great thinker Edward Said say in one of his last public lectures before his death in 2003, "is only one thing." Appreciation for the profundity of Said's seemingly commonplace remark had to be fought for. Crenshaw's interventions regarding the importance of intersections were, like CRT, designed to get a hearing in court. She coined the term in the context of DeGraffenreid v. General Motors, a 1976 case in which Black women workers claimed discrimination victimized them. Here was a classic case of class, race, and gender operating simultaneously. However, US workers have scant room to litigate class grievances, and the court found significant discrimination against neither Black workers (aggregating males and females) nor women workers (aggregating Black and white). The court would not consider the specific plight of the Black women workers at the intersection of identities. Even more than in the case of CRT broadly, theories of intersectionality drew immediately upon earlier bodies of activist and scholarly knowledge beyond law. Such knowledge included efforts of activists to think about and create solidarities, from the ideas of Sojourner Truth in the nineteenth century to the radical Black radical feminist Combahee River Statement of 1977. Equally, intersectionality itself intersected with bodies of thought beyond law but in dialogue with it, for example in the work of the sociologist Patricia Hill Collins, the poetry of June Jordan, and the theory produced by bell hooks.

By 1995 the legal scholars Richard Delgado and Jean Stefancic could produce a fat compendium titled Critical Race Theory with lots of material to fill it and a firm sense that scholars in and beyond law would understand the title. Its dazzling introduction already used the initials CRT to describe "a movement [that] is a collection of activists and scholars interested in studying and transforming the relationship among race, racism, and power." They added that CRT "considers many of the same issues that conventional civil rights and ethnic studies discourses take up but places them in a broader perspective that includes economics, history, context, group- and self-interest, and even feelings and the unconscious." Surprisingly, the volume generously sampled my work, underlining how broadly the newly named area of inquiry sought to introduce new stories.

I ultimately met Bell in 1996, when he initiated a series of conversations after a talk I gave at the Columbia University Teach-In with the Labor Movement. The event celebrated the new leader of the AFL-CIO, John Sweeney, though my in my remarks I found the local union efforts to free the political prisoner Mumia Abu-Jamal to be more inspiring than what Sweeney was then attempting. My most scintillating discussions with Bell took place in Florida and included the Black scholar and preacher Jefferson Rogers, who had been Arthur Ashe's minister. In 1997, Delgado and Stefancic would edit the weighty, useful volume Critical White Studies, including in it my work along with Bell's. CRT and critical studies of whiteness enriched each other early and often.

Critical Study of Whiteness:
The Moment and the Misapprehension

If CRT developed initially in response to practical problems in courts, the critical study of whiteness gained audience and attention as the result of intellectuals and activists thinking about changes in US electoral politics. In particular, the consistent failure of the Democrats to capture the White House from 1968 through 1992, with Jimmy Carter's single term being the lone exception, brought great attention to the defection of the "Reagan Democrats." These were the working class, often trade union white voters who had supported the New Deal tradition and rejected Republicans through the mid-1960s but who were won over by Nixon, and then Reagan. They left the Democratic ranks partly on "social issues," as ideas about racial justice and reproductive freedom came to be understood. They switched loyalty too over economic issues, like taxes, that were interlaced with race issues and welfare policies. Wooing the Reagan Democrat became an obsession in the center-right of the Democratic Party, with eventual electoral success, but at great moral cost, as charted in the nineties by Clinton strategist Stanley Greenberg and discussed in my recent book, *The Sinking Middle Class*.

At the same time, a little intellectual space opened to make fathomable the consideration of the Reagan Democrat not just in terms of electoral calculus but as part of the broader ways in which a "white problem" precluded advances towards either racial or class equality. It takes a long time to think through, and then write, a book. It was thus a decade after Reagan's 1980 election that the spate of titles eventually grouped together as "critical study of whiteness" appeared. But essays came more quickly. By 1984, James Baldwin, as wonderful a nonfiction writer as he was a novelist, could write the most direct and clear short piece on the cost to everyone—decidedly including poor and immigrant whites—of what he called "choosing" to be white. He would place that seminal piece, "On Being White, and Other Lies," in the African American popular beauty magazine *Essence*, displaying his confidence that Reaganism had made possible an intelligible critique of whiteness that was both generative and popular. At about the same time, Baldwin would say, in the 1989 film *The Price of the Ticket*, to the dominant race in the US, "As long as you think you are white, there is no hope for you." If white America was not ready for such tough love, there was some room for considering the idea fathomable in universities and among white union activists, when they got to hear the arguments.

For good reasons I have resisted helping make the critical study of whiteness into either a media sensation or a distinct corner of academic research, even when someone I admire, like the historian and artist Nell Irvin Painter or the poet and critic Claudia Rankine, identifies me a founder of the enterprise. Indeed, I do not think that the critical study of whiteness ought to be a freestanding field apart from ethnic studies or CRT. Perhaps this is because I came to study whiteness through Black Studies, broadly speaking. Not only do I oppose any aspiration to have a center or an academic major on the subject of whiteness, but I have never taught a class that focused on it. I know great people who have successfully taught such classes, but for me the risk of re-centering whiteness in such a setting remains too great.

I regarded as suspect claims that any small group of people—in press accounts often all-white—suddenly invented the study of white identities and interests in the early nineties, when such generalizations first appeared. My reservations reflected how thoroughly such a scenario flew in the face of my own experiences. Almost every insight I developed regarding what African Americans had long insisted on calling the "white problem" came from reading their words, from slave folktales and songs to the writings on whites of Harriet Jacobs, W.E.B. Du Bois, Ida B. Wells, Langston Hughes, Elma Stuckey, James Baldwin, Richard Wright, and others. Even in the nineties the leading figures in studying whiteness decidedly included Black, Latinx, and Indigenous authors such as Toni Morrison, bell hooks, john a. powell, Cheryl Harris, Neil Foley, and Vine Deloria Jr.

The remarkable ability to miss all that was clearly put on display when the New York Times Magazine devoted a lavish spread to "Getting Credit for Being White" in 1997. The article, by the essayist Margaret Talbot, suffered from having a hook—first there was "porn studies" and now there's "whiteness studies"—that precluded its author learning anything much. (Indeed, Talbot's use of writing on sex workers to epitomize frivolous and ephemeral academic and political writing proved as wrong as her singling out critical studies of whiteness.) She interviewed me for her article, and our conversation alarmed me by its emptiness, especially when Talbot cheerfully remarked at the end that she was now done with her research. When I asked whom she had interviewed, she named only white scholars. I protested that in its origins and best contemporary practices the critical study of whiteness was a project animated by those for whom whiteness was most urgently a problem. I thought she became enthusiastic about hearing from Cheryl Harris and Morrison.

A few days later the brilliant Twin Cities photographer Keri Pickett called to set up a time to shoot photographs for the article. When we met, she remarked that the assigned photographers, located in the several cities where interviewees lived, had all received the same odd instructions regarding camera settings. When I asked what the effect on the images would be, Pickett explained first in technical and then in lay terms. It would, she said, make the subjects in the shots whiter. The article was published shortly thereafter, without Morrison or Harris. Talbot wrote as if it were scholars who described race in a self-interested way. She wrote that "whiteness studies" engaged "inevitably, in a journey of self-discovery in which white people's thoughts about their own whiteness acquire a portentous new legitimacy."

At almost the same time, in 1997, the idea that the critical study of whiteness was self-aggrandizing surfaced in the news coverage of a huge conference on the subject at the University of California at Berkeley. The conference billed itself glitzily as the first of its kind. It would bring together participants under the title "The Making and Unmaking of Whiteness," producing excitement as most of us writing on the topic would meet for the first time. But it also generated a media buzz unheard of for a scholarly conference, based on a spectacular misapprehension.

The mid-nineties had produced a high tide of bipartisan white identity politics in which the presidential administration of William Jefferson Clinton joined Republicans in "ending welfare as we know it," increasing incarceration, and making the death penalty more "effective." In California in 1994, the Proposition 187 ballot initiative to keep those whom the proposal called "illegal aliens" from accessing state services passed in a landslide. The two major political parties vied for being the best listeners to what were cast as the grievances of "middle class" whites. In such a context it became possible to completely misunderstand the Berkeley conference as an act of self-assertion by those labeling themselves and their interests as white. Some in the large crowds came expecting as much, creating tensions.

The press warmly adopted the notion that the event expressed a desire by whites to gain, as Talbot had uncomprehendingly put it, "standing in the multicultural paradigm they have never before enjoyed." The fact that the conference occurred at Berkeley, understood as a citadel of historic left protests, made the narrative that identity politics were being challenged in their stronghold irresistible. The day before the conference began, a staffer from *Nightline*, the then-popular late-night national news show, called to ask me if I'd appear. When it became clear that he anticipated onboarding a white intellectual wanting to sit at the table of identity politics, I pointed out that I and certainly most of the conference presenters believed that concern for white interests already took up far too much political and intellectual oxygen. Moreover, the real, even dire, problems of ordinary people racialized as white did not get easier to address when defined as grievances born of being white. We supported the "unmaking" of whiteness. "Oh," the *Nightline* booker replied with admirable clarity and finality, "we wouldn't be interested in that."

Writing Critical Whiteness Studies before It Existed

Turning to my own work at this early juncture seems necessary to allow this chapter to remain one of intellectual autobiography and insider account. To do otherwise threatens lapsing into a review essay. Speaking from my own experience does not imply that I accept the role of "guru" or even founder of critical studies of whiteness.

When I switched in graduate school from African American history to labor history, I imagined I'd continue to write articles on the former but books on the latter. Strike support work promised to bridge the two. A turning point came in the summer of 1981 when the Professional Air Traffic Controllers Organization (PATCO) struck. I was back in Chicago and spoke in support of the walkout, digging in with others for a long struggle. The task suited me since one key demand, now largely forgotten, of the walkout was a 32-hour workweek, just the kind of renewed struggle over the hours of labor that Phil Foner and I had been predicting in our studying of the working day in US history. Nevertheless, the strike's defeat was swift, total, and symptomatic. Newly elected US president Ronald Reagan simply fired the strikers and hired permanent replacements. The labor movement, down from representing over a third of all workers in the fifties to just more than a fifth in 1981, had no response. Reagan's example emboldened private employers to hire permanent replacements when workers dared strike. Between 1980 and 2020 the percentage of workers in unions halved yet again, and the numbers of strikes slipped even more precipitously. PATCO, an overwhelmingly white and male union, had supported Reagan in the 1980 election, when he ran on a salad of code words appealing to whites: welfare queens, busing, crime, taxes.

With PATCO smashed, white workers nevertheless again voted in their majority for Reagan in 1984. I anguished more over the fate of unions than that of the Democrats but began to follow debates about what had produced the Reagan Democrats' rightward drift. I'd always known plenty of conservative white workers, without having to leave my family. They were Republicans on my dad's side and Southern (Illinois) racist Democrats on my mom's. The old left line terming capitalist politics a bird with two wings—the Democratic and Republican parties—applied in my experience to white supremacy as well.

But when I looked for guidance on race and working-class conservatism in labor history, my field at the time, the pickings proved slim. There were some useful heroic accounts of Black-white unity in the US, less still on the exclusionary practices of unions and hate strikes, and next to nothing that addressed conservative white workers and their racial fears and commitments. That dearth sent me to look again at what I'd read in independent study classes with Sterling Stuckey in graduate school. Those courses, labeled as history classes but also distinctly interdisciplinary Black studies ones, gave me the beginnings of a framework for discussing the "white problem." When I argue that the study of whiteness grows out of ethnic studies, I am, at the very least, right that this describes my own experience.

For the enslaved and for radical intellectuals of color, the white problem involved practical questions of how to survive affronts and often terror. The production of such knowledge, I soon realized, motivated the "John and the Master" folktales of the enslaved that had captivated me on a different level a decade before. African American folk stories, music, novels, poems, manifestos, sociology, and history rendered the white problem as a moral, political, aesthetic, gendered, and even historical one, showing great curiosity from slavery forward about just when and how some people came to define themselves as white. What defined modern critical studies of whiteness at their best was exactly this curiosity about how the white problem could be apprehended and addressed.

The debt of my best-known historical work on whiteness to the Black radical tradition caused me in 1998 to collect over fifty representative pieces—including work by Adrian Piper, Langston Hughes, Chester Himes, Derrick Bell, Toni Morrison, James Baldwin, Jacob Lawrence, Harriet Jacobs, Frederick Douglass, Ralph Ellison, Claude McKay, Richard Wright, bell hooks, W.E.B. Du Bois, and Sterling Brown—into the edited volume Black on White: Black Writers on What It Means to Be White. All towered not only as important artists and writers on the Black experience but also as leading students of the white problem.

I remained more specifically interested in the "white worker problem" and the ways in which poor and laboring whites offered allegiance—not perhaps more than whites in other social locations but more tragically—to a system that exploited them. Here too the lessons I'd learned from Stuckey informed everything. My point of departure was the realization that whiteness presented problems for Black workers and for white workers wanting to act on class grievances. Chester Himes wrote of a Black character's bad day in If He Hollers Let Him Go: "The white folks sure had brought their white to work that morning." I left that line on my desk for a long time, puzzling over its meaning. These were the days before we talked about microaggressions.

Du Bois wrote the passage that gave Wages of Whiteness its title. Of all the re-readings I did in the eighties, his Black Reconstruction stood as not only the most profound but also the most frequent. After 1985, I taught Southern history at the University of Missouri and assigned it at every opportunity as not only the best book in the field but also the best historical study produced in the US. White Southern laborers "received a low wage" after Civil War, according to Du Bois. But additionally, they "were compensated in part by a sort of public and psychological wage . . . because they were white." They accumulated "public defer-ence and titles of courtesy" and accessed the best parks and schools. Law enforcement workers came from "their ranks" and courts sometimes kept them from prison. Also necessary for me was Du Bois' unsparing clarity in stating that white labor did not just err here and get misled there but also stood against freedom at critical junctures during and after Reconstruction. Even in holding that "color caste [was] founded and retained by capitalism" he insisted that it came to be "adopted, forwarded and approved by white labor." His work emboldened me to think I could move from teaching about white labor one day and race another to writing about their relationship.

By 1989 I had published two articles on related subjects—one in *New Politics*, an independent socialist journal, and the other in *The Year Left*, an annual publication issued as a book by Verso, under the editor-ship of Mike Sprinker and Mike Davis. Especially in the latter, bearing Marx's formulation "Labour in White Skin" as its title, I argued that labor history as a field could benefit from more tough-mindedness in its approach to white labor organizations' record where race was concerned. Such an approach would pay attention to the rare instances in which a moment of beautiful antiracist unity flies like a swallow into the dismal general story of refusals by white workers to engage in solidarity. But it would also attend to how often the swallow was mistaken by writers of working-class history for an antiracist spring. Mineworkers especially received attention as having a good record of interracialism, but I knew that the most famous of their struggles near where I lived ended in the creation of a sundown town. Lines were very quickly drawn, and many labor historians feared that an emphasis on racism would make the past of the unions seem less "use-able" and alienate union officialdom. One bright and senior writer on the working-class past took me aside at a conference to warn against "airing dirty laundry." As labor history declined as a field one easy move was to regard "whiteness studies" as its nemesis, even though some of the most-cited labor historians came to be those who wrote on whiteness and class.

Lonely Writing: Not a Circle Nor Even a Proper Triangle

If the conditions for rethinking the "white worker" existed by the late eighties, the knowledge that others were doing so came to me very slowly. Writing *Wages of Whiteness* was a lonely pursuit. If any of us producing what came to be called critical studies of whiteness conspired, we did so by the twos or threes. "Soros money" never arrived. The experience of being so alone in writing, and of being so without a field to write for, was exciting, but also anxious.

I knew Noel Ignatin (later known as Ignatiev). The first event at which I felt completely at home and inspired as a sympathizer of the Chicago Surrealist Group came while doing work in Chicago in support of the bitter strike among US miners of bituminous coal in 1977–78. The surrealists hit on a stroke of genius in picketing the coal mine, itself a pro-coal industry publicity gimmick, that tourists visited in Chicago's Museum of Science and Industry. The museum had installed an actual mine, brought up from southern Illinois, when Peabody Coal was attempting to burnish its image around the 1934 Chicago World's Fair. The museum's mine, polished to a fault and upbeat in its view of coal-mining work counted almost as an amusement park ride. I'd loved it as a grade schooler. Our 1977 picket attracted some meaningful conversations and good publicity because it brought awareness of the strike to a large group of museum goers and raised questions about the cultural work the exhibit itself performed. We left the museum feeling pumped about the outcome.

Within a few blocks of walking towards the legendary Seminary Co-op Bookstore in Hyde Park, we happened into Ignatin, a Chicago revolutionary who took the edge off my bliss. Noel was about a dozen years older than I. The gap served as a good illustration of the difference between being part of the New Left at its start and coming in late, as I had. On hearing our account of how things had gone, he deadpanned, "So you spent your day picketing on behalf of a white supremacist organization," meaning to my amazement the United

Mine Workers. The long-time surrealists were ready with a deflection: "That's Noel." But I was 25, from a union family, and in the process of becoming briefly a more-or-less standard-issue labor historian in search of a "useable past." That meant scouring the historical record of white workers, and their white-led and sometimes whites-only unions, for the best, rare moments when "Black and white. Unite and fight" actually were words to live by. The UMW furnished a fair share of such moments—I knew most—alongside much else. I was unforgiving of Noel's remark in the moment.

Noel subsequently sometimes dropped into Red Rose Books, bringing in literature from the Sojourner Truth Organization, which he helped to lead while working in a steel mill. I discovered how likeable he was. Among the factory-working revolutionaries who'd abandoned universities—in his case leaving Penn—for industrial jobs, he told the best stories and appeared to best listen to workers. *Acceptable Men*, his posthumous book capturing life at US Steel's Gary Works shows these qualities. He rejected direct political lessons in favor of an insistence that the shop floor empowered workers while it made them miserable. I found Noel to be an uncommonly funny revolutionary. He loved political arguments, the fiercer the better, but with no strong desire to excommunicate those who disagreed. In those moments he could seem almost boyish, stretching to find the easiest posture, cracking wise, provoking, and hoping for the best in the long run.

My own politics on race broadened as I studied at Northwestern with Stuckey and informally in St. Louis with George Rawick. With the former I read W.E.B. Du Bois systematically and with Rawick, C.L.R. James. I'd known Noel's sixties and early seventies writings on the white worker, pieces done with and without Ted Allen. I had especially appreciated his 1974 *Radical America* piece "Black Workers, White Workers," which theorized white workers' consciousness as being distorted as the result of a "sweetheart agreement" between "themselves and their bosses," embracing a common whiteness. This was controversial stuff even on the left. The editors at *Radical America* ran the piece but prefaced it with a critical preamble. I admired the ideas of Ignatin and Allen but without feeling on first reading any need to take on the full import of their conclusions.

That changed when I read Du Bois and James and when I came to terms with the festive support Chicago Nazis could command in Marquette Park. I did not come to think the miners organized for white supremacy but did come to know that their practice, a great film like John Sayles' *Matewan* notwithstanding, too often failed to break from it. Over the years, the great fighter against employment discrimination, Herbert Hill, the labor secretary of the National Association for the Advancement of Colored People, became a friend, driving over from his home in Madison, Wisconsin for visits in the Twin Cities. Hill, by the way, spent part of his youth in the Socialist Workers Party and considered himself not only to have once been a surrealist but to have remained one, expressing not entirely jovial pique at not being invited to participate in group events. As much as I liked the great labor historian Herbert Gutman, Hill seemed to me to have much the better evidence in his critique of Gutman's writings on the extent of interracialism in the UMW, not to mention in his responses to the assessments of the steelworkers' record on race offered by Judith Stein. At the very least, learning from Hill made me realize that Noel was not only trolling that day on the south side.

By 1981, when the STO published a special issue of *Urgent Tasks* on James, I wrote for it on C.L.R. James' book on Herman Melville, *Mariners, Renegades, and Castaways*. Not long after that, Noel and I both left Chicago, he for Harvard and a doctorate in history, achieved under the name of Noel Ignatiev, and I for work at the University of Missouri. We had come to know one another, we later reflected, too little in Chicago. But later a mutual love of James and of Rawick joined our converging roles in critical whiteness studies to bring us together frequently. In 1990, Noel sent to me his wonderful little essay "Whiteness and American Character," published in novelist Ishmael Reed's journal *Konch*. It was through that article that I and others discovered Baldwin's "On Being White, and Other Lies."

Following Baldwin and Allen—and indeed Reed as well—Noel and I both became interested in the transformation of racially suspect Irish immigrants into more acceptable whites in the antebellum US. Noel engaged that history with more drama and evidence than I had in *Wages of Whiteness* in his arresting 1995 book *How the Irish Became White*.

That book's debt to Baldwin was as profound as mine would be in the subsequent *Working Toward Whiteness*, a study of race, whiteness, and the so-called "new immigration" from Southern and Eastern Europe from the 1890s to the 1930s. The most intriguing attempt to introduce the critical study of whiteness to a popular, if highbrow, audience, my late curator and art critic friend Maurice Berger's *White Lies*, owed Baldwin fundamentally as well.

In 2011, when the leading US historian Nell Irvin Painter published her own superb *The History of White People*, she twice emphasized that two works stood as "foundational" to what she called critical white studies. One was my book, *The Wages of Whiteness*, and the other was Noel's *How the Irish Became White*. She hit upon a connection profound enough that for once I did not try to wave away the idea that I am a founder of anything by replying that the profound thinkers among the enslaved population founded the study of whiteness. I acquiesced partly because I liked being mentioned alongside Noel.

Noel and I often disagreed. One example involved an error on my part. In the early nineties, as Noel and others launched the brave and important journal *Race Traitor*, they asked me to sit on its editorial board. I was still rightly (but too sternly) crusading for an emphasis on the fact that knowledge of whiteness has always come mostly from its direct victims, and I fretted that the name *Race Traitor* overly identified opposition to whiteness as a project among whites. Would African American radicals, I wondered, identify with the name? This literalism on my part came to seem less defensible when the Black radical intellectuals John Bracey and Robin D.G. Kelley rapidly joined the board. I had missed how the clear call by *Race Traitor* to abolish the white race clarified and advanced our arguments in a way that, like Baldwin, invited white workers to be something better than white. I wrote frequently for *Race Traitor*, including in its spectacular special issue on surrealism and whiteness. I also helped bring into print the book Noel edited for Kerr Publishing, *The Lesson of the Hour*, a collection of the abolitionist revolutionary Wendell Phillips' words.

The only other writer about whiteness whom I knew when writing *The Wages of Whiteness* was the brilliant historian and cultural studies scholar George Lipsitz. Lipsitz's deeply influential and incredibly smart article "The Possessive Investment in Whiteness" appeared in 1995, preceding his book by the same title by three years. Lipsitz and I were longtime friends. We'd both been in St. Louis at about the same time in the early seventies, though micro-generational differences had him, just a bit older, running through experiences before I did. In one account of his career Lipsitz allowed that he'd "enrolled in graduate school hoping to learn enough about labor history to understand [the] failure" of his labor solidarity work. I identified with that.

Lipsitz and I mutually admired, in my case idolized, George Rawick, the St. Louis–based Marxist historian, whose 1972 classic *From Sundown to Sunup* closed with an extended meditation on the origins and costs of whiteness. Lipsitz—I'm feeling like using the first names but want to avoid confusing the two St. Louis Georges—even managed, while a doctoral student at Wisconsin, to serve as Rawick's teaching assistant at the University of Missouri in St. Louis. *Sundown to Sunup* inspired many of the best sections of *Wages of Whiteness* and I suspect it did so for Lipsitz's work on whiteness too. Rawick died in 1990, after a series of strokes and other setbacks. He read, or rather had read to him, the final draft of *Wages of Whiteness*, noting its professed debts to him, and communicating delightedly through a scribe, asking "Are you sure I wrote all that stuff?" That would have been the time for me to conspire with Lipsitz on "whiteness studies," while we were communicating around Rawick's health. But I did not know of Lipsitz's growing interest in the topic until later.

I met Stan Weir, the compelling left and labor organizer, and theorist of the role of "primary work groups" in organizing, through Rawick. Stan introduced me to West Indian food, and the meal inevitably led to stories of the role of that cuisine in his friendship with James Baldwin. But it was Lipsitz who ensured that Stan and I would stay in close touch. Every time I spoke in southern California, George would show up with Stan. We ended at a strip mall Asian restaurant where Stan invariably drank a little from a flask and, to claim a small free dessert, announced to staff that it was his birthday. I hung on all words from Stan as he reflected on his maritime and auto work, hoping those lessons would not be lost. They weren't, thanks again to Lipsitz, who gathered Weir's writings in the edited collection *Singlejack Solidarity*. Lipsitz's first book, *A*

Rainbow at Midnight, came out in 1983 and offered a thrilling history of the post-World War II US working class. The book is a model for how a new labor history might have gone further, including stories about everything from general strikes to Hank Williams, from roller derby to the Latinx workers in a poisoned industrial small town fifteen miles from where I'd grown up.

By 1993 Lipsitz and I would reconvene as co-thinkers who were making whiteness a problem. We appeared on the same platform at a huge session of the American Studies Association in Boston. He anticipated the ideas in his forthcoming *The Possessive Investment in Whiteness*, and I offered scattered comments about the word "wigger" or its variant "wigga." Both words had just begun registering on my radar, sometimes as a slur with which white young people critiqued other whites they deemed too interested in Black culture, sometimes as a term pridefully adopted by those very whites adopting Black style and music, and sometimes as a term of affection Black kids used to refer to whites pulling off such a stance creatively and inoffensively. I gave out my phone number to the hundreds of people at the event, inviting them to interview their children and report local and regional variations to me. A house phone in the hotel ballroom rang as if on cue, making for what looked like a well-planned stunt. Soon enough, I got calls on "wigga" from oral historians of their own kids.

The feeling of anxiety and isolation accompanying the writing of *Wages of Whiteness* persisted even after it was finished. With the book just out in 1991, I pined for reviews, needing reassurance not so much that it would receive praise but that it would not be thought of as incomprehensible, even unhinged, within US history writing. Early reviews in the British press, even glowing ones in big Sunday papers, only reassured me a little. My book so differed from other US labor history books that I thought there was a good chance it would go completely unreviewed or be totally hated in the US. Alexander Saxton's *Rise and Fall of the White Republic* had just come out and I had seen the proofs, as we were both Verso authors. But it hadn't been much reviewed either. In any case, Saxton already had a distinguished career—in fact two such careers, given that he had been a brilliant writer of proletarian fiction before becoming a fabulous historian.

Then the mail brought a fat envelope from Michael Rogin, whose work I loved for its efforts to synthesize Marxism and psychoanalysis, also a concern of surrealists. Rogin, who taught political science at the University of California in Berkeley and was among the best writers of history in the US at the time, had sent the page proofs of his long treatment of *Wages* for a review essay that was to appear in *Radical History Review*. His words presented my arguments more directly and memorably than I had. Sending me the draft was a real act of kindness. Some luster was lost, however, because every time my name appeared in the article—I'm guessing forty times—Rogin misspelled it as "Roedinger." The old line about there being no such thing as bad publicity so long as the critic spells your name right was stood on its head.

I did not then know Rogin personally at all. Time was short for corrections to the essay to be made before the journal went to print. Luckily a colleague had Rogin's phone number. Screwing up courage to call, I led with fulsome thanks and then asked if he might press the journal for last-minute corrections. Rogin laughed at length before asking if I saw what he'd subconsciously done: "I added the 'n' so that your name contained all the letters in mine. I became the father of *Wages of Whiteness*."

An edge framed Rogin's remark, although I only later appreciated it. His famous 1975 study of Andrew Jackson, *Fathers and Children*, began with a remarkable three-chapter section titled simply "Whites." That, plus pivotal later sections on "primitive accumulation," capital, and race made Rogin's account of Jackson an alternative site for the foundation of modern critical studies of whiteness. (His *Blackface, White Noise* and other later works on immigration, popular culture, and identity became widely seen as central to such inquiry). Rogin's laughing reaction to his misspelling also involved joking about his own reputation for pursuing what was then called, usually dismissively in labor history circles, psychohistory. But making such a joke nevertheless suggested how deeply immersed in psychoanalytic theory he was.

A Wider Circle

In graduate school I learned the fancy word *"prosopography."* Now, fifty years on, I get a chance to use it. It refers to research into the common characteristics of people belonging to a specific group, studying their characteristics, similar and different, and the trajectories of their lives. As the nineties proceeded and I met most of the early writers on the critical history of whiteness in the US, their similarities impressed me more than the differences.

This is not at all to say we agreed much. My introduction to a new Verso edition of Saxton's *Rise and Fall of the White Republic* in 2003 offered the observation that Saxton's book represented the state-of-the-art among post-Du Bois historians writing on whiteness. Knowing his regard for Saxton's work, I thought Noel might concur. "Oh no," he said, "that's Ted Allen's work." On the other hand, a story circulated that Noel once told a press to ask Allen to write a reader's report recommending publication of Noel's work on whiteness and the Irish, and Ted then wrote a negative report, terming it "incorrect." Ted Allen certainly wrote a searing, long critique of my work that circulates widely on the internet even now. I liked the piece, though it too initially spelled my name wrong.

Those of us writing on whiteness in the nineties represented a variety of political generations and commitments. But to an extent greater than any other area of historical inquiry, we were overwhelmingly on the left, often influenced by Marxism, and steeped within either factory labor or labor support, or both. It was in those realms that we learned to regard whiteness as a problem. That fact makes it hard to support the charge that critical whiteness studies wanted to change the subject from class to race, that we did not address class differences, and that we regarded the working class as hopelessly and particularly backwards.

Underestimating the Marxism of the critical whiteness studies project made critics overestimate the role played by cultural studies, and even what was being called the "linguistic turn." My work, for example, analyzes the usage of keywords like "boss," "master," and "white slave." This proved enough to cause one labor historian to attack it as mere "word play." In fact, those keywords are the very languages of class and represent an analytical framework derived from the British Marxism of Raymond Williams and the Russian Marxism of M.M. Bakhtin. I could make a case regarding the changing meanings of the terms "wage slavery" and "white slavery" before digitized newspaper searches were possible because of the generosity of the great US Marxist historian Herbert Shapiro. He sent to me, without us having ever met, his own extensive notes on such usages in the antebellum press.

Allen and Saxton had even longer left and labor experience than Ignatiev. Both were born in 1919 and dropped out of college in the Depression, the former seemingly after just one day. Both became active in the Communist Party and held working-class jobs as union activists. Allen worked as a musician, miner, schoolteacher, draftsman, factory laborer, and librarian. The last seemed a good setting in which to produce his epic studies of the "invention of the white race," which practical experience led him to regard as a world-historic problem for the labor movement. I helped Verso edit the two volumes of Allen's work that appeared under that provocative title.

Saxton, whose dad was a leading figure in the publishing world, was born in Du Bois' hometown, Great Barrington, Mass. He dropped out of Harvard (though he did, after delays, graduate from the University of Chicago) to enter wage work, mostly on the railroads and in construction, and to organize maritime workers. A leading writer of proletarian novels in his young adulthood, Saxton told me, after we first met in 1993, when he spoke at a textile factory turned national park in Lowell, Massachusetts, that when he wanted to write a novel on railroad labor he had to study other unions to find a model for an antiracist white union member, as the rails generated so few such examples. In a later get-together in Youngstown, Ohio, he remembered testifying to a committee in the forties on racial discrimination at work. They would not hear the views of Black workers, who supposedly had too much self-interest to be reliable. White workers were not seen as having the same self-interest.

Saxton connected such experiences with his urgent choice of race and labor as topics when he changed careers midlife, gaining a doctorate in US history from the University of California, Berkeley, where he worked in part with Rogin. A career at UCLA followed, as did his 1975 classic The Indispensable Enemy, another worthy candidate, retrospectively, for originating the critical study of whiteness in academia.

Examples of how activism in working-class struggles shaped scholarship on whiteness multiplied as the nineties wore on. These included the best account of the labor process and whiteness, Bruce Nelson's *Divided We Stand*. Nelson had left graduate studies at Berkeley and San Francisco Theological Seminary to become a radical labor activist for most of the seventies, working on a truck assembly line and with a New Communist Movement group before pursuing a doctorate. Venus Green's magnificent *Race on the Line* remains the most exciting study of how whiteness mattered where labor, gender, and skill were concerned in the telephone industry, where she had labored and organized long before completing a doctorate at Columbia. Before Karen Brodkin's *How Jews Became White Folks and What that Says about Race in America* came out in 1998, she published a wonderful anthropological account of multiracial struggles of hospital workers, one she offered as a contribution to solidarity as well as to scholarship.

Critics and Haters

CRT and the critical study of whiteness have so long provided whipping boys—I'm not sure of the gender-neutral alternative—for the right that bitter criticism of my work in those areas occasions little surprise. The shape and timing of that criticism do bear elaboration as they came, after some delays, also from the left and liberals, and especially from my own field of labor history. The conservative media critics appeared almost immediately, but I turned out not to be quite what they needed. For nearly forty years they have asked, in wave after wave of mock outrage, if I didn't want to drive unpaid to a far-away studio to be denounced for five minutes by a reactionary TV host, often on Fox. I was too lazy, and eventually too savvy, to do that even once and always advised others to skip it. Usually, the hook for the outrage consisted of the "news"—decades later it is still presented as news—that college classes studying whiteness exist. Since I never taught such classes I had an easy out, even when the request came from more moderate outlets, like *Nightline* or Brian Williams' interview shows. In truth, I was also protected from far-right attacks by Noel Ignatiev's genius for soundbites. Both "abolition of whiteness" and "race traitor" attached to him, even though my follow-up book to *Wages of Whiteness* bears the title *Toward the Abolition of Whiteness*. On the other hand, the full-on white supremacists, especially at *Stormfront*, did single me out as an enemy of the white race.

Within the mainstream, and especially within labor history, the attackers were slow to come, then they gathered impressively. To say as much is not, with one exception, to complain about ill-treatment. For scholarship so self-consciously dissenting and irreverent, critical whiteness studies enjoyed a fair reception overall in academia and my own work in the area for a long while attracted almost alarming praise. In a kind of perfect storm, great initial responses in the English and Scottish press and the incredibly perceptive better-than-the-book review by the late Mike Marqusee in the *Times of India* allowed Verso to present the book as a big success. Steve Fraser's review in *American Historical Review* championed *Wages of Whiteness*. So did Catherine Hall's lengthy *New Left Review* essay on it, along with Rogin's in *Radical History Review*. Those who may have been tempted to write dismissively of the book were led to test the winds for a time, perhaps.

No sharply negative reviews came out until the Organization of American Historians awarded the book the Merle Curti Award. *Labor History*, then my field's flagship journal, ignored the book until it ran a negative review a full nine years after *Wages of Whiteness* first appeared. By then I longed for critical exchanges, knowing that the political differences within labor history were profound, and thinking, maybe wrongly, that such issues deserved airing. Loyalties to labor official-dom seemed to limit an open debate about labor and racism, at first generating reticence, and only later charges that studying workers and whiteness papered over social divisions among whites, or even "blamed" workers or trade union leaders (or maybe labor historians) rather than positioning all of them (including myself) as caught in a long-standing social tragedy.

The moment at which critics in the mainstream of labor history attacked critical whiteness studies perhaps came with a vengeance because it came so tardily. It arrived in 2001 and the venue was the relatively staid Cambridge University Press journal *International Labor and Working Class History*, called ILWCH (pronounced as "ill-witch" by the initiated). The publication regularly ran exchanges in which an idea was contested under the heading "Scholarly Controversy." The forum on whiteness took its title from the very long lead essay by the historian Eric Arnesen, "Whiteness and the Historians' Imagination," with imagination here counting as a bad thing. Answers came from an all-star cast including Eric Foner, Adolph Reed, and Barbara Fields. Arnesen wrapped up with a response. The absence of input by anyone centrally involved in the critical study of whiteness was total. Jim Barrett did contribute an even-handed piece, Victoria Hattam a characteristically intelligent one on race and ethnicity, and David Brody a kind if critical one.

But it remained a debate with one side represented by an empty chair and the debate suffered for it, lapsing into caricature. Arnesen's charges would not have been so incoherent if he'd known they'd be better challenged. The section on Du Bois and whiteness is a case in point. The article cannot decide if Du Bois' ideas on the "public and psychological wage" accruing to whites were traduced by myself and others or were so mired in "Marxism-lite" as to be themselves part of the problem. It takes both positions. Arnesen would have co-thinkers far to his left sharing his vacillations on Du Bois in the writings on *Wages of Whiteness*, especially in critiques published by the International Socialist Organization, many of whose leaders I helped acquaint with Marxism while teaching at Northwestern.

The historian Judith Stein introduces the Arnesen exchange with a piece barely a page long but bearing the title "Whiteness and US History: An Assessment." In it she rationalizes the fact that the ILWCH editors set up a one-sided debate. They reacted to a reality that they found unfortunate: "Whiteness studies have their sturdiest roots in labor history." Sought out were writers who had written about race and labor "but not about whiteness per se." They could "assess the work." Stein added that critical studies of whiteness reflected a shift in the political lexicon from racial discrimination to "white privilege," bringing politics into a hitherto objective field. Her crew, on the other hand, traded in "conceptual precision and evidence."

I did not know the ILWCH publication was in the works, learning of it only after it appeared, from a graduate student who agitatedly said, "That's directed at me, to shut down my work, not at you. You already get to write what you want." When I read the pieces, I had to agree. Several seemed snide but also strangely inconsequential. I've spent lots of time trying to figure out from where the forum's self-righteousness originated. From the Ivy League is only part of the answer. I asked my mother, then in her 70s, what she thought. She said maybe some people are just haters, which I massaged in responses to questions at public talks to imply she'd said "player haters." But I stopped retailing that line, cheap laughs aside, knowing the problems went quite beyond careerism and jealousy.

Working-class history was a field in crisis, bound to lose traction and jobs as the labor movement itself lost members and militancy. Nothing, Sweeney notwithstanding, showed signs of fundamentally interrupting that decline. *ILWCH* itself, an editorial board member later unabashedly told me, had been discussing ending its run when the buzz generated by the whiteness articles reenergized things. We all do our part. Labor historians, including those of us in both labor history and the critical study of whiteness, did not have an answer to the field's eclipse. It was unjust. The field had, at the University of Illinois Press, the best book series at a US academic press at the time but scant recognition. Perhaps it helped a little to imagine that the problem lay with historians whose work was making a popular impact or that the solution lay in excommunicating them. All that said, recent developments in labor history have impressed me.

Regrets and a Real Quandary

However defensive of the critical study of whiteness I became when it suffered attacks, my own early work in that area embarrasses me at times. It surely required critique. Insofar as we wanted to connect attacks on white privilege—I usually say white advantage—to other social movements, we largely failed. We lost out to diversity experts in defining the goals. My own embarrassment begins with the subtitle of *Wages of Whiteness*. Even given publishers' desires to oversell the breadth of content, *Race and the Making of the American Working Class* promises more than a short book can deliver and is wrong. The book is actually about the North and does not directly treat the enslaved and free Black working classes. Nor are women workers central, although my early writing connecting whiteness with manly independence attracted overly generous reviews where gender was concerned. I also do not use American when meaning US any longer. The "American Working Class" is then on many levels not the subject matter of the book. It was only later, in collaborating with Betsy Esch on *The Production of Difference*, that some of these deficiencies were remedied, and I fully realized that we do not need to choose between approaches to race growing out of Marxism and those originating in ethnic studies.

With regard to the body of the book, a mind-changing conference of the Australian Critical Race and Whiteness Studies in Queensland in 2005 called some certainties running through *Wages of Whiteness* very much into question. In particular, the idea that the white worker's identity formed against a Black other now seems to me only part of the story. I went to Brisbane to deliver a keynote at the invitation of Aileen Moreton-Robinson, the celebrated Aboriginal scholar who is part of the Goenpul people within the Quandamooka nation. She had shown the importance of the study of whiteness to its direct victims. Attendees widely knew my work. So did a group of workers at the hotel.

But Moreton-Robinson was also developing a profound critique of the US literature on whiteness and brought me to Brisbane so that I would hear that critique. Her writings, her talks, the presentations of others at the conference, and above all the weight of white oppression in Australia made me question how it was that a white identity so familiar to me could develop in a place without African slavery, the touchstone of whites defining themselves against an "other" in my reckoning of US history. By then I had also taught around spectacular Indigenous scholars at Minnesota (including Jean O'Brien) and Illinois (including Jodi Byrd and Robert Warrior) and picked up some knowledge.

When I published *How Race Survived US History* in 2008, I finally registered the extent to which whiteness in the US also formed around rejecting Indigenous claims, around acts of terror and dispossession, and around what Moreton-Robinson calls a "white possessive" occupation of land. Rogin's gentle point that his writing on settler whiteness could be considered foundational to critical whiteness studies had become legible to me, though the thrust of Moreton-Robinson's critique remains too little answered in both the critical study of whiteness generally and my own work in particular.

A real quandary has to do with the range of very differently focused activities that have long taken place under the banner of fighting against white privilege. Peggy McIntosh's "White Privilege: Unpacking the

Invisible Knapsack" first appeared in 1989. In it, McIntosh, a feminist scholar who had long encouraged concrete appreciation of all the ways that males received privilege, challenged herself and other whites to enumerate the many ways in which they were advantaged. She offered weighty examples like "I can choose public accommodation without fearing that people of my race cannot get in or will be mistreated in the places I have chosen." More light-hearted examples included one pointing out that flesh-colored bandages approximate the color of "white" flesh. In various ways "Invisible Knapsack" underlines how the normative and naturalized status of the dominant race keeps us from naming it, and spells out the advantages adhering to such status. The article became an instant classic in antiracist education. Google Scholar counts now over 7,000 citations of the much-reprinted piece.

Ignatiev and I differed on how to react to such initiatives. They clearly differed from the revolutionary intellectual work that we hoped we were doing. He sometimes professed opposition to "anti-racism" as certain to end in racial liberalism. I disagreed. I came from a place and mostly taught in places where people really needed to be reminded that race was socially constructed and involved unconscious bias.

At the time we first argued the point, thirty years ago, there was not a layer of paid Diversity, Equity, and Inclusion consultants. Many antiracist trainers had come out of the movement and some working on antiracist education were unpaid and consulted with unions, student organizations, and leftish church groups. I worked on such activities for Twin Cities social workers, steel and auto workers' schools, and even in one Sunday school. I was no expert and had at best middling success outside the labor audiences. But I did see "microaggressions" before I'd heard the word, and I thought it was important for whites to examine them. In 1998, when the oversized Twin Cites literary magazine *Hungry Mind Review* published a special whiteness issue with our assistance, the critical race theorist john powell and I devised a centerfold questionnaire for readers to fill out. The questions bore the influence of McIntosh. But they also included provocations like john's "When are you white?"

Another way to get at the quandary involves realizing that we were navigating between educating about race in general as a social construction and discrediting whiteness as a specific and costly lie. Just after *Wages of Whiteness* came out, I was teaching in the Western Cape in South Africa, mostly to a small group of former guerrilla fighters who'd lost educational opportunities as they served the movement. There had been an academic boycott of apartheid South Africa. But by 1991, with Mandela released and liberation groups being re-legalized, the African National Congress and unions invited some guests. I did not go to teach about race in the US so much as listen and learn. But over-enthusiasm still brought me to a mistake and a teachable moment concerning the need to think about when to intervene about race and when about whiteness.

The spur was the widespread use in the freedom movement of the term "so-called Coloured," a phrase employed especially by activists whom the apartheid regime put in the "Coloured" category of mixed-race people. In adding "so-called," fighters for a non-racial South Africa meant to underline the constructed, divisive, and state-sponsored nature of such a designation. I had first heard "so-called Coloured" as a self-designation from my friend and former Northwestern colleague Dennis Brutus, the late poet and activist. I heard it lots in South Africa in part because I was based at University of the Western Cape, which apartheid educational authorities regarded as a Coloured university but which was attempting to transform itself into an African one. "So-called Coloured" also got at something running through the history of the category of whiteness. I began to say glibly "So-called whites." Veteran activists in Cape Town found that not nearly as useful as I did. They recognized that to term the social position of a dominant group as constructed invited some to conclude that it was "merely constructed" at the very moment when emancipation was being hopefully conceived of as needing to take race and past racial oppression seriously.

The problem, all these years later, is not just that Tim Wise isn't funny anymore or that Robin DiAngelo is too scripted to have much to say that radicalizes anybody. It is that the two sides of anti-white privilege efforts—on one hand the revolutionary, structural analysis pole and on the other the therapeutic approach addressing problems by moving clients through individual stages of racial liberal self-improvement—no longer exist in anything like rough parity. We lost influence and the therapeutic approach has now been professionalized and capitalized, often delivered in corporate captive meetings.

The problems created by this moment can't be solved by magnifying their extent. It does not help to suppose that the diversity bureaucracy—itself now under attack—is an all-powerful if wildly under-specified professional-managerial class, somehow key to reproducing capitalist rule. They, often well-meaning and sometimes products of left movements, are problematic enough as much smaller fries than that. But they complicate our efforts to develop antiracist and anti-white advantage strategies from below.

Interlude Three

BRUSH WITH GENIUS:
TONI MORRISON AND ANGELA DAVIS

Toni Morrison's brilliant account of whiteness in US literature, *Playing in the Dark*, appeared in 1992, a few months after my *Wages of Whiteness*. Nevertheless, my work had already benefitted from some of the insights of that Morrison book as she had previewed its ideas in a 1988 lecture published as "Unspeakable Things Unspoken" in the *Michigan Quarterly Review*. I certainly recognized her fiction as offering profound insights into white identity. To be discussed in the same breath as Morrison provoked anxiety but joy too. By 1994, I had begun to assemble *Black on White: Black Writers on What It Means to Be White*, a massive undertaking just at the level of figuring to whom copyright permissions requests should go. I wanted to re-publish sections of *Playing in the Dark* as well as an incredible discussion of Herman Melville from "Unspeakable Things." I suspect Morrison's long association with Random House, my publisher on the project, made figuring out how to contact her possible. In any case, the negotiations proved simple, with no money changing hands, as I recall. She knew my work and when *Black on White* finally appeared, she contributed a glowing back-cover endorsement.

Morrison kept in touch, proposing things on which we might work together. In 1994, Princeton celebrated both her 1993 Nobel Prize for literature and Cornel West's work with the spectacular "Race Matters" conference. It hosted scholars such as Stuart Hall, Angela Davis, Patricia Williams, Howard Winant, Kendall Thomas, Kim Crenshaw, Neil Gotanda, Evelyn Brooks Higginbotham, Rhonda Williams, and many others. In her editor's introduction to the eventual book gathering essays from the event, *The House that Race Built*, Wahneema Lubiano called the collective endeavor an attempt to address race "on the ground."

Almost certainly my invitation came through Morrison. I went early, having only seen Princeton briefly before and having found it a little dislocating. Meeting Morrison calmed me and impressed me in many ways, not least in coming to know how engaged she was as a working, teaching faculty member and a too-often disappointed fighter for Princeton's recruitment and retention of Black faculty.

Morrison's talk to welcome the conference, the night before things began in earnest, became the essay "Home" in *The House that Race Built*. The talk undid any settling in I had managed. She spoke, as she did every time I had heard her in a lecture setting, from a polished text. Moreover, she reflected on how hard it is to produce such a text, dwelling on the choice of a single word in the closing of *Beloved*, a word she agonized over at length.

Many of us who were presenting had plans for drinks after the talk. I think all scurried back to hotel rooms instead, needing another round of editing, in my case with every individual word now in question. The proceedings the next day carried a similar edge. They occurred in an elegant, large, old hall, packed to overflowing. To look out on the crowd from the stage was to see Morrison front and center. Speakers who had long ago quit smoking started back up. And yet the warmth and gravity Morrison brought to the proceedings made it the most—picking a word carefully here—pleasant academic event I have ever attended.

In 1996, Morrison visited Minneapolis to deliver an endowed lecture profoundly reflecting on relationships of literature and history in a big hall at the University of Minnesota, where I then taught. Even her acknowledgement of her introduction taught me a great deal. The introduction fell to a younger member of a family donating to the university. At best it meandered self-indulgently. Its worst was truly awful, reflecting on the fact that Morrison was Black, a woman, and without great resources growing up, stopping at each juncture to marvel that she nevertheless had become a great writer, a Nobel laureate. Good grounds existed for ignoring the introduction, and better ones for responding to it in a way that would delay her own talk. Instead, she disposed of the condescension in seconds, saying gracefully that she considered those very identities central to what made her a writer, not as obstacles overcome and transcended. At the end of her stay in the Twin Cities, Morrison visited our house for a time, leaving for the airport with a police escort that ensured she could see Mall of America and still catch her plane. If the point was that nothing human was alien to her, I wasn't ready for it yet. The Mall remained alien to me. When the great British scholars Paul Gilroy and Vron Ware visited and also wished to see it, I reconsidered my position a little.

As O.J. Simpson's trial after the 1994 murder of Nicole Brown Simpson proceeded, Morrison recruited me to write a piece for a collection on the case, which would later appear as *Birth of a Nation'hood*. I worried that my co-author, the journalist and cultural studies scholar Leola Johnson, and I would never find a topic fit for the book. Morrison believed Simpson to be innocent of the murder and envisioned a book focused on his trials. We had neither that certainty nor much appetite for details of forensics and litigation. We ultimately settled on the ways the marketed Simpson and the cultures of US capitalism came together during his athletic, broadcasting, and advertising careers. In those realms he came to be imagined as a figure and commodity beyond race but one embodying an appealing African American style and masculine presence. Our delays, mostly my delays, and the great New York City snows of 1996 gave reason for Morrison to call often during times when going outdoors held little appeal. At the deepest part of the blizzard, our younger son Donovan answered her call and yelled with a certain tone of grievance, "Dad, it's that Toni Morrison again." The conversations with her were great for me, both in thinking through the Simpson article and in learning how organically Morrison came to address whiteness as a problem. She especially appreciated Elia Kazan's film *America America* for its acuity on immigrant/African American interaction and how learning "race talk" empowered poor new migrants from southern Europe, at least in comparison to Blacks. I never heard a good word about Kazan, anathema to the left for his informing on Hollywood comrades. I confided that I also thought that even his *On the Waterfront* had insights into working-class self-activity.

Our conversations sent me hunting for a 1989 Morrison guest column I'd clipped from *Time*. She'd written of immigrants, "When they got off the boat, the second word they learned was '[the N-word].' Ask them—I grew up with them." I had written in the margin of the clipping "What was the first word?" Morrison riffed in that passage on an old Black joke. Most people know it from the afterword of Malcolm X's autobiography. He and his collaborator Alex Haley are in an airport and looking at a beautiful white family arriving in the US for the first time. Malcolm notes that they will soon learn their first English word, the N-word. It's Malcolm's joke but also one in the African American tradition, before and after Malcolm. But the second word?

I had my notes ready when Morrison called the next day. I reminded her of the passage and asked, "What was the first word?" She laughed with such delight that she could hardly get the punch line out. Then she replied, "The first word was 'OK.'" The hilarity flowed in part from our both knowing that, among other derivations, "OK" was a so-called Africanism—that is, a US English word with at least partial origins in an African language. The foundational learning of power relations in the US thus included Africans on multiple levels. The wicked humor only increases the great weight of Morrison's observation. This joke did for Morrison what James Baldwin's insistence that learning to identify with whiteness represented "absolutely a moral choice" for white ethnic immigrants but also one made under "a vast amount of coercion" did for his analysis of the "lie of whiteness." There was little choice but to learn to say OK to immigration officials, cops, landlords, and employers. There was a choice regarding learning race talk, but it came in a context in which securing a foothold above at least one victimized group could seem irresistible.

Morrison later surprised me when she scoffed privately at the idea of those most intensely experiencing World War II as the "greatest generation." I agreed, too eagerly thinking she was crediting the activists of the thirties, the greatest generation for me. No, she objected, it was the sixties. She registered not only the civil rights, women's, and antiwar movements but also, and a little unexpectedly, the counterculture. I was half-persuaded.

The last time I saw Morrison a dismal day in Princeton ended well. The university sponsored a lavish mid-nineties conference on conservatism in the US. Sean Wilentz, the center-right (and therefore in the US, liberal) historian on that campus invited me, mentioning a handful of invited presenters whom I liked. With visiting Morrison as a possibility, I did not follow up with questions reflecting due diligence. As conference panels were populated, it became clear that conservatives would mostly tell their own stories. Hidden—from me anyhow—agendas abounded. Apparently, Princeton had some reason to want National Review's conservative publisher William Rusher to know how appreciated he was. The liberal and left window-dressing only made the event more suspect.

I spoke on the first plenary, responding I thought to a pre-circulated paper by the historian of slaveholders, Eugene D. Genovese. He was quite a figure, moving or perhaps careening from the Marxism of his youth to an eventual political home on the far right. I misread him consistently. His work, even as a self-avowed Marxist, seemed deeply conservative in its political implications and cultural strictures. Gene spent so much time denouncing "history from the bottom up," appreciating the principles and seriousness of slave masters, and courting favor from elite liberals in the history business that I felt certain he'd leave the left any day. But he hung in there for a long time, and I supposed he might just stay among us doing work that was more confusing than actively harmful. He'd written for the conference some paean to master class religion and sent it to me to comment. I had decided to be as nice as possible.

My luck ran bad, though. In his presentation Genovese tossed notes aside and spoke instead of his embrace of a Roman Catholic position on fallen humanity, defending the notion that no good society was possible without a firm belief in original sin. I had to toss my notes aside too, given that I'd written not a word on original sin. The day before I travelled, something had made me photocopy pages from National Review, in which the publication had retailed its deeply reactionary stance against the civil rights movement. I pulled those out and said that since we were off-script I'd just be reading them as illustrations of what conservative tough-mindedness can look like in practice.

Things proceeded downhill from there. Genovese had brought a supply of—go figure—Cuban cigars that he tried to get people to smoke with him during breaks. I think he succeeded only with Wilentz; the National Review crowd seemed not quite ready to embrace their new co-thinker. The day turned more rancorous as the few left presenters spoke. The ethnographer Kathy Blee gave a great paper on her studies of racist skinhead women. Some on the right reddened perceivably. Shortly after that, Morrison, having finished reading microfilm to gain historical background for her eventual novel *Paradise*, stood in back of the not very crowded lecture hall for a bit, found me in the crowd, gathered me up and said, "Let's get out of here."

I had met Angela Davis a few months before Morrison brought us both to the Race Matters conference at Princeton but it was, in my case anyway, the sheer impact of that conference that made us friends. The initial encounter was at the California Humanities Institute, where Davis was a fellow in 1993. We then found chances to meet at her university (University of California at Santa Cruz) or mine (especially when I was at University of Illinois) or elsewhere. We socialized over a pretty wide set of political differences, initially at a time when attitudes toward the Soviet Union's social system seemed to occupy center stage in defining one's left politics. I retained, even after the fall of the Soviet Union, the view in which I had been educated politically; I saw the Soviet Union not as a socialist experiment but a state capitalist one. The worldwide Communist campaigns for Davis' freedom when she was under threat from the US state, her considered beliefs, her regard for the Soviet role in defending the Cuban revolution and supporting African liberation movements—all had her coming down differently than I on what was somewhat ponderously called "the Soviet question."

The occasion where we most nearly talked in depth about these matters was the 2011 International Marcuse Conference in Philadelphia, held amidst unseasonable early snowstorms and at the height of the Occupy movement. She spoke as Marcuse's most famous student and I as a longtime fan and the keeper of a small flame of mutual support between him and the Chicago Surrealist Group. Davis and I arrived early for the conference, and others had travel delays. We ended up being able to sit in the hotel bar and talk for two or three nights, with the Cardinals' final wins over the Texas Rangers in the World Series the perfect backdrop. (I was, by that time of the year, a Cardinal supporter, the Cubs having finished a distant 25 games out of first place). I tried out the view that it was completely understandable, but nevertheless unfortunate, that she joined the CPUSA. We agreed to disagree, with the game providing a particularly good diversion.

In every meeting Davis impressed me in some unexpected way. In Irvine she spoke on her developing work on prison abolition, then brand-new to me, and reflected on the irony of having so much trouble getting access to the incarcerated for research after the state had earlier spent so much energy trying to put her into jail. At the Marcuse conference, after giving a long and passionate keynote, she walked far in the snow to visit the Occupy encampment. In Illinois, she awed the restaurant's wine expert whom she asked to pick our bottle. She then identified it so learnedly, without seeing the label, that I thought the whole thing was set up in advance as a parlor trick.

When we both talked in New Orleans at an early conference on race, class, and gender she risked losing the crowd by saying she opposed the death penalty even for the racist murderers of James Byrd. I also came to understand after that talk just how thoroughly surrounded she often was by admirers, in that case well into the evening after an afternoon event. We, with the Asian American revolutionary Bob Wing, ducked in to see Spike Lee's then-new film *Bamboozled* for a respite. In Santa Cruz, where she taught, she'd spend much of a day reading files on appeals of tenure and promotion cases—necessarily confidential and kept in a locked room—realizing that the hard work involved in serving on appeals committees for such decisions was an important task for radicals. In this she reminded me of Morrison, who could clearly have functioned as a writer-in-residence at Princeton but chose to participate fully in the daily work of the English department there, even when outcomes were dispiriting.

7

CARING FOR THE HISTORICALLY WHITE FAILED STATE UNIVERSITY

Recently, country singer Maren Morris announced she would leave the business, after a lonely battle to open it up to queer content. If this book had epigraphs, her exit line would serve perfectly for this chapter. "I thought I'd like to burn it to the ground and start over," she said of the industry. "But it's burning itself down without my help." I'm not leaving universities, not for a bit anyhow, but Morris' line works perfectly for my evolution as a worker in higher education.

As I was writing this book, the US Supreme Court outlawed affirmative action in college admissions. It ruled in one case involving Harvard and another involving the University of North Carolina that to account for race in choosing students violated the equal protection clause of the US Constitution. UNC's defense of its affirmative action practices included especially sophisticated and uncommonly frank expert historical evidence. It detailed how its own long, brutal, and impactful practices had furthered white supremacy. It insisted Black exclusion had long been policy and specified how relatively short and partial were attempts at redress. This strategy gained no traction. Considering race was to indulge "stereotypes." Chief Justice John Roberts' majority opinion, joined by five other justices, maintained that "Eliminating racial discrimination means eliminating all of it," swallowing the idea that race-based strategies to achieve racial justice are no different than those that produce inequality.

The decision was totally unsurprising, as was the fact that it leaves room for further litigation when universities are sued for "workarounds" attempting to maintain the meager levels of racial diversity now in place. It does not address, though its logic dooms, affirmative action in other university practices, such as scholarships and employment, nor in non-university businesses and government jobs. Nevertheless, the decision registers how weak a case for racial justice in higher education we have been able to make. Even though the *New York Times'* *1619 Project*, which examined centuries of US white supremacy, wins journalistic awards, Roberts' view—that the forty-five years of higher education admissions based on attenuated affirmative action policy was plenty long to set right centuries of discrimination—is the law of the land. Universities are the weak link that have been the first loss to affirmative action, without a public campaign to defend them. Polls at the time of the decision suggest widespread support for the Roberts opinion, with the Democratic party not having won even a majority of its own supporters to the idea that it's necessary to defend race-based initiatives, whether in pursuit of justice or to maintain a political coalition.

The 2023 Supreme Court decision provided an apt closing bracket for my career as an academic worker seeking to stem the decline of the university, in part by making it face its racial past. The majority's chilling recital of precedents reminds us how uphill that battle has been and how slender is the hope for even moderate reform. As I wrote my doctoral dissertation at Northwestern in 1978, the Supreme Court decided in Bakke that affirmative action in higher education could proceed, but within narrow parameters of white self-interest. These could not include pursuit of racial justice but would rest on a circumscribed and scrutinized plan for, as Roberts summarized, "obtaining the educational benefits that flow from a racially diverse student body." It wasn't in 2023 that this pretense that the US legal tradition was a "colorblind" one was articulated, but 1978. It was then, not twenty-five years after the Court countenanced Jim Crow, that Justice Lewis Powell wrote "Racial and ethnic distinctions of any sort are inherently suspect," for reasons somehow "rooted in our Nation's constitutional and demographic history."

When the Supreme Court decided Grutter in 2003 my career was—we'll see—about half-done. I was at the University of Illinois, whose chancellor had been at the University of Michigan when Barbara

Grutter, an unsuccessful law school applicant there, challenged the school's affirmative action in admissions. There was some liberal rejoicing when affirmative action was weakened, but not abolished, in Grutter. Some gloried in the genius of a strategy of stressing that not only the university but US corporations and the military benefitted from educational diversity. Nonetheless, the decision, and a defeat for affirmative action in a companion case, closed already slender possibilities. Justice Sandra Day O'Connor, writing for the Court's majority, set twenty-five years as a reasonable possible period before affirmative action could be retired.

There was talk of the policy gaining breathing space, but *gasping* space proved closer to the mark. Roberts mentioned O'Connor's timeline in his 2023 opinion, but the end actually came only twenty years after Grutter. By that time, the ranks of passionate believers who thought affirmative action would deliver a new day of justice had dwindled greatly, despite the successes of Critical Race Theory in showing how defending the policy took us to fundamental issues of power and history in the US. In none of the big state universities where I taught did affirmative action deliver student bodies that look racially anything like the US people. And yet even knowing how little affirmative action in college admissions had transformed things, and how inevitable was the policy's demise, I stayed sad for days after the ruling.

This closing chapter aims to discuss my teaching career in a way that speaks to the crisis of US public universities. It connects the university's record of failure on racial justice, despite moralizing around the issue, with higher education's broader failures while also examining universities' business and managerial practices. Racially liberal self-satisfaction tethered to acceptance of neoliberal austerity make for institutions sadly able to regard their decline as blameless, even virtuous, victims. The chapter winds its way toward thinking about whether public universities can survive, even in the short to medium term, and how campuses are situated in the rural areas that these schools often occupy.

The Author at Work

Lots of us who work in public universities suffer with an unpaid side job. We study universities' policies, linger over their budgets, and note how their restrictions on dissent coincide with their attacks on job security. We worry about their futures, however much we deplore their present, and we know they have a past of exclusion and elitism. This fretting over what I call "failed state universities" extends to the many professors who believe that the faculty shares governing power and who seek a voice in policy decisions—a seat at a table of administrators, trustees, legislators, and foundation executives. The likewise large number of us—I'm one—who seek a union to stem the speed at which the institutions slide—many are also active in governance—likewise read turgid prose looking for ways to challenge the "there is no alternative" mindset prevailing. Some of us subscribe to the *Chronicle of Higher Education*, a kind of trade paper for the higher education business that includes just enough investigative reporting to hold faculty interest. Some drop other research to study the crisis of colleges instead.

Nor does the study of universities by workers end with faculty. Unions of graduate students, far more successful than those of faculty, have produced a big, healthy layer of activists who study the university as a site capable of incredible opulence in spending on buildings and sport, and sophisticated poor-mouthing in contract negotiations. The staff—and surely the most acute crisis in universities today stems from loss of knowledgeable staff—weighs trends to see how deep the cuts will be. They try to judge at what point the congeniality of a more loosely bossed, less dress-coded university job no longer compensates for lower pay. Workers who maintain buildings and grounds or prepare food listen for news about whether their jobs are to be contracted out to private vendors and, after that happens, whether vendors will change overnight.

You won't get critical universities studies, as the new field studying higher education is called, in this chapter. Or rather, you'll get plenty of the critical but less of the studies. Only brief research excursions on universities—for example on the land-grant colleges, on guns on campus, on Covid policy, and on academic repression—have found their way into my writing. Nor am I choosing to do much new research on the fly here, settling instead for a critique based on my experience, labor, and pain. What I know enough to write about specifically is the decline of the Midwestern "flagship" university, the largest of the universities in that region. "Failed state universities" suggests both that the institutions have failed but also that the apparatus of government—the failed neoliberal state conducted on the cheap and on behalf of those on the make—has failed them. Even when spending has grown, what the geographer Ruth Wilson Gilmore has called the "anti-state state" has directed allocations in a way that discredits the very idea of a public good.

To write exhaustively of this sad story would mean also writing exhaustingly—both to myself and to the reader, who has signed up for an autobiography. I've probably read about universities for five hours most weeks for forty years, but in response to emergencies, not in systematic study. I will therefore spell out what has led me to dire conclusions about higher learning via small examples, elaborated into broader concerns: the story of law, of a mystery, of some facts about shifting university and household budgets, and of faculty trying to find a personal balance between disgust and heartbreak.

I write from a particular, even peculiar, set of experiences. While earlier sections of this autobiography on critical whiteness studies, the Kerr Company, and surrealism sketch my political and intellectual trajectory, it is worth adding a brief employment history for this one. In the nearly forty years I have had a tenure-track or tenured job, all my paychecks have come from Midwestern "flagship" state universities: eight years at Missouri, seven at Minnesota, fourteen at Illinois, and now eleven and counting at Kansas.

At Missouri and Minnesota, I had an average humanities salary, one not too different than the pay of friends who worked for the phone company or at the big auto plant near my hometown, especially when they worked overtime. As higher education obscured the general decline in the pay of its professors, it developed a small layer of highly paid "star" faculty alongside a bigger, more overpaid layer of administrators. From the aughts on, at Illinois and Kansas, I have fallen into the star category, making double and more the salary of peers. (The process is often startlingly crass; Kansas, I learned after arriving, feared it needed citations of professors' writings to stay in the good graces of the Association of American Universities, a group regarded with great awe by institutions worried about losing their places in it. I had the citations, and I became their man). My time at Minnesota and Kansas included long stints as department chair. At Illinois I founded and directed for its first two years the Center on Democracy in a Multiracial Society, a project well-funded by administrators embarrassed by their failure to deliver on other social justice promises.

There were things to like, especially early on in my career. Three of these long-term workplaces nestled in middle-sized regional cities near fields of corn or wheat or soybeans or sunflowers, very like the rural town where I grew up but better for being near a university. All three brought modernism, science, arts, bars with music, and occasionally left ideas, into nearby small-town life that I'd grown up seeing as bereft of all those things. Three of the four—all but Kansas—began as "land grant colleges," and their extension programs served the surrounding areas, tutoring me on what to plant to attract local birds and butterflies.

These Universities Never Fooled Me

I fit poorly among scholars who feel betrayed by how the university disappointed their hopes that it might be a great force for social transformation and for pure knowledge, free from the interests of commerce and state power. Even in my undergrad days at Northern Illinois it seemed to me far-fetched to think a "people's university" lay on the horizon. Today I remain unmoved by theorizing of the "undercommons," insofar as it suggests that universities are potentially promising places for radical movements to graze. To be clear then: What follows in this chapter does not simply mourn the public university. Nor do I hope to conjure into being a utopian model for higher education. If such were in the cards, I would champion it. But even knowing that it's not, I find it worth critically defending the crappy, underfunded, corporate, compromised public universities that we have against the forces dismantling them.

The economist Thorstein Veblen originated heated denunciation of the university, branding it as the purveyor of high ideals in its self-promotion and tawdry deals in its practices. I read Veblen's *The Higher Learning in America* when I was 20. It recently turned 100 and still reads like an exposé on contemporary universities. Today the things it gets right—not everything, and scarcely anything concerning race—ring truer than ever. Veblen's long-ago diagnosis of the university could serve as the explanation for the unabashed catering to property rather than people that guides the operation of the giant endowment, for example, at the otherwise starving University of Kansas. Veblen wrote:

> a "university" has come to mean . . . an aggregation of buildings and other improved real-estate . . . [T]he pursuit of learning is a relatively obscure matter. The academic work is, after all, unseen . . . Current expenditure for the prosecution of this work, therefore, offers the enterprise in advertisement a less advantageous field for the convincing use of funds than the material equipment, especially the larger items, [such as] assembly halls [and] grounds for athletic contests.

Veblen reserved his most venomous and wickedly memorable lines for describing how things like fraternity and sorority life, school spirit, anti-intellectualism, athletics, and what his subtitle calls "the conduct of universities by businessmen" robbed higher learning of its vision and grandeur.

I returned to *The Higher Learning in America* when teaching at the University of Missouri because Veblen himself, on the faculty there from 1911 till World War I, lived a few blocks from where I later did. He was said to have despised and outraged the university town of Columbia. His most picturesque line regarding it found Columbia to be "a woodpecker hole of a town in a rotten stump called Missouri." The line may be gentler than it is now read. (I'd say the same—cherishing woodpeckers and their habitats—about Lawrence in comparison with Kansas as a state.) Missouri was at the time he produced *The Higher Learning* the most recent stop in Veblen's star-crossed university career.

In revisiting the book as a faculty member, I was again moved but I could never share Veblen's animating rage. That required imagining a better, nobler university system, perpetually betrayed by philistinism and the "pecuniary." I have never seen universities, including the state universities at which I've taught, as separable from their roles as capitalist workplaces, imperial projects, and sites of the reproduction of class and racial hierarchies. In that sense, my views are more similar to those of the novelist Upton Sinclair, whose neglected 1923 non-fiction work on higher education *The Goose Step* was less ready to see a good university even in its ideals than Veblen was.

I began as an undergraduate to oppose the presence of the military and police on campus and to see the handwriting on the wall that universities would be inaccessible, or accessible only through great debt, to most people from my background. I have not so much resisted temptation to be wistful about universities as I have simply never felt it. When I first began to think about "the university" as an institution, my commitments to Marxism were sufficiently crude that they precluded supposing that big, rich institutions could under capitalism avoid serving that system at the end of the day. The obverse also applied in part as a reflection of my mother's trade unionism as a teacher. That is, as interesting as the ideas and relationships on offer at universities undeniably were, those universities pressured their own workers horrendously.

Nothing in my forty-five-year teaching career changed that view. Much reinforced it. When I began, work in classrooms fell overwhelmingly to those tenured or on a track possibly leading to such status. They suffered anxiety, not the least around gaining tenure and policing who else got it or didn't. Some of the most successful proved the most tense. Salaries eroded in the face of inflation and underfunding. Today those miseries are magnified. Less than a third of student credit hours are delivered by such relatively privileged tenure-stream faculty. The casualized labor of the great majority of instructors places them outside of the protections of academic freedom, of job security, of health insurance, and often of a living wage. It is not the rare Marxist ideologue on campus that tells us the political economy of higher learning demands such misery. College managers routinely bring just that news as if it is fresh, secret wisdom that only they are brave enough to share.

Higher education seems to me best thought of as just another workplace. It is no worse than the quarries, offices, switchboards, printing plants, grade schools, warehouses, labs, morgues, soda fountains, and refineries where my relatives had worked. But also no better. Those family members also found lots to admire in some coworkers and sometimes preferred one boss over another. I never heard any of them say that they had a great job or a perfect boss. University labor seems to me a variation on the same theme, made worse by a sense that it can pretend to be different. It pulls critics into its gears.

My training as a labor historian makes me add that these overarching similarities between the work of professors and that of others also apply at the level of how the faculty's work and some staff labor is managed. The ideology of "shared governance" in which faculty and staff believe that their university senates have power, even though it is their managers who bear the title of CEO, seems exotic and, I once would have said, petty bourgeois. But it is surely more like than different from a long history of company unionism and more recently of Quality Control circles that create a feeling of "jointness" between labor and management and bedevil attempts at independent organization by workers in factories and offices.

Nor are others of the supposed benefits of university work, even for small numbers of tenured professors, anything like what they seem, either in their bounty or in their supposed differences from what workers in general want. Sabbaticals—traditionally a year off every seventh year—are now very often just for a semester and come competitively, not as a standard benefit. The steelworkers' union bargained for sabbaticals during its heyday. The vaunted "summer off" is in fact a time of retooling courses and of research and writing, necessary to secure tenure, access merit raises, and pass post-tenure reviews. It is unpaid, with this arrangement so fetishized that until two years ago the University of Kansas would not even offer the choice of dividing a nine-month salary into twelve parts to have income in summer.

Tenure is likewise, on one level, a provision of job security like those sought by industrial unions when they had power. To complete the short list of similarities, the stark divisions between tenure-track faculty and those without the protections of tenure matured in universities over the last decades alongside the disastrous acceptance of "two-tier" contracts treating new workers far worse than senior ones. A tenured job, even in a flagship public university, is not (leaving aside those paid as stars) a particularly good job except in comparison to the shameful way that untenured workers and staff are treated.

A second matter further blocked any chance of my imagining the good old days of the university or an institution able to mend itself.

Much of the New Left had put forward a critique of higher education as being complicit with militarism and empire. Even before I went to college I read about the University of California's attacks on free speech, met anti-ROTC activists in St. Louis, and reflected on the deeply unsatisfactory responses of universities to the murders of students by repressive forces at Kent State, Jackson State, and South Carolina State. One of the hardest-hitting polemics informing my views, Carl Davidson's 1968 *New Radicals in the Multiversity*, became one of our better-selling reprints at the Charles Kerr Company from 1990 onward. The massive resistance to integrated universities was part of the mediascape of my youth. The gaping inequalities in access to higher education that I witnessed at universities over decades of teaching best fit into a narrative emphasizing the continuation of bad old days.

Commitments to Fellow Workers and Public Universities

But there were people to love. I'll extol just one here. My favorite colleague, Susan Porter Benson, overlapped with me for six years at Missouri. A brilliant labor and women's historian, she taught the same introduction to US history course I did. I attended her classes to learn, having never taught so many students. She held herself, far ahead of the times, to the standard of discussing class, gender, and race in every lecture, emphasizing that they mattered simultaneously. Apart from Sterling Stuckey, I'd never seen such a compelling lecturer. She taught me little tricks and big ideas suited to mass teaching, and I learned to love it. I've ultimately taught over 15,000 undergraduates and counting in such survey classes, 700-plus per class at Minnesota and almost that at Illinois. A colleague at Northwestern had once described his classes as geared to keep privileged young conservatively inclined students from becoming fascists. Sue saved me from such cynicism and made the task of deciding just what to try to impart in thirty hours of contact with a student in such a course come alive as generative work. Sue also taught me how to mentor doctoral students, in part through our sharing some advisees and letting me watch what she did in balancing rigor and loving support. I'm now nearing my fiftieth doctoral advisee. Each has benefitted from Sue's example, even from her rigor.

When student course evaluations became available, Sue insisted we look at them together for both of our classes. I was shocked, knowing which class was better, that mine were more highly rated. She wasn't shocked and made that a teachable experience, pointing out what should have been apparent to me and is now well established in studies. That is, the clarity of setting classroom responsibilities and procedures—one of the things I emulated from her teaching—struck a fair number of students as controlling and—their word—"bitchy," coming from a woman. Until then I'd treated student evaluation as something like a report card—high score wins. But between Sue and sharp questions from the Africanist Jeff Holden on why anyone would want uniformly adulatory results, I learned to see them as guides to know where to push.

Sue, along with the peerless historian of the Atlantic world Peter Linebaugh, believed more deeply in the history of ordinary people than anyone I have known. I was with her in Connecticut when she died of cancer, far too young. The day before her death she described the state of an unfinished manuscript using archives from the Department of Labor's Women's Bureau to reconstruct working-class family dynamics in the interwar US. (Jean Allman and I posthumously joined others to finish it, published as Household Accounts from Cornell University Press.) In those last hours she became most animated in seeking out everyone's views on whether it showed the most respect to those whose lives she brought to light to use their real names or pseudonyms.

Sue glued together a fabulous, if short-lived, group of left professors that made Missouri the closest thing to the Northern Illinois department that I have since experienced. They included Sundiata Cha-Jua, Kerby Miller, Tani Barlow, Ted Koditschek, Eli Zaretsky, Dina Copelman, LeeAnn Whites, Susan Flader, Jean Allman, and Holden. The fascinating Marxist historian Donald Lowe often came around to visit Tani. Undergraduate majors in history, active in anti–Gulf War, anti-apartheid, and antiracist movements, included the now distinguished Korean American filmmaker Grace Lee and the deeply creative African Americanist Minkah Makalani. I mourn for our little Missouri group, soon dispersed.

Even given my skepticism regarding universities, a soft spot left me sentimental in one limited way. The large public state university has long seemed to me a great idea. I had liked my high school trips to regional campuses like Eastern Illinois, Southern Illinois, or Illinois State. Such visits mostly avoided the beautiful University of Illinois flagship campus straddling the cities of Urbana and Champaign, perhaps because its students were higher-performing—at least in terms of standardized test scores—and it cost more, though the campus impressed me when I went there for state athletic tournaments. As I became a political radical, my mother's championing of public education became mine, and University of Illinois seemed its epitome.

Specific moments attracted me greatly. At the University of Illinois, I loved the summers when, without students, the cities seemed crazily overbuilt in terms of public facilities, especially for sports and live music. But the return of students in the fall offered its own excitement—the central appeal of the large public university—as some of the most inquisitive young people from an entire state, and to an extent from the world, came to meet each other. The flagship state university remains a terrific aspiration, however undermined by its tragic white- and empire-serving past and present as well as by its current impoverishment. My faculty peers and even I warily cherish its possibilities far more than our managers do. Nowhere is this clearer than in the astonishing alacrity with which administrators take apart athletic conferences and rivalry games with many decades of tradition. Sadly, many of those managers emerged from the New Left, or at least the racially liberal sixties, and retained radical flourishes as they presided over the accelerating decline of higher education.

Since my first days at Missouri, with but two exceptions, I never seriously applied to, nor considered offers from, anything but a state university. A love of what's now called "outlaw country" music and a consequent desire to at least think about living in Nashville drove one of the exceptions. I gave a job talk and endured an interview at the request of Vanderbilt University, which was bringing nobody else in as a candidate for a job search in US history. They wisely opted for nobody else. The other exception reflected a nearly mystical desire to live in New Orleans so as to be part of the rebuilding of the city after Hurricane Katrina. So convinced was I that this was fated that I responded for the only time in my life to an invitation to apply for a dean's position, in arts and sciences, at Tulane University. I did manage to attract an endowed chair position at the flagship Louisiana State University after the storm but decided Baton Rouge was too far from New Orleans for me to build a useful life in both cities.

This commitment to the public school was not wrong when I made it. Nevertheless, it did turn out poorly. If the turn to an insecure, poorly paid teaching labor force became one hallmark of state universities during my career, the reliance on tuition as a source of university funding was its mate. When conservatives attack state universities, they depend on the schools not having staunch defenders. My arrival at college in 1970 roughly coincided with the advent of austerity-oriented policies regarding social spending. These came to be termed "neoliberal." Public university budgets, especially if we include endowment funds, did not so much shrink as surround themselves with market-worshipping rubrics that sent funds to construction, to financial capitalist firms managing construction, to attendant loans, to coaches, to a few star faculty, to many more administrators, and to the patent-generating disciplines. The curricular moves away from a broad liberal education became self-fulfilling prophecies. Students gained little experience of history, English, and ethnic studies classes, for example, as they learned to be consumers of vocational credentials.

Such student "choices" were conditioned and constrained at every turn by policymakers, especially where the massive growth of student debt is concerned. When I began teaching at the University of Missouri in the mid-eighties, tuition accounted for less than a quarter of funds public universities used for educational expenditures. By the time I reached Kansas three decades later that proportion had doubled to just less than half of total educational expenditures. During the same period, median family income grew by less than 25 percent and public university costs by 160 percent. These trends generated a massive increase in student debt, which the Education Data Initiative pegged at $1.75 trillion in 2023. The average debt of a public university graduate totaled more than $31,000.

The tuition/debt crisis made a broad, deep education seem a luxury, even a frivolity. So much is this the case that some right-wing proposals to reform student loans seek to index eligibility to borrow by majors, penalizing those who choose what are regarded as unmarketable specializations. Sometimes sociology, sometimes anthropology, and very often ethnic studies and women's studies become the targets. Amidst rising costs, the product worsens, with steep rises in student/teacher ratios accompanying high tuition in the years that I have worked at Kansas. Colleges seem a raw deal to ordinary people in large part because they increasingly are just that. They are perceived as failing to open minds because they are not set up to do so.

Here again economic policy issues collide with questions of racial justice. The turn to austerity happened at just the moment when public higher education was mandated by both law and changing student demographics to serve a somewhat more diverse student population. Inclusion, as Chris Newfield has shown in studying the University of California system universities, coincided with withdrawal of state support. Strapped public universities struggle to compete with wealthy private universities to attract and fund students of color.

The Moral Overconfidence of the Historically White University

The most nationally recognized University of Kansas building, Allen Fieldhouse, takes its name from the school's legendary basketball coach Forrest "Phog" Allen. Through almost all of his thirty-nine-year coaching career at Kansas, Allen helped make certain that the university fielded all-white teams, although it did have a few Black students. As athletic director after World War I, he was one of the administrators instrumental in replacing the practice of having a cafeteria and intra-mural and varsity sports open to Black students with policies of either segregation or total exclusion. He welcomed the outreach efforts of the Ku Ku Klub, a student organization cresting alongside the Ku Klux Klan in the twenties, as they performed racism at games. Allen himself performed in blackface minstrel shows, as a white interlocutor.

The ear-splitting venue bearing Allen's name is undergoing a $49 million renovation, up from the $20 million originally budgeted. It regularly receives attention in national basketball telecasts as the very temple of the sport. "BEWARE OF THE PHOG" adorns countless t-shirts and a banner in the arena's rafters. In this time of questioning the memorialization of racists with monuments and building names, Allen's past is not unknown, but it remains almost unmentionable. He is beyond critique. Cursory defenses offered turn on the old white chestnut that almost everyone was racist "back then." Or it is pointed out that Allen changed just before his mandatory retirement at age 70, albeit when Kansas was recruiting superstar Wilt Chamberlain, who was appalled by Jim Crow in the university and the city.

The inability to process the life of Phog Allen does not keep Kansas administrators from issuing the most extravagant, if toothless, statements on "Jayhawk Nation" values and how they are breached by the behavior of the cops in Minneapolis or the Russian invaders in Ukraine. The righteousness of such pronouncements is, especially where race is concerned, self-righteousness. Neither Kansas nor any of the other flagship campuses where I have taught have worked to face their past or transform their present enough to claim to embody an antiracist "nation" of sports fans. The ease with which such claims get made requires explanation. The relatively well-known ways that Jim Crow and its halting end created what I am calling the Historically White University deserve emphasis in accounting for such hubris. So too does the selective appropriation of the heritage of the land grant university, one which I first intuited and later understood based on a fabulous new body of educational history scholarship.

Managers at the University of Kansas recently faced a grilling from state officials regarding its faculty's alleged teaching of Critical Race Theory. The request came in the context of some in the state's conservative movement warming up to insist that Kansas higher education fully join the ranks of the red state universities by banning CRT. I understood but opposed the university's response. They searched course descriptions and reported finding only one specifying CRT as central to its content. The university could then reassure all that CRT was no problem on its campus. This doubtless seemed a deft, perhaps even a liberally intentioned, strategy. Nevertheless, it implied that if CRT were frequently taught, scrutiny would be necessary. At Kansas and nationally the liberal stance became that CRT is marginal to the modern university—that it is only an arcane sub-specialty in law schools—and that therefore no policy measures designed to censor were needed. I turned myself in at Kansas as a second Critical Race Theorist, thinking it important to own unapologetically whatever little bits of antiracist intellectual ground we have gained.

And yet and as usual, the far-right's exploitation of what it is tempting to regard as the non-issue of CRT works intersections between economics and race in higher education more effectively than moderate college administrators do. Equally, the moderate impulse to offer no substantive defense of CRT, or even of free expression, leaves opportunities for further demagogy, especially at the K–12 level of schooling. More importantly for the agenda of this closing chapter, the hesitancy to call upon CRT and critical studies of whiteness in thinking through the crisis of universities impoverishes our understanding of the lack of progress toward racial justice in higher education and of the vulnerability of public colleges to attacks from enemies. It contributes to managers believing in their own illusions.

A central insight of CRT holds that moves in the direction of equality under the law leave in play historic inequalities and the current structures that reproduce them, requiring a systematic remedy. Higher education provides examples by the bushel. When I began teaching at University of Missouri in the mid-eighties that school was not even fifty years removed from losing a US Supreme Court case in which it tried to maintain its practice of providing legal education only to white students. Throughout most of its existence, the university had conspired to deny opportunity to aspirant Black lawyers. Its late shift toward inclusion could not create the networks of admissions, the endowments, or a curriculum serving the needs of minority lawyers and communities. For that matter, the university still operated under a court injunction in the Adams decision, litigation unfolding in the seventies and eighties addressing a very recent past of racial exclusion.

More generally, in about 1970 many state universities responded to student protests by recognizing the legitimate place of ethnic studies as an interdisciplinary field. However, the new programs emerged at a time when austerity-based and supposedly market-driven budgets directed money away from resources for faculty with secure jobs and away from the humanities and social sciences, where many who studied people of color taught. Administrators did not allow ethnic studies programs to flower like those of the traditional disciplines long recognized as legitimate, nor could they grow like the newly anointed initiatives in computer science, petroleum extraction, and agribusiness. Ethnic studies remained small and precarious as evaluators from outside universities judge programs by numbers of majors, so crudely in the Kansas case as to not even take size of faculty into account.

The insights of critical studies of whiteness would apply with force if universities considered them. The acronym HBCU carries some popular resonance now, in part because of Deion Sanders' brief attempt to build a top football program at Jackson State University. Spelled out, it means Historically Black College or University. It's been around a good while and is now supplemented by coinages including Hispanic-Serving Institutions and Tribal Colleges and Universities circulating in law and policy. We don't hear about Historically White Colleges and Universities though most US higher education institutions are just that. Within critical whiteness studies a language emerged that helped us to identify whiteness as a historical and practical problem needing investigation. HWCU would make an apt addition to discussions of racial justice in higher education, reminding us of wisdom straight out of CRT, namely that habits and structures of white advantage weigh on the present.

I began toying with the term HWCU in 2004 when Washington University's law school invited me to give a keynote at their conference on whiteness and the law. As it happened, one of my sons was studying law there. When I asked him if I should accept the engagement he said to do so only if the talk would hit hard and speak specifically to the pretensions of the host campus regarding its record on racial justice. I ended up speaking, then writing, about both Washington University and the University of Illinois law schools as historically white institutions burdened by histories of exclusion. In Washington University's case this took the form of self-promotion for its historic role in accepting a Black student in the nineteenth century while ignoring the long acquiescence to Jim Crow that followed, leaving the university all-white after schools in the South had integrated. Absent systematic efforts to redress inequality, the HWCU stays a White-Serving Institution as well.

The Hubris of the Land-Grab University

Another source of the unspoken assumption that higher education—and even diversity within it—should serve the interests of its white majority of students has longer roots. These lie in the connections among Indigenous dispossession, higher education funding, and facile claims that schooling was for the public good. It took me, and most of us, much longer to see this dimension of the formation of HWCUs within the history of the land grants that funded many of the big public universities. From 1985 until 2013, I taught exclusively in land grant universities at Missouri, Minnesota, and then Illinois. From almost the start, I noticed how often that heritage came up, especially from administrators introducing events. Sometimes they'd give a very short history of the 1862 Morrill Land-Grant Act, which introduced federal funding for a university in each state, one that would be devoted significantly to practical agricultural and mechanical knowledge. Over half of the so-called "flagship" state public universities benefitted from Morrill Act aid at their founding. Today's appeals to the act, and its Vermont sponsor Congressman Justin Smith Morrill, work in many ways to explain the priorities, or what administrators almost always called the "mission," of their institutions.

At Minnesota, invocation of such a mission dovetailed with a (also not unproblematic) self-definition as serving "citizens." At Illinois, Morrill Hall lay a short walk from the building named for Abraham Lincoln, who signed the land-grant bill, and who typified what one historian has called the "right to rise" that the act was said to underwrite. Everywhere the Morrill aegis proves capacious enough to signify outreach to the community and an orientation towards agribusiness, engineering, and corporate interests generally. I had mostly tuned out of land-grant rhetoric until the education I was receiving in Indigenous history from colleagues at Minnesota and then Illinois and eventually from Australia sparked new connections. I first asked, "Whose land was granted?" under my breath when Morrill was championed but then asked publicly.

Before that I had lectured in survey US history courses on the Morrill legislation merely as part of a package of pro-development legislation passed when the Confederate states left the union. It was of a piece with grants to transcontinental railroads, higher tariffs to protect US industries, and the Homestead Act, putting the topic in a different lecture from that on brutal and breakneck expansion into trans-Mississippi Indian territories after the Civil War. Those lectures soon became one. The Morrill Act funded fifty-two universities with lavish foundational subsidies of Indian land. The grants amounted to an eighth of the land-grant bounty famously subsidizing the railroads. The law concretely placed its beneficiaries within worlds of dispossession and real estate as much granted land quickly went on the private market. It linked the practical and the progressive to the transfer of land as a commodity to white ownership. It made changing the land and water educational priorities, not infrequently with the disastrous long-term consequences under which we suffer, Kansas being a prime example.

Thanks to "Land-Grab Universities," the spectacular project of research and mapping coordinated by *High Country News* and released in 2020, we now have precise answers to the question of "Whose land?" at our fingertips. The maps connect specific universities, in beautifully rendered cascades, to the specific parcels of Indigenous land that funded them. With reference to places I'd worked, the University of Minnesota and the University of Missouri both link to parcels within the state, benefiting from dispossession close to home. Whites in Illinois had already expropriated Indigenous land before the Morrill Act, ethnically cleansing the state with deadly attacks and forced migrations. Thus, the University of Illinois speculated further afield, taking tracts from tribal nations in Kansas, Colorado, Nebraska, Minnesota, Iowa, and California. The schools benefitting from land grants currently enroll Indigenous students at less than a half a percent of total student population—more than a five-fold underrepresentation relative to Indigenous presence in the US population. The ways in which such Historically White Universities never have to say they are sorry—or more recently can lavishly say they are sorry without having to think through how the Land Back and other demands of Indigenous movements apply to higher education—connect powerfully to distortions in Morrill Act history.

Almost Noir: A Momentary Insider and
a Settler Colonial Song-and-Dance

For what seemed like health reasons, I started writing a novel twenty-some years ago. It was projected as a mystery, designed to let me process rage regarding the deep and depressing commitment of my workplace, the University of Illinois, to its faux Indigenous mascot, Chief Illiniwek, generally portrayed by a dancing white fraternity member. An excellent history, by Carol Spindel, had neither dislodged the Chief nor shaken the excuse that the deeply inauthentic performance somehow paid tribute to the tribes ethnically cleansed from Illinois. More great nonfiction work was on its way from Jennifer Guiliano, whose superb doctoral dissertation on the subject I co-supervised. Even Jay Rosenstein's searing documentary film In *Whose Honor?* could not move the university's trustees nor, in truth, many of its students and alumni. I did not believe a mystery would do the trick either but at the least I could get the red-face impersonator playing the Chief killed off in the book.

The story of how the mystery almost happened requires background. It takes us to the heart of how deeply difficult transformation, even modest change, is bound to be in the public flagship universities in even nominally liberal states. The Chief, as almost everyone familiarly called him, had disgraced the sidelines of Illinois sports for many years by the time I arrived to teach at Illinois in 2000. I'd grown up in Illinois thinking the mascot—the university later denied he was a mascot because to admit as much detracted from the gravity and high educational purpose that was being claimed for him—was silly and unimpressive.

When politicized, I switched to seeing the mascot as offensive and embarrassing but nevertheless unlikely to be removed. That changed in the later eighties when heroic Indigenous graduate students in art mounted an energetic challenge to Chief Illiniwek. One leader of the protests, Charlene Teters of the Spokane nation, gave visibility to the anti-Chief campaign by appearing at Illinois games with a small sign reading INDIANS ARE HUMAN BEINGS. Soon Kwame Ture (formerly Stokely Carmichael) came to campus to deliver a high-profile speech on his life and Black liberation. The celebrated freedom movement leader yielded a chunk of his time to Teters. At the time, I was still at Missouri but would soon be visiting the University of Illinois area lots in the nineties for solidarity marches with the A.E. Staley lockout and other labor struggles in Decatur, Illinois. I very much knew of the heroism of Teters and followed the ongoing anti-Chief initiative. When I took a job at Illinois in 2000 practically the first thing I asked was how I might be useful to that struggle.

I spoke soon at a packed Board of Regents meeting as a voice in favor of "retiring" Chief Illiniwek. I positioned the talk as that of a son of the soil of downstate Illinois whose fathomable values made him fully anti-Chief. The talk came complete with a Biblical injunction to "put away childish things." The regents listened to the talk, unmoved, but the student protesters heard it enthusiastically. Surprisingly, so did administrators who, having been promised by regents action to get rid of the mascot, sought outspoken allies and a way to re-frame the Chief question. Challenging the narrative of sophisticated cosmopolitans opposing the Chief and hayseeds in support of him seemed to them fascinating, because novel. More broadly the episode speaks to a dimension of the crisis in higher education seldom broached. Culturally, administrators are often at sea in the rural settings surrounding their universities, finding little success in connecting with ordinary small-town life beyond country clubs. They are prone to believe highly questionable things about rural residents.

At Illinois, for example, I ran into the chancellor at one point outside a demonstration that had briefly occupied the administration building. The issue may have been the Chief or perhaps it was collective bargaining rights for graduate teaching assistants. Spring break loomed, and there was scant chance that the protesters were going to lock themselves for long in an office when they could be on a beach. But the chancellor nevertheless pled with me and another professor she thought also had the ear of the demonstrators to help talk them into leaving. She mentioned that some believed there was a threat that townspeople from small surrounding places would come and dangerously confront the students. I thought I'd misheard, then thought this was caginess from someone wanting calm, and then realized she took the threat seriously, and probably had heard it discussed by others in her office. The chances that furious townspeople from tiny Homer or Arthur or Sidney, Illinois, were on their way to campus was zero. In 2018, when University of Kansas' chancellor ordered a piece of interesting but not very edgy public art be taken down in response to conservative political pressure he cited "public safety concerns" in justifying the censorship. Here the calculation probably outweighed the actual fear of the countryside, as the lone phone call raising the issue was later characterized as more harassing than threatening.

To compensate for the endless deferrals of the promise to get rid of Chief Illiniwek, administrators briefly included me in plans designed to make the university look good on other questions of race. With mixed feelings, I participated in such efforts while continuing to agitate against the mascot, for bargaining rights for the graduate students, and ultimately in favor of a faculty union. I'd long taken various leadership roles, for example in the writing-across-the-curriculum program at Missouri and as chair of the terrific program in American studies at Minnesota. However, I stopped well short of the Dean's office pretty much because my mother would not have been a principal nor my uncles foremen.

I liked some administrators, coming especially to value a straight answer, even if a negative one. I realized some of what I did as department chair implicated me in the daily life of the declining university. For example, I celebrated when money materialized to hire a contingently employed lecturer, even knowing that this was part of a move away from secure jobs on the part of universities. The level of dinner partying, advisory meetings, and personal closeness with administrators for a time at Illinois was different from anything I'd experienced before or since. The insider/outsider role I played caused me considerable anxiety and eventually pain but it did provide some excitement along the way.

Veteran University of Illinois professors who seemed to understand what was possible and impossible there put me in a leading role on a committee looking at racial justice broadly. My friend Joe Feagin, the superb sociologist of race, visited us, bringing a back-of-the-envelope plan for a center studying multiracial democracy, one that he'd tried and failed to implement at universities where he taught. The plan was ours to work with as we liked, he added. Among many virtues, Feagin's vision centered on production and dissemination of new knowledge, defining itself as an intellectual initiative associated with justice. The plan also spelled out that such a center could not depend on grant funding for basic operating funds, though we did soon get a substantial amount of support from the Ford Foundation. We had a planning committee in months and opened the Center on Democracy in a Multiracial Society in 2002. I agreed to serve as founding director but for just two years, and a national search was to be conducted in the second year for a permanent director. Nothing was fully easy. We'd assumed that the name would be the Center for Democracy in a Multiracial Society but "for" became "on" after a bizarre push-back.

With a course release for me and for an associate director—part of the time the extraordinary Puerto Rican scholar and great friend Pedro Cabán—CDMS also benefited greatly from another dimension of the rural setting of many flagship universities—an asset today being squandered. With a large pool of office workers, typically women, possessing great skills, few credentials, and few better job choices locally, colleges have long run on the knowledge and judgment brought to departments by local people. The intellectual challenges plus opportunities to complete a degree little-by-little and to have somewhat flexible schedules helped to retain these workers. (Now, lagging staff salaries have begun to undermine retention of such stalwarts as they also bedevil efforts to keep key tech staffers). At CDMS and in chairing at Minnesota and Kansas I learned to rely on the expertise regarding detail of these staff people and on the fact that they'd be among the brightest colleagues and the most committed to democratizing universities.

In the case of CDMS, I persuaded a very experienced office manager, Aprel Thomas, to come from history to direct operations, and she recruited an equally stellar co-worker. Building on their work, the beginnings of CDMS showed how incredibly much could be done with modest but consistent support. The university housed the program in a building of its own, an edge-of-campus former private home on the national historic register for its place in the inauguration of residential air conditioning. It provided a space perfect for seminars and small art exhibits. We spent about $400,000 a year, overwhelmingly to fund faculty research, to recompense departments for course releases, and to have both junior and senior colleagues join graduate students to mount local conferences with outstanding national and international figures joining Illinois scholars. The university kept some faculty of color longer than they would have otherwise because of support from CDMS.

In short order we welcomed to campus such important writers and agitators as Ruth Wilson Gilmore, Vijay Prashad, George Lipsitz, Ramon Gutierrez, Rose Braz, Paul Buhle, john powell, and Dell Upton, as well as prominent cultural figures including the artists Adrian Piper and Suk-Ja Kang, the film director Warrington Hudlin, and folk-singing historian Michael Honey. The topics ran far ahead of their time, with major events on race and space, on incarceration and education, on Chinese diasporic identities, on sports and capital, and on the rights of migrants. The chancellor and the provost regularly introduced conferences—and stayed to listen, now a fully lost practice. When Angela Davis spoke, the chancellor begged to introduce her but settled for introducing the introducer. Thousands of people came to CDMS events those first two years with many doubtless thinking that the administration as well as the Center was inviting them.

Unexpected successes provided as much satisfaction. When one branch of the Immigrant Workers Freedom Ride passed through Illinois in 2003 on the way to Washington, D.C., its leaders asked if the large busload of protesters could stop overnight and park near the Center. We not only held a huge picnic in the yard but, through good relations with hotels, secured rooms so that there could be a night of showers and real beds. That same year, when recently exonerated Illinois Death Row inmates could celebrate their release, CDMS hosted them, along with Joe Moreno of the Campaign to End the Death Penalty. Perhaps the most successful initiative, a very informal study group on the critical study of whiteness, seldom had a budget exceeding a few dollars for snacks. It brought together scholars from history, art, journalism, landscape architecture, English, counseling psychology, African American studies, and more. Its systems of mutual aid changed several scholarly lives and produced, at book length, the first comprehensive bibliography for that area of study.

As much as this stretch of activity represented a high spot in my university work, it could not last. I accepted being asked to found CDMS and direct its first two years. However, I believed the search for a long-term leader should weigh affirmative action in its choice. It weighed on me that the greater the center's profile was, the more it functioned as cover for interminable, hurtful delays in addressing Chief Illiniwek, after so many signals that action would finally be taken. So great were the disappointments that that Chancellor Nancy Cantor came out publicly against the mascot, after long patiently working behind the scenes. A vicious campaign against her developed, the nadir of which were billboards calling for the "return" of Cantor, who is Jewish and a New Yorker, and to keep of the Chief.

At the center, we re-doubled efforts to oppose the Chief, supporting demonstrations, bringing Charlene Teters back to campus, and directly speaking to the impossibility of taking a center on racial justice seriously with the mascot still in place. In the CDMS newsletter, named in W.E.B. Du Bois' honor as *Reconstructing Democracy*, I wrote of "Multiracial Democracy in the Shadow of the Chief." As we were searching for a new director, word came that Cantor had resigned, moving a little less than laterally to a similar position at Syracuse. The new leadership had generally supported the center's existence in their former roles, but we'd lost the leading advocate of its vision. The problem of dissonance between the Chief and multiracial democracy went unsolved. We'd burned some bridges, and a fair share of faculty thought that any difficulties we had validated their view that you can't go too far too fast.

The Chief situation encouraged a certain desperation, as we had run out of tactics. In 2005, Illinois recruited an elite basketball prospect, Eric Gordon. Purely as a stunt, the distinguished biologist Stephen Kaufman and I fashioned a public letter to Gordon encouraging him to be aware that a racist mascot divided our campus as he considered his final decision on where to play. Against all odds, Gordon did drop his commitment, not at all because of our letter but because Indiana University had hired Kelvin Sampson as its coach. That Sampson is both Black and Indigenous added to the brew. Thousands of students and fans signed petitions calling for the firing of Kaufman, who was already retiring, and myself.

The same desperation provides the context for my undone mystery novel on the murder of the Chief, which never went far but did teach me something again about the local setting of flagship universities. I'd read hundreds of mysteries. Much of their appeal lay in how often attending to material interests—following the money—led to the culprit. But I needed to think more about what specific material interests explained the Chief—about what money to follow. I had bonded with an upper administrator at Illinois, out of mutual disgust at the continued presence of the Chief. I took the idea for the detective novel to that administrator and asked what money I should be tracking.

The administrator urged me to think about which firm had perennially won the contract for an important process within almost every major construction project on campus for decades on end. It turned out to be a company from just down the road in a still smaller city, signaling that for all the ties of a leading university to transnational agribusiness, state-of-the-art computer engineering, and high finance, its sports decision making and its construction budgets remained very much in the orbit of local and regional capitalists. The organized pro-mascot forces were far more likely to include car dealers, beer vendors, and mobile home sellers than those near the commanding heights of the economy. Chief Illiniwek danced as the mascot of something that might better have been called Central Illinois State University than University of Illinois.

In 2007, the National Collegiate Athletic Association put an end to my whodunit writing. Its moves to punish teams with racist mascots finally backed the University of Illinois away from the Chief, albeit in the least principled way possible and with elaborate efforts to pretend that we should forever remember the mascot as well-meaning and educational. I put the manuscript aside, not because there'd been a satisfactory solution—the university retained the "Illini" name and the faux-Indian music of the school band—but out of tiredness.

Red States, Blue States, Dire Straits

When my partner Elizabeth Esch and I moved to the University of Kansas—she from teaching at Barnard College and I from the University of

Illinois—in 2013, skeptical friends questioned the sanity of moving to a Republican "red state" and working in one of its public universities. I had never lived in such a state, Missouri having been a different place in the eighties from its current scarlet coloration. Indeed the red-versus-blue distinction seemed not to have been drawn back then. It has taken a good while for the meaning of the colors to sink in for me, in part because it seemed counterintuitive that red identified the right. The move to a conservative state did not worry me greatly. My general political orientation held that the two parties shared more than they divided on.

Many in Minnesota had told me on my arrival that the state was run by a farmer and labor party under the banner of the Democrats. But the two governors during my years there were Republican or independent, the latter pro wrestler Jesse Ventura. The university administration, viewing itself as impeccably progressive, outrageously tried to abolish university-based tenure procedures in 1996, joining with a hotshot anti-labor law firm, and enabling us to almost win a union election. The difficulties at Illinois, as rehearsed above, occurred in a blue state. Things worsened just after I left, when the administration succumbed to pressure by reneging on a job offer to Steven Salaita, the Palestinian American scholar who had earned a tenured appointment in American Indian studies. Censure of the university by the American Association of University Professors followed. In victimizing Salaita, the administration allowed the dismantling of that world-class department, the creation of which had been the lone attempt to repair the damage done by clinging to Chief Illiniwek. It was in Illinois that my books suffered banning. I hazarded that the University of Kansas could scarcely be worse.

But timing is everything. Kansas has proven worse, at least in degree, despite the presence of remarkable colleagues. About half the states in the US are red states. The twenty-five states that Trump carried in 2016 and won again in 2020 provide a rough roster. Even if we put legislatures, governors, and laws aside, they would be hard places to fund strong, secular public universities. They are less wealthy, less unionized, less populous, less productive, less taxed, less educated formally, and more religious than the blue states. Kansas fits snugly in these demographics, though not on taxation.

The relative lack of resources makes extreme austerity seem logical. So does the fact that the relatively small state underfunds three sizable universities, Wichita State and Kansas State as well as Kansas. So much was austerity accepted as a fact of life that year after year the lack of raises at KU went completely unremarked. I'd been at state universities that received such meager appropriations that salaries remained flat for a year but this state of affairs at least received publicity and sometimes even complaint in a way it did not at Kansas. In the view of many Kansas faculty, the university administration is the victim of the legislature, much as administrations are now to be thought of as victims of the Supreme Court where affirmative action is concerned. Many begin with great sympathy for those presiding over the university's decline.

However, campus leadership has also chosen its path to declining numbers of faculty and to salaries not nearly keeping pace with inflation or with those offered by competing institutions. When they began, quite prior to Covid, to project a still longer and deeper trough of austerity, administrators explained the need for sacrifice by pointing to a not-on-their-watch spending spree on buildings, which were endowed but not completely so and secured by often unwise public/private partnerships with financiers. Just before I arrived at the University of Kansas, the annual outlay of a salary base for tenured and tenure-track faculty far more than trebled university debt service. By 2022 they were even, with all the trending growth on the debt service side. Debt skyrocketed as the salary base declined by roughly a quarter.

Here was the problem Veblen identified a century before and the one around which my abandoned mystery novel had hoped to construct a plot—the ease of uniting business and the university around appropriations for buildings rather than operating budgets. In KU's case, the buildings often did not even prioritize classroom space. There was a temple to house the original rules of basketball, a second student center, increasingly fancy dorms amidst teardowns of older ones, a welcome center for prospective students, and lavish new athletic facilities for practice and housing as well as for games. A highly subsidized research park—the subsidies come at the expense of the city of Lawrence too in the form of massive tax abatements—became the focus of what a transformed university would look like.

Greater shortfalls in state appropriations make such ventures still more attractive as they are increasingly the only games in town. Not long ago I consulted at the University of California's San Diego campus in an ethnic studies department I had visited lots. On a break, I went to a landing in the building to see a beautiful view of the ocean. Instead I saw cranes and new construction obscuring that view. The University of California system was dead broke at the time, mired in a much-publicized crisis. How, I asked hosts, can a big new structure be going up, given those constraints? They explained that the building was an upscale new dorm, financed as a profit-making "public-private" venture. There was money for that.

The Covid pandemic clarified how resources get channeled. Kansas is a cash-poor university with an endowment of over two billion dollars. Already engaged in a campaign to make austerity—cheerfully called "rightsizing"—central to its mission, the managers of the university did not let the crisis caused by the disease go to waste. Short-term enrollment declines occurred, especially when classes could not safely meet in-person in a state where vaccinations could not legally be required and regulations undermined contact tracing. This was exactly the sort of temporary crisis that a huge endowment could help to bridge. Instead of showcasing the confidence of an institution that might have helped to retain the best campus workers, the messaging was frantically couched in the language of "emergency," mixing the effects of Covid with supposed fall off a "demographic cliff" in prospective student numbers to come. In fact, having lost a big chunk of its faculty, Kansas now has record-size entering classes.

Campus leaders not only further trimmed hiring but instituted a temporary salary cut for campus workers. The Board of Regents offered all universities in their system the opportunity to fire tenured faculty. Most campuses immediately declined to let any tenured professors go, or pointed out that union contracts prevented them from doing so. The University of Kansas neither acted on the offer from the regents nor rejected it. The university kept the possibility alive for many months as a threat and finally decided not to use it only after so many faculty left that massive savings had already been achieved. The talk of emergency did not move the endowment to provide emergency support, except in the case of special campaigns to cover shortfalls in the athletic department. The endowment has separate tracks for sports and is separate in its legal standing from the university itself. As Veblen outlined: Donors will fund physical assets (and perhaps some scholarships).

Covid also clarified just what the University thought it sold—an experience, not an education. Kansas administrators registered utter panic when students could not come to campus. Their genuine fears came not only because public/private partnerships required that they have parking, dorm rental, and dining revenues to pay their partners. Panic further ensued because they saw not learning, nor even a degree, but experiencing "being a Jayhawk" as the commodity KU delivered, a goal said to be proven by "market research." The university's online presence beckons students with "Explore the home of the Jayhawks."

In much of the US the public university has become a battleground in which dwindling state support nevertheless entitles lawmakers to investigate Critical Race Theory, to impose anti-trans policies, and to promulgate vague, sweeping policies prohibiting social media speech that may be "contrary to the best interest of the university." All these instances come from the recent past at the University of Kansas, and all feature political pressure from conservative political forces in the state. The Board of Regents tossed into the mix a claim to be able to fire tenured professors without cause. With campuses lacking reputations as either a bargain or a place of cultural ferment, the public university absorbs blows from far-right politicians as a convenient punching bag pummeled when it is desirable to produce rage amidst a base not so much of voters as of far-right, small-time activists.

The notion that even a staid place like University of Kansas harbors sex and socialism means that whether a policy will hurt it counts for little in political debates. In 2015, two years after we arrived, the ultra-conservative governor Sam Brownback, happily now un-electable anywhere, dug up an order by one of his predecessors protecting LGBT state employees from job discrimination. He splashily countermanded it, championing such bias. This unwarned attack of course discredited state universities greatly in the eyes of many of their current and prospective employees and students. The next year Brownback signed into law a bill that explicitly mandated public universities to provide normal funding to student groups even if they discriminate against gays and lesbians.

At the national level the draconian attacks on immigrant rights, before and during the Covid pandemic, hurt universities. Financial planning had included projections of international student enrollments, soon undermined by both concrete exclusionary policies and the ways in which those policies enhanced the global image of the US as too xenophobic to be a good a place to study. Little response pointed to the specifically anti–higher education ramifications of such xenophobia. The right in Kansas and other red states has succeeded in silencing debate on such issues in part because it has built a constituency, or at least a cadre of activists, that accepts that universities deserve to be hurt.

Administrators and a fair share of faculty hope such attacks will just go away, imagining ordinary Kansans as unfathomable, and not worth appealing to regarding what is being done in their names and to their universities. Open opposition to right-wing culture wars in Kansas can be politically risky and there should be debate about when faculty, staff, and students take the lead and when administrators' statements might be useful. But especially after the landslide statewide referendum victory for abortion rights in Kansas in 2022—a success shocking even to activists in Lawrence—there's room for those in universities to help others in the state to challenge the idea that rural working people are hopeless.

The clearest example of red-state impact on the university has involved the almost infinite array of "gun rights" in Kansas. The day I first met with the former chancellor to be recruited to the university, she was preoccupied with responding to ginned-up complaints regarding a professor's pro–gun control tweets after a mass shooting in a workplace, the Washington Navy Yard. I understood her to be saying that finessing the issue by giving right-wing legislators much of what they wanted was the wisest course. The resulting social media policy did that. I had no basis on which to doubt that judgment at the time but soon did. The professor, David Guth, suffered harsh discipline—seven months away from teaching—purely for speaking freely outside of the classroom.

The haphazard media policy acknowledged freedom of expression only to balance it against "the interest of the employer in promoting the efficiency of the public services it performs through its employees" and against any tendency to "impair discipline by superiors." The American Association of University Professors, whose own language regarding free expression the university selectively sampled in its policy, found the new social media policy "a gross violation of the fundamental principles of academic freedom."

Just as I accepted the job at Kansas, the state legalized the right to carry concealed weapons on public university campuses, including in classrooms. Each institution could apply for a four-year exemption, and all did, making 2017 the effective date for the coming of the guns. That seemed to provide a respite for administrators to argue against the policy, but the actual public efforts to prevent its taking effect fell to faculty, staff, and students. Those groups, polls showed, were overwhelmingly against the armed classroom. We built a remarkable fightback, participating in the Kansas Coalition for a Gun-Free Campus, testifying, demonstrating, creating art, and educating, especially regarding work on suicides among young people and the availability of guns. We were outgunned from the start but did contribute to the decision not to include the medical campus as a venue for concealed carry. Administrators, silent in public on the issue, seemed to want credit for not enforcing another 2013 Kansas law, necessarily opaquely drawn for constitutional reasons, against use of state funds to influence "the enactment of legislation before the federal government, state legislature, or a local government legislative body relating to gun control." Faculty, and especially junior and contingent faculty, took implied threats seriously.

The Stakes: Can Flagship Universities Survive?

I have long wondered if the public university as it exists deserves to survive even while rooting for it to figure out a way forward. Only in the past five years did this cross over into a clear question about whether it will last, even for a few more decades, at least in the form of the flagship or main state university campus, where I have spent almost my entire working life. That question crystallized in a specific setting and again around a policy regarding racial justice. Not long before the Covid pandemic, I went to a catered dinner party in the lavish

condo of an up-and-coming University of Kansas academic administrator. The bash entertained distinguished professors, who have jobs
carrying more salary and less teaching responsibility. These "chairs"
had long existed but grew wildly as the position and condition of the
faculty as a whole declined in recent decades. What gets called a "star
system" papered over the decline of stable, secure faculty jobs with a
few enticing stories of success, although the pay-offs for the faculty's
chosen few remained far less than for those for those moving up in
the burgeoning administrative sector of universities.

I'd been to quite a few such meetings of top academic managers and
distinguished professor groups at Illinois and Kansas. Not surprisingly,
individual dissenters notwithstanding, bodies of such favored professors
tend to be hyper-identified with understanding the need for austerity
and to cherish access to personal contacts with decision-makers who
sometimes offer opportunities to socialize.

Distinguished professor groups function mainly as conservative
bodies, however much almost all members think themselves liberal
because, as a wise business school friend says, they get news from the
New York Times and not the Wall Street Journal. Legendarily invested with
a responsibility for looking after the future of the university, they are
nevertheless skeptical of unionization and respectful of the desire of
administrators not to be put on the spot. At Kansas, just before the
dinner at the condo, I'd worked for many months to get the mildest
of statements from the distinguished professors group against the new
Kansas policy that allowed students to bring guns to classrooms. I'd
even been willing to be elected as chair of the steering committee of
the group to move things along. Late and tepid, the ensuing statement
missed its moment.

Going to the dinner at Kansas broke my vow not to waste time on
such matters. I had two reasons for attending, three if you count that
I knew who was catering. First the host sort of interested me. He'd
recently arrived, trying his hand within an administrative job market
characterized by constant pronouncements of loyalty to place and
mascot but also by a permanent candidacy within searches elsewhere.
He came from a professorial career devoted to research carrying a
great possibility to ease human suffering. Making the choice to trade

research on addiction to manage the decline of a university fascinated me. He had sometimes showed good instincts, for example in rejecting for a moment the university's leap into the madness of Academic Analytics as a subcontracted data and managerial service. However, his stronger instinct turned out to be one for knowing what positions it was impermissible to hold, and he quickly moved into the Academic Analytics fold.

At least he was different. During the guns-on-campus controversy he came not to, but near, our demonstration, head on his hand like Rodin's Thinker, while taking no position on the issue. Few others in the administration even struck a pose. He also came, early on anyhow, to academic events, listening to talks about ideas, putting him in a vanishing minority among top administrators. Personally irreverent in a way that hovered between being a personality trait and a marketing niche, he seemed worth watching, if only to observe whether he was destined to soar or implode within university systems. So far, it's been a rise with two better jobs already far beyond Kansas.

I also came to the dinner to learn what form anticipated new policies on what was increasingly being called diversity would take. The distinguished professor group, itself impossibly white and male, had to its credit made the issue its focus that year, even contributing personal funds to diversity initiatives. We anticipated hearing something of the secret diversity plans administrators were making with considerable fanfare. After dinner, we heard a breathless description of a breakthrough allegedly making faculty diversity central to the budget process regarding hiring lines. In a 100-point schema, diversity was to count negligibly, not nearly enough to counterbalance the wholesale defunding of those parts of the university accounting for most of its faculty and students of color. As a British friend once observed about Tony Blair's reign as prime minister: "I had very low expectations and yet I was severely disappointed."

The policy, which I think the administrator honestly regarded as a bold one, astonished me for its very sincerity. I thought the soundtrack for the dinner had become Fela Kuti's "Beasts of No Nation," especially the line "Dey wan dash us human rights." The interim provost was sticking with it being "We Can Make It Happen," maybe the Prince

Charles and the City Beat Band version. I could not get past one over-whelming thought: wondering how long university leaders supposed things could continue on a course so mismatched to the gravity of the problems. My response in the discussion following was something like: "I have taught for many years at places whose downward trajectory made me wonder what they'd look like fifty years from now. Kansas is the first place where I'm now thinking instead about whether the campus can survive fifty years." I specifically talked about the loss of staff as the canary in the University of Kansas coal mine, announcing its maturing crises.

Tellingly, the dinner's host did not reject the prediction out of hand. Even as he maintained that the tiny changes that he proposed on diversity occupied the visionary edge of what was possible, he allowed that the bigger question of whether there was a viable future for the university consumed him late into nights, and he agreed that the staff crisis was where it presented itself most urgently. It turns out, colleagues elsewhere tell me, the possibility of major state universities disappearing is a pressing question beyond Kansas—unless we are ready to equate universities with stadia, tax avoidance, and research parks.

If the research parks/malls fail and connections between college sports and colleges are severed— at Kansas to an important degree they already are separate, in terms of budget and fund-raising—it is hard imagine that the state's three major public universities would not be consolidated into one in twenty years, if any survive in a recognizable form at all. For now the University of Kansas persists, with big athletic facilities and research park-cum-shopping mall public/private projects, in perpetual crisis regarding what Veblen called "working capital," and with a self-image buoyed by a vague commitment to diversity that is increasingly illegal.

Afterword

WHAT GOOD IS BEING FATHOMABLE?

My cellphone is beaten-up enough, and the word "fathomable" is unfamiliar enough, to invite confusion. Once this took the form of a friend being shocked that I, after so many years of neglect, had come around to the position that it is important to be *fashionable*. This brief afterword gets that straightened out and thinks about the ways in which it matters to know that currents in ordinary lives of those racially labelled as white imperfectly steer toward a questioning of inequality as well more insistently to its acceptance. I'm asking: What good is it to know that dissidence from whiteness is fathomable? What can we build from recognizing that those who bear the advantages of whiteness sometimes come to think about the unfairness of that fact and the harm it does to everyone by structuring a society based on hierarchy and irrationality? What does it achieve to find among those with white skins a critique of whiteness that opens onto a broader attack on misery?

One short, correct answer to those questions is that it does not do nearly enough, given the crises we face. Everyday life, also and often, leads ordinary whites to exclusionary conclusions and sad failures of imagination that expose the limits of supposing that mobilizations among whites, and least of all as whites, hold the key to either survival or transformation. Those failures are not just fathomable. They are expected. The lessons of my life do not lead to thinking that the harm done by people living as whites is not as bad as we had thought. If anything, the realization that whites sometimes nearly break out of the cage of whiteness makes the massive reproduction of conservative white identities even more tragic. My singular life story, and the way it is framed here, permit no epiphanies in concluding, no sense that the key to everything is now on offer.

However, a second answer, less grand, to "What good is it to be fathomable?" also exists. It emphasizes that seeing how a critique of white advantage grows organically within some parts of everyday white lives offers small insights that can be measured without lapsing into grandiosity that again re-centers whites as historical actors. The extent to which these moments provide tentative ways of inching struggles a little bit forward, or at other moments of getting pushed back a bit less, makes such little bits of good news worth gathering up. Most of this afterword accents the limits of being fathomable, but some last paragraphs suggest what the fathomable white—who at her best is poised to also be anti-white in the sense of opposing the ideology of whiteness that glues together reactionary political alliances and liberal inaction—might modestly offer.

A Necessarily Pessimistic Framework

About a dozen years ago—I was 60—a persisting lump in my neck led to a cancer diagnosis. The Bangladeshi American doctor whom I consulted recognized it as chronic lymphocytic leukemia, or CLL, and pronounced my fate a little bit too jubilantly for my taste at first. It was "absolutely the best cancer to get." What he meant was that—though there is no cure—it is often beaten back for extended periods and even repeatedly by relatively benign treatments. His prognosis: you will live a long time and die of something else completely. I said that's kind of what I'd planned anyhow before the bad news. And—minus that dying of something else part—that's how it has worked out so far without symptoms and even without side effects during two periods of brief treatment.

Still the mere fact of having cancer, which coincided more or less with my mother's having a stroke at 88, made me think about whether life required some kind of summation. I did for a time resolve to speak up more but realized I did so already to such an extent that continuing to add more would annoy everyone, including me. Since I speak up by counterpunching, the idea of setting out to speak up interrupted my rhythm. Moreover, as a believer that even structures of oppression are responsive to the unpredictable struggles of living labor and its aggrieved allies, such final words must often include "it all depends" for me. With regard to the issues I have studied and struggled around, my summative opinions remain disturbingly consistent with what I have argued since the seventies: That meaningful change comes from below, that there is no serious US study of class that does not also take full measure of race and gender, that the way to nonracialism is through the consideration of race—not around it but through it—that we need more imagination and less polling data.

Considering questions of aging and mortality has made me pay more heed to one specific kind of discourse. It is the senior left spokesperson's valediction to keep on keeping on, to stay the course, to remain optimistic. When such is said, often in retirement speeches or interviews summing up a life on the left, I cringe a bit, especially if the testimony is offered by someone I know to be wonderfully acerbic in other, private moments. I get the goal of hope talk but I don't support it. Even the familiar quotations from the Italian revolutionary Antonio Gramsci that often accompany the cheeriness—we are urged to nurture "pessimism of the intellect" but "optimism of the will"—don't convince me.

I fear such talk rings false to young people being told in other moments that the planet will soon be beyond repair. It also risks seeing hope as a matter of individual psychology, unmoored from material realities.

The logic of championing hope is, I suppose, that we don't have another way to keep movements struggling without over-egging the optimism. But to say as much is to admit the gravity of our situation. I think we are better off owning up to it. A variant of the optimistic position has it that we cannot "afford" pessimism with the stakes so high. But can we afford optimism if it leaves us thinking in terms of redoubling our efforts along the same failing political lines instead of reexamining all of the left's habits in light of climate change and genocide? My pro-Grinch position—the early, pessimistic Grinch—might not seem easy to sustain, but we do have long examples showing an ability to enter the struggle between socialism and barbarism on the side of the former, even knowing the latter is winning.

I grew up in social movements with the seeming luxury of believing we would outlast our oppressors. From Cuba we heard "History is on our side," southern Africa and elsewhere gave us the wonderful folk wisdom reminder that "Time is longer than rope," and Dr. King promised that the "bend," however slowly, of the "moral arc of the universe" leads "toward justice." My grandkids may not be able to gain solace from thinking of liberation in the historical long run, nor even to know with certainty that there is to be a long run for humans on an Earth being despoiled.

We might as well acknowledge our social tragedy and hope that doing so frees us to inquire as to whether keeping on can really be our strategy. I am old enough to remember early seventies moments when cranky veterans of the left would react to florid, fanciful speculations—sometimes my own—about the new day's imminence by calling for a "dose of astringent spray." To deal with the much more half-hearted and half-baked proclamations of hope in the liberal university we'd need whole vats of astringents, producing at least a little healthy stinging and sanity.

Two Things at Once

In 2016, after Donald Trump won the presidency, Wisconsin commanded attention as one battleground state that delivered his razor-thin margin of victory. Despite a storied progressive heritage, Wisconsin preferred Trump over Hillary Clinton by a few thousand votes. Aware that the county of exclusionary "sundown towns" in which I grew up went big for Trump, I wondered if the virtually all-white towns in Wisconsin registered the same preference. Did they make a winner of Trump? Kathryn Robinson, a graduate research assistant, and I pored over the returns from Wisconsin, at that juncture most available at the county level. We compared the counties that had a sundown town as a county seat—almost all such counties also had overwhelming white populations overall—with counties having a county seat not sharing sundown patterns of expulsion and exclusion. Two facts stood out. First, what we came to call "sundown counties" accounted for an astonishing 58 of Wisconsin's total of 72 counties. Second, though largely small and rural, the sundown counties did deliver enough votes to put Trump over the top. He lost the non-sundown counties by 230,000 but won the sundown ones by 256,000, squeaking by in overall totals. We had a good story and planned to publish it in the left muckraking venue

Counterpunch, under a title something like "How White People with Almost No Experience of People of Color Elected Trump."

But something made us not part with the article. We began to look at vote totals for the mostly white but not sundown counties collaring Milwaukee and they—sometimes upper middle class—contributed proportionately more votes to Trump's margin of victory. I wondered what James Loewen, the historical sociologist of sundown towns, would think of the article and sent it to him. He encouraged its publication but added that he had just been to Calhoun County, near where I grew up in Illinois, and found out something surprising. The county, a northern place named for the pro-slavery Southern politician John C. Calhoun and the home of sundown towns, kept that name even through the Civil War, and still retains it. Having many poor white people, Calhoun County voted, Loewen reported, for Trump by a huge majority. None of that was surprising but what Loewen said next was. Calhoun County had voted for Obama in 2008. Astounded, and a little alarmed by the assumptions I had made, I looked up 2008 election results for those sundown counties in Wisconsin. Many voted strongly for Obama. *Counterpunch* was kind enough to let us have a little higher word count, making possible a more layered story than an exposé of the blameworthy ordinary rural white.

After all these years of living with and studying ordinary white people, I came very close to letting us play oversimplified blame games that find them to be the singular source of what ails us. Robinson and I almost sent off an article doing just that. We would have hardly been alone. In its immediate reaction to Trump's 2016 win, the *New York Times* thought it knew the story ahead of the data. Trump won because of a hidden coalition of "mostly blue-collar and white working-class voters." Such rushes to judgment were sometimes challenged and even walked back but they are as regularly walked forward again. The names of the culprits shift slightly from indictment to indictment, depending on which academic, pollster or politician is speaking, but the "deplorables," those clinging to guns and giving us Trump, have come to be seen as white workers, losers of rustbelt jobs, and, now more than ever, those left behind to nurse their "white rural rage" in the countryside. These are more or less the people I grew up with. I recognize them in some of the caricatures and certainly do not deny that a great many whites made miserable by poverty and overwork support Trump. That even a few do would qualify as tragic, but many do. To name-call and saddle them with the responsibility for electing Trump is nevertheless both counterproductive and wrong. Many of the rageful don't vote and, again in Wisconsin, upwards of 40 percent of voters choose against the far-right. When and where Trump has won, he has commanded wide white support across class and geographic boundaries. Rural whites are complicated in their motivations and can change positions from election to election.

Ordinary whites are more than the sum of their own received prejudices and furies, however much political appeals to them assume they can only be convinced by courting their worst impulses. Republicans make direct appeals to xenophobia and racism. The dominant forces in the Democratic Party have since the nineties explicitly argued that the "white middle class" and the "white working class" are to be won over by doing less to address racial justice issues rather than by doing more to erase poverty and challenge corporate power. It may be that national electoral politics offer one of the worst places to find ordinary whites acting on their best impulses. Perhaps the early victories for a new labor movement, especially in the South, will make us see anew that white workers can contribute to seemingly unfathomable things. The idea that many experiences, not all leading to reaction, give ordinary whites chances to break from ordinary whiteness deserves to be one small part of how we think about changing the world.

Finally, to think about the ways in which life among working-class whites informs, animates, and makes fathomable dissent is healthy as personal reflection. There is a tendency for the academic worker, the antiracist, the socialist, and the credentialled among us to imply that an "up from" plot captures our life stories. Sometimes that makes for a certain precision but as often it separates blue-collar from white-collar workers, professionals being immiserated from their parents, and brothers and sisters from each other. The voguish rubric for separating the working class from the middle class—no college versus went-to college—tends to create self-fulfilling senses of division. At its worst it makes antiracism itself seem like a product of higher education, even of Diversity, Equity, and Inclusion initiatives and "woke" teachers. If it were, we wouldn't have a chance.

I like to think that some of the questions this book pursues stem from reflecting on my near miss of joining in simplistic blame games targeting poor and working-class whites as the specific source of our woes. Blame, even shame, and guilt have an understandable place in the history of white supremacy, but that place does not always sit productively at the center of that history. As James Baldwin so eloquently taught us, guilt is a poor substitute for whites feeling angry after realizing that they have been made bereft by the racial system that they inherited and reproduce. Clearly, such is the case where generating desires for repair of injustice are concerned. It is knowledge—often incomplete, fleeting, and contradictory—of what whiteness separates whites from—a vital labor movement, an even rudimentary welfare state, a critique of empire and settler colonialism, meaningful planet-saving political coalitions, and humanity.

Further Reading

Chapters One and Two

On East St. Louis, Cairo, and Columbia, see Jennifer Hamer, *Abandoned in the Heartland: Work, Family, and Living in East St. Louis* (Berkeley: University of California Press, 2011); Andrew J. Thiesing, *Made in USA: East St. Louis, the Rise and Fall of an Industrial River Town* (St. Louis: Virginia Publishers, 2003); Kerry Pimblott, *Faith in Black Power: Religion, Race, and Resistance in Cairo, Illinois* (Lexington: University Press of Kentucky, 2017); Christopher K. Hays, "Way Down in Egypt Land: Conflict and Community in Cairo, Illinois, 1850–1910" (PhD diss: University of Missouri-Columbia, 1996); Fletcher Martin, "'We Don't Want Your Kind': Segregation in Illinois," *The Atlantic* (October, 1958); Preston Ewing Jr., *Let My People Go: Cairo, Illinois, 1967–1973* (Carbondale: Southern Illinois University Press, 1996); David Roediger, "Remembering Black Hawk," *Boston Review* (March 2, 2022) at https://bostonreview.net/articles/remembering-black-hawk; James W. Loewen, *Sundown Towns: A Hidden Dimension of American Racism* (New York: Touchstone, 2005).

My book, *The Wages of Whiteness: Race and the Making of the American Working Class* (London and New York: Verso Books, 1991) contains material on Cairo and Columbia in my youth. On the role of sports in helping me reach revolutionary conclusions, see Roediger, "Wanting to Be Like Ashe" in Arne Dewinde and Lieven Van Speybroeck, eds., *Crossing the Line: Arthur Ashe at the 1968 U.S. Open*, with photographs from the John Zimmerman Archives (Furnes, Belgium: Hannibal Publishing, 2018) and "Sports, Surrealism, and Subversion," *Cultural Correspondence*, 12–14 (Summer 1981), 56–58. For more on my mother and family see https://www.leesmanfuneralhome.com/obituaries/Mary-Roediger/#!/Obituary

Chapters Three and Four

On Students for a Democratic Society in its post-glory years, see John F. Levin and Earl Silbar, eds., *You Say You Want a Revolution: SDS, PL, and Adventures* in *Building a Worker-Student Alliance* (San Francisco: 1741 Press, 2019) and Alan Adelson, *SDS: A Profile* (New York: Charles Scribner's Sons, 1972). On the Northern Illinois University Department of History and radical history, see James Livingston, "The New Left at Northern Illinois University in the 1960s and 1970s," (forthcoming). For the Chicago Surrealist Group, see Kate Khatib, "Surrealism's America: Notes on a Vernacular Epistemology" (PhD. Diss.: Johns Hopkins University, 2013); David Roediger, Kate Khatib, and Paul Garon, "The Surreal Life of Franklin Rosemont," *Counterpunch* (April 16, 2009) at https://www.counterpunch.org/2009/04/16/the-surreal-life-of-franklin-rosemont/. See also The Chicago Surrealist Group, "*Three Days That Shook the New World Order: The Los Angeles Rebellion of 1992*," *Race Traitor*, 2 (Summer 1993), 1–17; Roediger, "Plotting Against Eurocentrism: The 1929 Surrealist Map of the World," *Race Traitor*, 9 (1998), 32–39 and Roediger, "Radical Culture without Surrealism," *Race Traitor*, 13–14 (Summer 2001), 75–90.

On George Rawick, see David Roediger and Martin Smith, eds., *Listening to Revolt: Selected Writings of George Rawick* (Chicago: Charles H. Kerr Publishing Company, 2010). On Fred Thompson, see Thompson with David Roediger, *Fellow Worker: The Life of Fred W. Thompson* (Chicago: Charles H. Kerr Publishing Company, 1993). On the Iranian student left in the US, see Afshin Matin-Asgari's superb *Iranian Student Opposition to the Shah* (Costa Mesa, CA: Mazda Publishers, 2002).

On the long history of the Kerr Company, see Allen Ruff, *"We Called Each Other Comrade": Charles H. Kerr & Company, Radical Publishers* (Urbana: University of Illinois Press, 1997) and David Cochran, "A Socialist Publishing House," *History Workshop Journal* (UK), 24 (Autumn 1987), 34–38. See also "History Against Misery: Penelope Rosemont & David Roediger on the History of Kerr," *The Charles H. Kerr Podcast* (December 9, 2020) at https://soundcloud.com/kerr-podcast/episode-one-penelope-rosemont-and-david-roediger-on-the-history-of-kerr.

Interlude One

The many sides of the genius of C.L.R. James are difficult to capture at once. Most successful in doing so is the special issue of *Urgent Tasks* from the summer of 1981. See especially the articles by John Bracey,

Ferruccio Gambino, Franklin Rosemont, Richard Small, Sylvia Wynter, George Rawick, Peter Linebaugh, and Robert A. Hill.

Chapter Five

See David Roediger, "The Making of a Historian: An Interview with Sterling Stuckey," Journal of African American History 99, no. 1-2 (Winter-Spring 2014), 88–105; David Roediger, "An Interview with Elma Stuckey," Black American Literature Forum 11, no. 4 (Winter 1977), 151–53. On Foner, see Hyman Berman and David Roediger, "Obituary of Philip S. Foner," OAH Newsletter (February, 1995), 37–38.

Interlude Two

Sean Burns, Archie Green: The Making of a Working-Class Hero (University of Illinois Press, 2011); Mike Honey, Sharecropper's Troubadour: John L. Handcox, the Southern Tenant Farmers' Union, and the African American Song Tradition (New York: Palgrave Macmillan, 2013) and Douglas Wixson's Worker-Writer in America: Jack Conroy and the Tradition of Midwestern Literary Radicalism, 1898–1900 (Urbana and Chicago: University of Illinois Press, 1994). H.L. Mitchell tells the story of his own life and his union in Mean Things Happening in This Land: The Life and Times of H.L. Mitchell (Norman: University of Oklahoma Press, 2008, originally 1979).

Chapter Six

For the story of this chapter told with citations and fewer good stories see David Roediger, "Accounting for the Wages of Whiteness: U.S. Marxism and the Critical History of Race," in Wulf Hund, David Roediger, and Jeremy Krikler, eds., The Wages of Whiteness & Racist Symbolic Capital (Berlin: Lit Verlag, 2010), 9–36. See also Franklin Rosemont, "Surrealism: Revolution against Whiteness," Race Traitor, 9 (Summer 1998), 19–29.

For attacks on the critical study of whiteness see Margaret Talbot, "Getting Credit for Being White," New York Times Magazine (November 30, 1997), 116–19; Eric Arnesen et al., "Whiteness and the Historians' Imagination," International Labor and Working-Class History, 60 (October 2001) and Sharon Smith, "Race, Class, and 'Whiteness Theory'," International Socialist Review, 46 (March–April, 2006).

On Theodore Allen, see Jeffrey Perry, "In Memorium: Theodore W. Allen" (2002) at https://credo.library.umass.edu/view/pageturn/mums1021-s02-i009/#page/3/mode/1up. See also my contribution to Noel Ignatiev, *Treason to Whiteness Is Loyalty to Humanity*, edited by Geert Dhondt, Zhandarka Kurti, and Jarrod Shanahan (New York: Verso, 2022). Alexander Saxton's incredible life is captured in Robert Rydell, "Grand Crossings: The Life and Work of Alexander Saxton," *Pacific Historical Review* 73, no. 2 (2004), 263–85.

Interlude Three

The two articles that I wrote or co-wrote as parts of projects in which Toni Morrison was involved were (with Leola Johnson) "'Hertz, Don't It?' Becoming Colorless and Staying Black in the Crossover of O.J. Simpson," in Toni Morrison and Claudia Brodsky Lacour, eds., *Birth of a Nation'hood: Gaze, Script, and Spectacle in the O.J. Simpson Case* (New York: Random House, 1997), 197–240. "White Workers, New Democrats, and Affirmative Action," in Wahneema Lubiano, ed., *The House That Race Built* (New York: Random House, 1997), which also includes Morrison's lead essay "Home," the published work based on her talk to the Race Matters conference.

Chapter Seven

On college admissions and the critical study of whiteness, see David Roediger, "What's Wrong with These Pictures? Race, Narratives of Admission, and the Liberal Self-Representations of Historically White Colleges and Universities," *Washington University Journal of Law and Policy*, 18 (2005), 203–22. See also Elizabeth Esch, Megan Jones, and David Roediger, "Academic Freedom under the Gun: A Report from Kansas," *Journal of Academic Freedom*, 9 (September, 2018). On land-grant colleges, see, amid weightier contributions by others, my "Morrill Issues and Academic Liberalism," *NAIS: Journal of the Native American and Indigenous Studies Association* 8, no. 1 (Spring 2021), 92–96.

On international comparisons shaping my views of race, class, and education, see Aileen Moreton-Robinson, *The White Possessive: Property, Power, and Indigenous Sovereignty* (Minneapolis: University of Minnesota Press, 2015), which includes a searing critique of the absence of indigeneity in Critical Whiteness Studies in the US, and Moreton-Robinson, Mary-rose Casey, and Fiona Nicoll, eds., *Transnational Whiteness Matters* (Lanham, MD: Lexington Books, 2008); Jeremy Krikler, "Lessons from America: The Writings of David Roediger," *Journal of Southern African Studies* 20, no. 4 (December 1994), 663–69; Duncan Money and Danelle van Zyl-Hermann, eds., *Rethinking White Societies in Southern Africa 1930s–1990s* (New York: Routledge, 2020), which includes my foreword. For impacts of the Black British Left, see my "Small Internationalisms and Fugitive Thoughts: An Appreciation of *Race Today*," in Paul Field et al., eds., *Race Today Anthology* (London: Pluto Press, 2019).

For an analysis relating failures of universities to the economy and politics in which they exist, see Neil Kraus, *The Fantasy Economy: Neoliberalism, Inequality, and the Education Reform Movement* (Philadelphia: Temple University Press, 2023). For the University of Kansas as a representative, if dire, example of the crisis in higher education see *AAUP Prof Notes*, 82 (September 2022) at KUAAUP_Newsletter_4_15_22a.pdf (storage.googleapis.com)

Afterword

On pessimism, see Rosie Warren's "Some Last Words on Pessimism" on the *Salvage* website (January 4, 2016) at https://salvage.zone/some-last-words-on-pessimism/. See also Roediger and Kathryn Robinson, "The Sundown Town Vote in Wisconsin: Race-ing the Trump Victory," *Counterpunch* (November 29, 2016) at http://www.counterpunch.org/2016/11/29/the-sundown-town-vote-in-wisconsin-race-ing-the-trump-victory/. For some of the broader political arguments here, see Roediger, *The Sinking Middle Class: A Political History of Debt, Misery, and the Drift to the Right* (New York: OR Books, 2020).

David Roediger is Foundation Distinguished Professor of American Studies and History at University of Kansas. His books include *The Wages of Whiteness* (Verso, 1991), which won the Merle Curti Award from the Organization of American Historians and *Class, Race and Marxism* (*Verso, 2017*), which won the Working-Class Studies Association's C.L.R. James Award.